IF I LIVE UNTIL MORNING

A True Story of Adventure, Tragedy and Transformation

This work is non-fiction. The names of a few individuals have been changed.

Front and back cover and pg. 85, *Mount Whitney in late afternoon clouds*
Photo credit: istock.com/pleum

Photos of Orland Bartholomew, pg 5,
with permission from Phil Bartholomew

Photo of the north face of Mount Whitney, page 68,
with permission from Dirk Summers

Cover Design: VajraSky Books

Printed and bound in the United States of America
Second Printing April 2018

ISBN-10: 0-692-95581-X
ISBN-13: 978-0-692-95581-9 (paperback)

Library of Congress Control Number: 2018902467

Published by VajraSky Books
P.O. Box 3136
Estes Park, CO.

DEDICATION

To those who seek wild open spaces
To those who turn dreams into action
To those who heal dark inner places
To those who spread love and compassion

May this book inspire others to heal
through sharing their most difficult untold stories

A Note to Readers

In its larger context, this memoir is about the human spirit's capacity to overcome adversity. I shared my journey to transform my personal tragedy into something meaningful for myself and others.

I hope this story will give readers the courage and strength to transform their own life's challenges—and the inspiration to realize their greatest dreams.

PART I

A GRAND
AND
REGRETTABLE ADVENTURE

*....I was coming down from the hard, bitter region of whiteness,
where gusts of sleet were swirling and storms were building up.
I knew that all too soon various things would keep me from returning
to that celestial country of jagged ridges dancing in the open sky...*

René Daumal, *Mount Analogue*

1

MERGING DREAMS

"More morphine! More morphine!" I screamed at the top of my lungs. My cries pierced the silence every four hours. "Someone help me, please! I need morphine *now*!"

The painkiller subdued all physical sensations. My body responded to the medication like a volcano on the verge of an eruption. Whenever the drug faded from my bloodstream, I shrieked in agony as pain surged up from my broken spine and spread like molten lava through my muscles and damaged nerves. The physical torment and helpless desperation was unbearable; waiting for the next injection felt like an eternity.

Eventually a nurse would rush into my hospital room clenching a needle and a small glass bottle filled with the pain-numbing opiate. I didn't know if her hasty arrival was out of obligation or a desire to silence my wails. It didn't matter. Once the morphine was delivered, I relaxed again into a hazy oblivion.

Earlier in the week I had a different mantra: *I am going to live, I am going to live, I am going to live.* I repeated this over and over, day after day, hoping to convince myself that it might be true. But now, I yelled for medication to end my misery.

My inner world had turned into an immense black hole. Where had meaning and purpose, the light of life, gone? I often gazed out the window near my bed for inspiration. The purple mountains on the horizon evoked a pendulum of emotions. A regretful sadness pervaded my heart like a shadow dwelling deep inside of me. Still, my mood wasn't entirely dark. Occasionally joyful memories bubbled up from my soul like the fleeting light of fireflies. It had been a grand adventure, but now I worried about the future.

The High Sierras had just become my personal symbol for calamity and conquest. They deserved respect. These mountains had given me an appreciation for the human spirit's capacity for enduring hardship. I had just survived five days of hell. After lying helplessly in a tent, I dragged my severely injured and nearly dead body out of the mountains. My companion and I descended over 4,700 vertical feet through rugged terrain. With my broken spine and pelvis, we crawled over jumbles of rocks, crossed a high mountain pass and sank into thigh-deep snow. Then we negotiated a narrow canyon with cliffs, rocky ledges and a snow-clogged stream. By the time we reached the road my strength and vitality were depleted.

Still in the shadows of Mount Whitney, I welcomed the stark contrast of being in a tiny hospital in the small town of Lone Pine, California. My once-fit body was now frail and full of shattered bones. I rested in a warm bed while blood transfusions and IVs dripped into my thirsty veins. I was safe now. Hunkering down in my bloodied sleeping bag with a winter storm raging outside the tent was just a memory.

I quickly discovered that getting out of the mountains alive wasn't the end of the journey. Instead, it was the beginning of a long and formidable path to finding my own guiding light.

The day after I checked into the emergency room at the Southern Inyo Hospital, Dr. Donald Christenson, a silver-haired man wearing a white lab coat, entered my room and slowly approached my bedside. His eyes expressed the soft gaze of compassion and indicated that he had something important to say. Before speaking he placed his hand gently on my shoulder.

"Tomorrow you will have surgery. We need to remove the blood clots, necrotic tissue and bone fragments in your left buttock. Afterwards, it will take several weeks to drain the fluids from your wound," he informed me in a calm voice.

I was stunned. It didn't seem possible to have gangrene in 1982. Wasn't that something that killed soldiers back in the Civil War? In my opiate-induced confusion I nodded with acceptance. My mind was too numb to contemplate any future implications; at twenty-two years of age, I was just grateful to be alive.

An innocent conversation a few years earlier had brought me to this critical moment. I was with a handful of students on a warm autumn day in 1979. We traveled in the back of a white pickup truck piled high with overnight camping gear. Our group was on a weekend rock climbing outing with San Diego State University's Recreation Club. Classmates eagerly exchanged their summer memories as we drove towards Jacumba in the desert. A quiet young man with brown eyes and curly dark hair sat across from me. He introduced himself and started up a conversation.

"What did you do this past summer?" Ken asked.

"I worked at a lodge in Yellowstone National Park. I did quite a bit of hiking and fishing on my time off too."

"That sounds like fun," he responded.

"Yeah, it was. I especially enjoyed sleeping out under the stars every night in the sage brush. How did you spend your summer?"

"I backpacked the John Muir Trail."

My eyes lit up. My interest was piqued.

"That's awesome! My boyfriend and I had talked about hiking the JMT this past summer. He wasn't able to go, so I went to work in Yellowstone instead."

Ken's shyness disappeared momentarily. My genuine interest in his trek filled him with excitement. He quickly became animated. He lifted his chest, his eyes grew wide and he raised his voice. He then provided an enthralling account of his solo 211-mile hike. His path traversed the Sierras through some of the most rugged and spectacular scenery in North America. I was captivated. I listened intently as the wind blew through my long brown hair and the truck drove east on Interstate 8. After Ken finished recounting his memories, he paused and then divulged his real aspiration.

"My dream though, is to ski the entire John Muir Trail during the winter. But I need someone to do it with," he added while looking at me with an intense and direct gaze.

Ken's remark surprised me; it gave me the impression that I had just been invited on his expedition. In that moment our two dreams had just merged. In time, the two of us would embark on an epic winter journey on skinny cross-country skis with three-pin bindings.

Ken went on to tell me that his idea came from reading the story of a little known, adventurous snow surveyor, Orland Bartholomew. Ken had read about him in Eugene Rose's book *High Odyssey*, which was based in part on Bartholomew's diary. "Bart," as he was known, was essentially the John Muir of winter. His work as a snow surveyor for the Southern California Edison Utility Company required him to roam throughout the Sierra Nevada Range when the mountains were buried in snow. I later read *High Odyssey* for myself and reflected upon what I'd learned about Bart's trip.

Bart was an experienced outdoorsman. His personal ambition was to ski from the southern end of the Sierras to Yosemite Valley. During the summer of 1928 he hiked into the Sierras and strategically placed his supplies. With the help of pack mules, he stashed nearly 800 pounds of provisions. Each of his eleven caches contained fifty to sixty pounds of film, supplies and food. It was enough to support Bart and his companion Ed Steen for several months.

Later in the year Bart's friend had financial problems. Desperate for employment, Steen opted out from the journey. Bart did not give up easily. Next, he invited a famous mountaineer of the time, Norman Clyde, to accompany him. Clyde declined Bart's invitation; he was confident when scaling peaks, but his skiing skills were insufficient for craggy terrain. Since Bart's only option was to go alone, he quit his job and made his final preparations.

Bart started his expedition near Cottonwood Pass in the midst of a blizzard on Christmas Day, 1928. He traveled on six-foot long hickory skis and he used ski poles that were crafted from the shaft of a garden hoe. Inside his seventy pound wood-framed pack he carried a down robe for a sleeping bag, a canvas tent, a cast-iron skillet, a double-bitted ax and canned and dried food. En route to Yosemite Valley, he planned to record wildlife activity and photo-document the Sierras in winter. He also hoped to make the first winter ascent of Mount Whitney.

Orland Bartholomew

From listening to Ken describe Orland Bartholomew's adventures, I could tell that both men had a love for exploring wild, mountainous terrain. I did too. I felt that Ken and I were fated to be friends from the moment we met in the back of that truck. Nevertheless, our relationship got off to a slow start.

Weeks passed after our trip to the desert before we crossed paths again. I rarely saw Ken because we frequented opposite ends of the college. He was over in the Mathematics Department while I studied geography. When I finally ran into him on campus, he paused briefly to say hello. Our short conversation quickly faltered. Ken seemed to be trembling inside with the fear of rejection. I sensed that he wanted to ask me out for a date, but he didn't know how. He was simply too shy. I believed that it was too early for me to start another relationship; I had broken up with my boyfriend just a few months earlier. Nonetheless, I felt sorry for Ken. During this encounter I mentioned my plans to ski at Rock Creek, just north of Bishop, over Christmas with the Recreation Club. Then I suggested that he sign up for the trip too.

A month later we headed north with another group of students. Since the Sierras were engulfed in a storm of swirling wind and snow, nearly everyone spent the weekend next to the lodge's crackling fire place. Ken and I were the exceptions. Each day we skied through a scene reminiscent of the plastic snow dome that I had as a child. Our life-size private bubble of wilderness didn't require shaking to change the weather. Fluffy white flakes resembling delicate feathers fell incessantly from a slate sky, and the green boughs of fir trees sagged under the accumulating snowfall. Abundant fresh powder made the woods utterly quiet. We shattered the deep silence of winter with a loud and joyful squeal each time a tree branch released its load and sent cold snow cascading down our necks.

During this weekend I discovered that Ken was a gifted athlete. He was an avid and dedicated runner, a long-distance bicyclist and a serious white water kayaker. He was especially agile in water. A few years earlier he had taken 6th place in the North American Cup, a kayaking race that had been held in Canada.

Ken and I were very compatible; both of us loved adventure and moving under our own power. We had our differences too. Ken was reserved while I was more out-going. Although he was uncomfortable interacting with others, I had a knack for putting him at ease.

Ken was most confident when tromping around in the high country. He was courageous, kind-hearted and a nerd. He was almost a genius and had a remarkable memory as well. Ken could solve complex math problems in his head and recite full lines from the books he had read back in junior high.

Once Ken got past his bashfulness, I discovered that he had a great sense of humor. We were both prone to outbreaks of deep laughter. When I visited him at his house, we often howled and rolled on the living room floor with fits of belly-shaking giggles.

After our Christmas outing, we frequently got together on weekends to hike or ride our bicycles. We also took special trips together. We skied in the mountains in winter and when the snow melted in the spring, we traveled to the west side of the Sierras for white water rafting.

After many months our weekend adventures came to a halt. I had accepted an internship at Glacier National Park for the summer of 1980. While working as a backcountry ranger, I lived in a remote patrol cabin fifteen miles from the nearest road. My experience in Upper Park Creek was pervaded by solitude—so much so that I counted each person that I met on the trail. By the end of the season I had interacted with only fifty-two visitors.

After leaving his job at a science lab in San Diego, Ken came to Glacier for a lengthy visit for the last part of the summer. We shared my rustic one-room log cabin furnished with a table, sawed-off stumps for chairs, and thin mattresses on a bunk bed made of rusty woven wires. During the day, Ken assisted me with sawing logs that had fallen over the trail and building backcountry campsites at Lake Isabelle. On our breaks we gathered wild huckleberries from the bushes, and later turned them into cobbler on my wood stove.

By summer's end our relationship had blossomed. We returned to San Diego and moved in together. Soon afterwards, we began plotting our up-coming journey, the *1982 Trans-Sierra John Muir Trail Cross-Country Ski Expedition*.

Our ski trip would traverse the rugged terrain between Yosemite Valley and Whitney Portal, the trailhead to Mount Whitney. En route we would make four detours to pick up our supply caches. While carving 223 miles through the snow, we would ascend over 48,000 vertical feet and descend another 43,600 feet. In all, we would cross a total of fourteen high altitude passes—eleven along the JMT, plus three additional passes to pick up our food caches. The grand finale would be to climb Mount Whitney, the highest point in the lower forty-eight states. It was an imposing plan.

It took years to transform our dream into reality. First, we honed our cross-country skiing skills. We skied in the Cascade Mountains around

Crater Lake and on the lower slopes of Mount Rainier. During college breaks we completed numerous trans-Sierra backcountry ski routes. On weekends we also skied in the mountains of Southern California. At home, we maintained a fitness program that included jogging, bicycling and roller-skiing on the pavement around Balboa Park.

Our first year out of college gave us the freedom to seriously pursue our dream. Ken's gifted mind was a great asset for planning. He calculated a myriad of details: travel routes and mileage, quantities of calories and food, and all the supplies and gear that would be needed.

Our equipment was also thoroughly inventoried and tuned-up. Since we couldn't find everything we needed, we resorted to making some of our own gear. One of our greatest challenges was creating outer booties to insulate our lightweight ski boots. For this, we used Velcro straps over neoprene booties covered with coated, heavy-duty nylon cloth.

Equipped for departure

Our plan was to travel as lightly as possible so we researched and then purchased the best lightweight tent on the market; a three and a half pound Gore-Tex climbing tent. It barely accommodated two people, our down-filled sleeping bags, inflatable mattresses and emptied backpacks.

8

The tent tapered from head to toe. It had three arched aluminum poles of decreasing height which made it impossible to sit up inside the tent. The only way in and out was by crawling through a flap in the door. In the months to follow, due to its size, I named our tent the "Gore-Tex coffin." Sadly, it nearly lived up to its name.

To familiarize ourselves with our route, a large section of our small living room floor was covered with USGS quadrant maps. Night after night we studied the green and white paper tiles. We analyzed the terrain and estimated the distance that we could ski each day. We concluded that the journey would take a month.

We also needed a well-thought out itinerary to determine our food needs. High-calorie meals would provide fuel for physical exertion during the day and keep us warm at night. Our menu included freeze-dried dinners, canned kippers, Pilot Biscuits, Tiger Milk Bars, powdered rehydration drinks, cheese, butter, powdered milk, peanut butter, jam and more. We also added some home-made treats. The delightful aroma of ginger, honey and molasses often permeated our kitchen. We baked nineteen pounds of high-nutrition granola and made ten pounds of trail mix.

Next we sealed our food in gallon-sized, heavy-duty Ziploc bags. Our supplies were distributed among four white plastic drums secured with duct tape. On top of each lid was a clear plastic bag with a note inside that pleaded others not to take our food; our lives depended on it.

The last preparation before starting our trip was to place our food caches in the mountains near our ski route. For this we drove north on Highway 395. It's my favorite drive in North America. For me, it was the highway to adventure. Even though I had learned to ski as a child in Colorado, the Sierras had become my preferred winter playground. My family often traveled to the Mammoth Ski Area for extended weekends when I was a teenager.

On every trip I was captivated by the juxtaposition of cobalt skies, jagged snow-covered peaks and the dusty brown Owens Valley. I loved the steep canyon walls divided by ragged lines of light and shadow. I would stare out the car window for hours. My eyes didn't part from the mountains until the peaks disappeared from the horizon. Once I became an adult, I left downhill ski areas behind and explored the backcountry of the Sierras on Nordic skis with Ken.

Author skiing into the sunset in Center Basin

We had four stops to make on this trip into the Sierras to deposit our expedition's supply caches. Each reserve needed to be strategically located: easy to retrieve and separated by one week's skiing distance.

Near the town of Big Pine we departed from Highway 395 and headed west towards the Palisade Range. Our weathered blue Toyota Corolla traveled up a long, steep and dry alluvial fan before delivering us into a forest of stately looking Jeffery pines. At the end of the road was a solitary inn adjacent to Big Pine Creek. The brown structure was a mix of rustic Western decor and European elegance with an inspiring backdrop of the dark craggy peaks and white alpine glaciers.

"Jeaner, maybe we should buy this lodge. We could run it as a base camp for climbers," Ken suggested as we pulled into the parking lot.

The scene was impressive, but his idea was mere fantasy. We would never be able to afford such a place. It was expensive enough just to spend the night here so that we could retrieve our cache during our expedition. Since we had called in advance for permission to leave it at the hotel, we just dropped off our food barrel with the inn's owner. Then we continued north to the town of Bishop.

Our plan was to leave another supply cache near Hutchinson Meadow. This involved skiing about twenty-four miles round-trip from North Lake over Piute Pass. Our trip was soon thwarted. Near Piute Lake we encountered a blizzard. The wind howled. Snow blew horizontally and pelted our faces with sharp icy crystals. Visibility was reduced to nearly zero. The grey sky and snow-covered ground were almost indistinguishable from each other. We were forced to stop at the base of Piute Pass. Squinting into the blowing snow, we could barely see the immense obstacle on top of the ridge—a massive cornice draped over the brink of the mountainside. The frozen wave of snow was deposited on the lee slope from strong winds blowing all winter. The current weather conditions made it impossible for us to determine whether the cornice covered the entire length of the pass.

Ken and I agreed that it was imprudent to continue; pushing onward risked triggering a life-threatening avalanche. After identifying a uniquely twisted tree on the northeast slope, Ken climbed up its trunk and wired our five gallon plastic drum onto a sturdy branch. It was the best option at the time. We would make another plan if the overhanging snow was still on Piute Pass when we came to reclaim our supplies. Neither of us were willing to repeat the experience that Orland Bartholomew had with a cornice on his trip.

While Bart was trying to cross the Great Divide between the Kings and Kern River Valleys, he encountered a massive cornice hanging precariously over a gap on Harrison Pass. Despite fierce winds, Bart climbed up a snowy slope to 12,600 feet. With ice creepers on his boots and his skis strapped to his belt, he looked over the edge in horror—a deep, fifteen foot eave of snow blocked access to a snow chute that led down his intended route.

Bart inched his way toward the edge. He moved cautiously and slowly, testing the snow with his poles. With immense courage and nearly frozen hands, he sliced through the lip of the cornice. With each swipe of his ax, chunks of snow broke off and tumbled down the mountainside. Eventually Bart hacked a slot through the wind-packed cornice, crossed the pass, and carefully cut footsteps down the other side of the slope.

After leaving our cache near Piute Pass, Ken and I continued north on Highway 395. Our plans were foiled again. A few weeks earlier we had called Tamarack Lodge near Mammoth Lakes and arranged to leave a supply drum with the managers. Now we were greeted by a "closed" sign hanging in the window. The door was locked. There was no information indicating when the resort might reopen.

"Now what do we do?" I sighed.

"Maybe we can convince the rangers at the Forest Service visitor center to store our food cache," Ken suggested.

"That seems like the only realistic option. Let's give it a try."

The forest rangers were sympathetic. They graciously agreed to keep our big barrel of food. After taking our cache into a backroom, they delivered discouraging news—the Sierras had a record snowpack, with deep snow and extreme avalanche danger.

Two disheartened souls then headed south on the highway. We laid our sleeping bags out in the open, next to a gated dirt road at the entrance to Onion Valley and then went to sleep.

In the morning we hiked up the closed road to the trailhead. Ken carried our drum of food in his backpack. As we ascended, the aroma of pine and fir trees gradually replaced the scent of desert sagebrush and the trail became obscured by snow. We donned our skis and continued up the mountainside, gaining over 4,000 vertical feet in just a few miles. Our calves burned from the effort. We paused to enjoy the view when we finally reached Kearsarge Pass. Golden-colored pinnacles laced with snow stretched out along the Sierra Crest. The backcountry of Kings Canyon National Park extended out before us as a jumble of steep snowy peaks.

The weather was now much calmer than on our previous trips over

Kearsarge Pass. Here on an earlier journey, we skied into a strong and steady wind. While I was standing at the summit a forceful gust slammed into me. One moment I was upright and the next second I was blown over. It didn't matter that I had forty pounds in my backpack; the gust pushed me over and knocked the wind right out of me. I was left dazed, lying on my back, draped over my pack, staring straight into the sky.

We had better luck on this day. The weather and the snow conditions were both excellent. With our ice axes in hand to regulate our speed, we sat on our butts and glissaded down the steeper portions of the pass. Once the terrain eased up, we skied the rest of the way down to Bullfrog Lake. The afternoon light highlighted our graceful ski tracks. Across the slope behind us were bright lines that resembled silver threads embroidered on the snow. Our tracks were the only human signs marring the pristine landscape.

Ken on Kearsarge Pass

We stashed our last cache near the southern edge of the frozen lake. Ken climbed up into a gnarled subalpine tree. Then I hoisted the plastic barrel up to him. Using nylon webbing and wire, Ken lashed the drum onto a gnarled branch. Then we skied back over Kearsarge Pass. The snow was perfect. We sculpted S-shaped turns and glided all the way down to the trailhead in just over an hour. We were fit and ready to go.

Once home, our new-found optimism faded in the face of obstacles. Snow continued to fall in the Sierras which increased the avalanche danger. Meanwhile, it rained heavily in San Diego. We hunkered down in our house and waited impatiently for the spring snowpack to stabilize. Then one night the water-saturated ground in our backyard collapsed inward, revealing an enormous hole where a septic tank had once been located. We spent Easter weekend shoveling eighteen tons of dirt into the cavern. The back-breaking work only strengthened us for the coming journey.

Just when we were ready to depart for the Sierras, heavy spring rains broke water and sewage lines in Yosemite National Park. Rocks up to two stories high tumbled down the hillside blocking the road into Yosemite Valley. To deal with the crisis park officials closed the entrance gates. Our trip was on hold again.

2

THE JOURNEY UNFOLDS

Our journey began a month later than planned. On April 14th we flew from San Diego to Fresno on a small commercial airplane. For most of the flight, I stared out the plane's tiny window. The Sierra Nevada Range stretched out along the eastern horizon as far as I could see. While I gazed at the serrated peaks cloaked in deep snow, the reality of our undertaking hit me. We were going to ski the length of those mountains on Nordic skis with ankle-high boots. Inwardly, I wondered if we could really do it. Then I quickly pushed all doubt out of my mind; if we were to succeed, I had to believe it was possible.

En route to the mountains we were conspicuously out of place. Overdressed in turtlenecks, wool knickers and ski boots, we sweated profusely on the city bus between the Fresno Airport and downtown. Next we endured countless stares as we toted our backpacks, laden with skis and poles strapped to their exteriors, across the transfer station. After a long wait we finally boarded a Greyhound bus bound for Yosemite National Park.

Our route traveled along curvy roads through lush rolling hills, dotted with oak trees and carpeted with lime green grass and patches of colorful wildflowers. The road into Yosemite had just reopened. Our timing couldn't have been better—our bus was the first vehicle allowed past the landslide that had recently closed the highway.

Excitement coursed through our veins as we approached our starting point. It was a poignant moment each time I entered Yosemite Valley. The imposing sheer granite walls always left me awestruck with a child-like sense of wonder. Time seemed to stand still from the joyful presence of being one with the splendor of nature. What human soul would not be touched by this magnificent scenery?

Perhaps no one has been more passionate about the beauty of Yosemite's landscape than John Muir. He was entranced by this glacial valley the moment he laid eyes on it in 1869. Soon he called Yosemite his home. Muir fought for Yosemite's protection after witnessing the rampant exploitation of natural resources throughout the West. His efforts and writings also helped to preserve other national park areas such as Grand Canyon, Sequoia, Mount Rainier and Petrified Forest. He wrote nearly a dozen books and hundreds of magazine articles. Each recounted his adventures from the Sierras to Alaska. Today his writings continue to inspire generations of outdoor enthusiasts. I was one of them. John Muir's stories of rambling through the Sierras sparked my interest in following the trail that was named in his honor.

That time had finally come. Before embarking on our journey, Ken and I spent the night at Sunnyside Campground. The next morning we filled out a backcountry permit form at a roadside drop box. Then we took the shuttle bus to the trailhead at Mirror Lake.

As I heaved my thirty-eight pound load onto my back, we crossed the threshold between dreaming and doing. We were now fully committed to our undertaking. During the first mile of hiking, I felt a tinge of unexplainable apprehension behind the rush of excitement. Nonetheless, I continued up the trail with my red cross-country skis strapped to the sides of my blue frameless pack.

Spring had already arrived in the valley. We felt hot while hiking at the lower elevations even though cool water flowed down the rocky trail in rivulets beneath our feet. It roared loudly as it gushed down the surrounding cliffs in long silver ribbons. Every drop of melting snow was destined to leave the high country and join the already overflowing Merced River at the bottom of the valley.

The Snow Creek Trail switchbacked up 3,000 vertical feet in just three miles. As we hiked upwards wearing ski boots, small blisters appeared on our heels. There wasn't enough snow to ski until we reached a dense forest higher up on the valley's rim. Our pace quickened as soon as we could kick and glide across the snow and through the trees.

We were concerned about our next goal—crossing Snow Creek farther ahead. On a previous trip when the snowpack had been lower, the bridge had been washed out from spring runoff. After a long search we eventually found a fallen tree large enough for safe passage across the swollen water. This year the snowpack was much deeper and rivers were raging with snowmelt. When we finally located the new and still intact bridge, Ken and I both felt an immense relief.

We continued through the forest until we reached the road leading to Lake Tenaya. The pavement was completely buried in snow and littered with chunks of snowy avalanche debris. The heavy rains had lubricated the nearby granite slabs, forcing the snow to peel off the glacially polished rocks.

Civilization was now far behind us. In a few months this place would be packed with people. For now, the area was pristine. Fog saturated the basin. Together with the snow, it hushed the landscape into a deep silence. The view was bewitching, both primal and tranquil. At twilight, an ephemeral mist painted the scene in pastels. Meltwater glistening on the granite domes reflected the dusty-rose sky above and accentuated the black streaks of water running down the cliffs.

Shortly before dark, we found our exact camping spot from a few years earlier. We took off our packs and performed our winter camping ritual. First, we packed down a platform for the tent. With our skis still on our feet, we stomped the snow into a firm rectangular pad. Then we staked the tent down with pegs, ice axes, or skis, depending on the snow's consistency.

Lake Tenaya was visible from our tent door. The lake was in the early stages of thawing; slushy, turquoise-colored ice covered its surface. Tracks from a fearless bear led across the sludge towards the other side of the valley. Since hungry bears had just emerged from hibernation, we took precautions to protect our food. After dinner we placed our fare in two large nylon bags, suspended the stuff sacks with a nylon cord, and then counter-balanced them over a high and long tree limb.

The first day of our two-person expedition had been easy. We covered thirteen miles and gained 4,500 vertical feet. Except for my right knee aching from the strenuous climb, the day had been perfect. Before the evening turned cold, we crawled into our warm down bags. The anxiety I felt during our morning departure was long gone. Now my heart was filled with joy—I was happy to be back in the wilderness. Here, my emotions were in sync with the rhythms of nature.

We took time to be leisurely the next morning. Before breakfast we shook the nighttime frost off our tent and draped our sleeping bags over a thin nylon cord strung between two trees. While waiting for our gear to dry, we sat on a rock in the soothing warm sunlight and ate breakfast.

As winter nomads we lived simply. Traversing through peaceful, scenic terrain nourished our spirit. We quickly rediscovered how little is needed to survive and thrive. While each day brought new adventures, the pattern of our daily routine was predictable. After breakfast, we packed up our gear and skied all day with a stop for lunch. At dusk we set up our tent, cooked our dinner and went to sleep. Some days were easy. Others presented more difficulties. Finding open water for drinking and cooking was consistently difficult.

En route to Tuolumne Meadows we skied beneath gigantic domes of granite. I was captivated and inspired by the lone pine tree growing out from the stark western face of Pywiack Dome. It was a testimony to strength and tenacity.

As we traversed along the snow-covered road, we chuckled about the irrelevant 35 mph speed limit signs—going that fast on skis was unlikely on the relatively low-angled highway. Other signs warned backcountry skiers that the road passed through avalanche-prone terrain. Just before we arrived at Tuolumne Meadows, we encountered two other skiers.

"Hi there! Where are you guys coming from?" Ken asked.

"We came from Lee Vining on Highway 395. We're skiing to Yosemite Valley. Where are you two headed?" one of the guys inquired.

"We're skiing to Mount Whitney. We just started our trip," Ken explained.

"Today's our second day on the trail," I piped in.

"Awesome!" exclaimed his companion, "Good luck on your trip."

After our brief meeting we stopped for lunch. To insulate ourselves from the frozen ground, we plopped our backpacks onto the snow next to the riverbank and enjoyed our meal sitting atop our gear. The meadow was buried under ten feet of snow and fringed by lodgepole pines. We skied upstream into Lyell Canyon for the rest of the afternoon and set up camp just before sunset

A roaring stove signaled that we were snug in our tent and ready to eat. To stay warm, we cooked our dinner just outside the tent door while lying inside our sleeping bags. For safety reasons, the stove had to be used outside of our shelter. Besides the obvious danger of flames, a buildup of carbon monoxide inside a tent can be fatal.

Since dehydrated food lacked what our bodies needed, we added extra cheese or butter to our freeze-dried meals. This time-tested strategy is used by high altitude mountaineers and polar explorers to increase caloric intake. A high-fat dinner kept our metabolic heat burning all night. During the day, our food was fuel to move us through the mountainous landscape. By the second night on the trail, we started a new evening tradition. We exchanged our food fantasies for the day. Pizza, enchiladas, guacamole and a fresh green salad were consistently on our list of desired entrees.

That night, the temperature dropped to 10 degrees Fahrenheit in Lyell Canyon. Coyotes were active in the area. They left abundant tracks in the snow and their howls punctuated the quiet night every few hours. Each time they barked, their wails echoed back and forth across the valley accentuating the feeling of isolation and wildness.

On the third day of our journey we crossed Donohue Pass, our first mountain divide on the John Muir Trail. Skiing from one major watershed into another required a lot of effort. Careful planning was also needed. We analyzed the directional aspect and angle of the slopes we intended to cross, paid attention to the consistency of the snow, and sometimes dug snow pits to evaluate avalanche conditions. This helped us determine our exact route and the techniques and equipment that were best for going up, over, and down the other side.

To get from the bottom of Lyell Canyon up into the high country, we had to cross a long steep slope. Before ascending, we took additional precautions to avoid triggering an avalanche. We removed our skis and tied them to the sides of our backpacks. Then we climbed upwards in a straight line, plunging the shafts of our ice axes into the snow and kicking steps into the slope. This was safer then traversing back and forth across the snow-laden incline

The views also changed as we approached Donohue Pass. Lodgepole pines gave way to mountain hemlocks. The summit of Lyell Peak dominated the skyline just beyond us. As we gained altitude the trees became sparse and stunted, and then disappeared altogether. Just above 10,000 feet we entered a bowl-shaped glacial cirque with intense sunlight reflecting off the steep snow-covered slopes. We were miserable. Besides suffering from the sudden increase in temperature, our eyes burned from the combination of bright light and beads of sweat mixed with sunscreen.

"I feel like I am baking in an over-sized oven," I complained to Ken.

He nodded his head and continued on. As the sun climbed high into the afternoon sky, the snow turned into slush. The climb was strenuous. It also aggravated my right knee. I skied at a turtle's pace but with a focused mind. Years earlier I had mastered a psychological approach to skiing up and over the high passes. To keep from getting discouraged by all the false summits, I set intermediate goals along the way. I fixed my attention on some part of the terrain ahead of me. Sometimes it was a tree or a cluster of rocks jutting out of the snow. At the higher elevations where the world is only white, I concentrated on reaching a subtle irregularity in the snow; a slight dip or bulge in the landscape. I ascended each mountain pass by connecting these imaginary dots.

Reaching the top was more than just a physical and mental achievement. The summit of a mountain pass can serve as a metaphor for the present moment; the gap between the past and the future. Our journey was connecting points in space and time. Behind us was the landscape that we had just traversed. Ahead was yet-to-be-explored terrain.

Near Donohue Pass there was abundant evidence of avalanche activity from a few weeks earlier. Huge chunks of snow and broken trees were scattered in long tracks running down nearby mountainsides. As we crossed the 11,000-foot pass, we left Yosemite National Park. The surrounding peaks were plastered white and Lyell Glacier was buried under a deep mantle of snow. The entire landscape resembled an enormous meringue pie with gigantic whipped peaks.

At the top of the divide, a pika scurried in and out of rock piles. He was raiding one of his stashes of food. These cute rock-rabbits spend their summers cutting and storing alpine vegetation to support an active winter lifestyle.

I reveled in the calm conditions. On a previous ski trip from Mammoth to Yosemite Valley, howling winds blew over Donohue Pass. The air was too cold to breathe. A wind-chill factor of 20 degrees below zero triggered my cold weather, exercise-induced asthma. Breathing heavily under a wool scarf caused droplets to condense and freeze onto my skin. It wasn't until later in the day that I discovered the damage. Frostbite had specked my face with black blisters. I was horrified to return to college after spring break with such a dreadful looking face.

On this trip though, Donohue Pass offered different challenges. Sastrugi covered the south side of the slope. These miniature waves of frozen snow were sculpted from high winds. The trough between each crest ranged from six to eighteen inches deep. Without metal edges on our narrow skis, it was extremely difficult to cut through the sharp edges on each frozen ripple. As we skied downhill, the undulating, hard-packed snow was also a tripping hazard.

From Rush Creek we skied up to Island Pass. The surrounding peaks looked different from the other mountains. Here, the Minaret Range was made of reddish volcanic and metamorphic rocks. Looming just ahead of us, Mount Ritter and Banner Peak were enticing.

John Muir had a harrowing experience while making the first ascent of Mount Ritter's 13,000-foot summit in 1872. He was overcome with fear half-way up—unable to move either up or down to the next set of holds. Certain that he would fall and die, he clung to the rock for dear life. Then something unusual happened. He felt the presence of a guiding force which allowed him to continue with ease until he reached the summit.

Before long I would know exactly how John Muir felt to be caught on the side of a mountain, unable to go up or down. My exploit however, ended with a very different outcome.

Soon Ken and I arrived at Thousand Island Lake. Just beneath the peak of Muir's conquest, we were baffled to see a single set of ski tracks heading off towards Mount Ritter.

"Where do you think that skier was going?" I asked.

"Who knows?" Ken replied.

I was intrigued by the lone and unknown skier. Coincidentally, my life would later converge not once, but several times in the future, with the maker of those mysterious ski tracks. The journal I kept on this trip later revealed that the skier's solo winter ascent of Mount Ritter occurred the day before our arrival at Thousand Island Lake. It was this yet-to-be encountered skier, Paul, who was destined to become my friend and later, to play a key role in my recovery from this very expedition. After pondering over the ski tracks, Ken and I paused to soak in the scenery.

I longed to see Thousand Island Lake during the summer when black rocky islands rise above the blue water. Strangely, I was only acquainted with the Sierras during the wintertime. Here, on a previous winter excursion, the small rocky islands had jutted out from the lake's frozen surface like black beads atop a mirror. That scene was reminiscent of the beauty and simplicity of a rock-filled Zen garden. The lake looked very different on this ski trip. This time the stony islands were nowhere to be seen; they were buried beneath a thick quilt of white.

The summit of Mount Banner was aglow with the last golden rays of evening light. Shortly afterwards the sun slipped behind the jagged horizon, the peaks turned grey and the temperature plummeted. The slushy afternoon snow quickly froze into a hard icy crust.

Just before dark we needed to refill our water bottles. There was no open water around us; everything was frozen. Whenever possible we avoided melting snow for drinking water. Besides wasting precious fuel, water melted on a stovetop lacks the fresh taste and vitality found in water that emerges naturally from mountain rivers.

To quench our thirst, we went to the lake's outlet stream. The ice was thinner here. With his ax, Ken carefully chopped a hole through the frozen skin. Then he dipped our water bottles below the ice and let the water trickle slowly inside.

Afterwards, we found a cozy campsite nestled in a small grove of trees. Ken unpacked his backpack and laid the tent poles on the slippery snow. An instant later we heard a *whoosh* sound as the poles quickly disappeared down the hill. A few moments of panic followed. Which way did the poles go? How far had they traveled? Would we ever find them in the dense forest below and in the fading light? After a long search we located the missing tent poles. They had traveled quite a distance down the valley. Later we went to bed pleased with our progress: we had skied seventeen miles that day and crossed two high mountain passes.

A relaxing morning followed. We enjoyed the views of the surrounding peaks while savoring our homemade granola. Shortly after our departure from Thousand Island Lake, we skied through a forested canyon next to the San Joaquin River. We mistakenly followed the stream too closely. Soon we were boxed in. A reddish-brown volcanic cliff rose about twenty-five feet above us on the other side of the canyon. Below us, a steep snowy bank dropped to the floor of the narrow gorge. The river at the bottom writhed loudly like an angry serpent. We watched in horror as large chunks of snow broke off from the frozen white bank. Once released, the blocks of snow swirled briefly in a whitish-green froth before being gobbled up by the river.

The fast moving water sounded like thunder reverberating through the confining gorge. The noise amplified my anxiety. I was scared. My heart raced as the warm flush of adrenaline surged through my veins. The slope was a patchwork of different snow conditions. In some places it was slushy and rotten, and in other places, slick and icy. As we skied rapidly downhill, we quickly assessed the surface of the snow to gauge how to respond on skis. Skiing with a heavy backpack increased the challenge. One slip would lead to an icy wet death; vanishing into the serpent's gaping mouth and into oblivion. For a few minutes the skiing was dicey and tenuous. Luckily, we found a ramp of snow that led us through the rocky band and above the stream to safety.

As we skied southwards, various tributaries of the San Joaquin River would be our companion for the next eighty-five miles. For now, the stream led us to Devil's Postpile National Monument, site of one of the tallest, most nearly perfect examples of columnar basalt in the world. They formed roughly 100,000 years ago after lava pouring out from fissures in Earth's crust created a deep lake behind a glacial moraine. When the liquid rock cooled, it contracted and then fractured into pillars of stone. This magnificent natural sight draws hordes of visitors each summer, but for now, we had the place to ourselves.

Although the tightly clustered black columns were fascinating, our eyes were drawn to the brilliant chartreuse-green lichens that dappled their dark surface. For us, the intense color was an exquisite contrast from the white monotony of snow.

At our camp in Red Meadows, we indulged by eating two freeze-dried dinners. Despite our plan to pick up our first cache the next day, we still had ample food left in our supplies. After our meal, we hung our food bags from a tree limb to keep black bears from stealing our goods.

Orland Bartholomew had been less fortunate when he camped at this same location. He was only fifty miles from the end of his historic journey when he discovered that most of his food cache had been eaten by inconsiderate trappers. Like us, he had put a note on his supply barrel with a plea to leave it untouched.

Our food was faring well but our gear wasn't. After only a few days on the John Muir Trail our equipment was already showing serious signs of wear and tear. The metal plate that attached to the three-pin bindings in Ken's boot had broken. The metal sidewalls on his ski bindings were also loosening, making it hard for him to control his turns.

Early the next morning we skied up to Mammoth Pass. We paused at the top to admire the view. The Minaret Range saluted the sky with gigantic blades of rock that resembled bayonets. During our descent we encountered an increasing number of cross-country ski tracks from skiers staying in Mammoth Lakes. We were overjoyed when we reached Tamarack Lodge on the outskirts of town and found it was open again.

A clerk greeted us with enthusiasm when we checked in. "Where are you two coming from?"

"Yosemite Valley."

"What a great trip!" she replied. "Is your car waiting here for you?"

"No, we are skiing the entire John Muir Trail."

"Really?" Lisa asked. "My boyfriend just left to ski the JMT too. He and a friend are traveling from south to north. Maybe you'll run into them."

Later, our conversation revealed that Lisa's friends were making their journey on skis just before starting their summer jobs. Like us, both of her friends were seasonal rangers with the National Park Service.

After our conversation, we moved into a toasty, pine-paneled room. We quickly adorned it with a white nylon cord strung between the walls. Soon the line was strewn with wet socks and damp clothes. With nearly a full day of light still ahead of us, we hitchhiked into the nearby town. The experience was bewildering. It was jarring to make the transition from a silent white wilderness into the hustle and bustle of California's most popular ski resort.

We had unexpected shopping to do. We needed more moleskin for blisters, sunscreen, glue, medical tape and aspirin for my knee. We also needed sun hats to shade us from the intense UV light and the bright reflection from the snow. We visited countless mountain shops, but none of the staff could repair the metal plate in Ken's boot. Eventually, Ken bought epoxy glue and fixed it himself.

Before returning to our lodge, we picked up our first food cache at the ranger station. Afterwards we called our parents from a nearby pay phone. Besides letting them know that we were doing fine, we wanted to express our appreciation for their enthusiasm for our expedition. I suspect they had no idea of what was involved in skiing through these rugged mountains. Perhaps it was better that way.

That night a hot shower felt even better than sleeping in a bed. We also relished not having to sleep with cold boots and water bottles buried inside our sleeping bags to keep them from freezing at night.

3

A GUT FEELING

We were brimming with optimism as we left Mammoth Lakes. So far, our journey had been smooth. In a short time frame we had covered many miles, and now we had a new supply of food. The climb out of town and up to Duck Pass was fast and easy. Avalanche debris was the only thing that slowed us down. It was tiresome and time-consuming to navigate through a labyrinth of broken trees and chunks of snow.

By afternoon we arrived at the camping spot designated on our itinerary, but since it was still early in the day, we glided onward. Just past Duck Lake something bright caught my eye; a long yellow object was careening down the mountainside. It was one of Ken's skis. His boot had popped out from his loosened three-pin ski binding. He quickly chased after the ski like an expert skateboarder, sliding downhill on only one ski. He managed to keep his balance by touching the snow periodically with his other foot. I watched the scene with amazement; transfixed by his skillful and speedy performance. I was astounded when he finally retrieved the missing ski several hundred feet from where he'd lost it.

The day dragged on as we skied towards Purple Lake. The bright sun was unmerciful and the temperature was hot. Our newly purchased sun hats protected us from the reflecting light, but now our lips hurt. Despite sunscreen and chapstick, they were dried, cracked and bloody.

The heat created other issues too. Large rocks buried under the snow absorbed the warmth of indirect sunlight. Each day when the boulders warmed up they softened the surrounding snow and created hidden heat sinks. These invisible booby traps were impossible to detect. While gliding across the snow, I sometimes heard a faint *thunk* beneath my skis. A split-second later, the rotten snow collapsed. With nothing to support me, I would fall waist-deep into a newly opened pit.

"Shit!" I yelled each time this happened.

Next was the ordeal of extrication. I couldn't see the skis on my feet; they disappeared under the snow with the lower half of my body. It wasn't as easy as just pulling my skis up and out to the snow's surface. The tips of my skis were usually trapped under the lip of dense crusty snow, or caught beneath the branch of a hidden subalpine tree. I grunted from the effort as I pulled my skis upward. More often than not, my skis hardly budged. It was maddening.

"Damn it! Let go of my skis." I pleaded with the snow.

I wiggled and squirmed, cursed and screamed. Then I slid my buried skis backwards and forwards to release them. When I found the offending boulder buried under the snow, I unsnapped my ski bindings, took off my skis and stepped onto the recently revealed rock. Then I reached down and rescued my submerged skis. Other times, I laid my poles on the surface of the snow in the formation of a cross and then pushed my hands down on the point of convergence. This gave me enough leverage to pull myself out of the hole. Helping each other was out of the question; if Ken came to my aid, he would simply fall into the snow pit with me.

These heat sinks took an enormous toll on our enthusiasm and energy. We skied tentatively between them, never knowing where the next booby trap might be. Most days we didn't encounter them on our journey, but when we did, it was like skiing through a mine field of large hidden holes.

As we approached Purple Lake I heard a loud rumble. It echoed through the valley. It was distant but booming.

"Whoa!—did you hear that avalanche cut loose?" I asked.

"What avalanche? That must have been an airplane."

"No, that was an avalanche," I disagreed.

Shortly after my comment, Ken skied across a large open slope and triggered a small snow slide. Although the slope was steep, the small avalanche, six by three feet across, didn't travel very far. Nonetheless, it got his attention.

As we skied onward, I felt a nagging and unexplainable tinge of apprehension. Sadness replaced the zeal that I had experienced earlier in the morning. By late afternoon I was so discouraged I thought about quitting our trip and going home. It was disheartening to acknowledge these feelings. After all, we had spent years planning and preparing for our expedition.

Near the shore of Purple Lake we found a perfect campsite, sheltered by a small grove of trees. Since we were camping in the high country we didn't hang our food for the night. Bears were more likely to be foraging lower down where the temperatures were warmer. Other worries consumed us over our dinner of macaroni and cheese.

"What do you think about these snow conditions?" Ken asked.

"The snow is wet and heavy. It's a lot of work to make any progress. I am mostly concerned about its lack of cohesion. I am worried about avalanches. There were times today that I just wanted to give up," I confessed.

We decided to continue to Silver Pass the next day. If the poor snow conditions persisted we would return to San Diego. I went to sleep longing for the magic that we had experienced at Purple Lake just a few weeks earlier on a three-day ski jaunt.

On that trip, we had witnessed an extraordinary evening. Above the Silver Divide a brilliant sunset painted the clouds with intense purples and reds. Later, a full moon rose in the eastern sky. Its bright light reflected off the snow, transforming the hoarfrost into a field of shimmering diamonds. Each facet of these super-enlarged snow crystals glittered with tiny specks of light in every imaginable color. Juxtaposed against the night sky, the scene was absolutely enchanting.

Now the moon was long gone. While we slept, the stars twinkled above our tent and the temperature dropped to 13 degrees. We welcomed frigid nights—they consolidated the snowpack, made us safer and gave us peace of mind.

The next morning was bitterly cold. We departed from our campsite at dawn. Our plan was to cross Silver Pass early in the day before the snow deteriorated and conditions became unsafe.

Before we could ascend the pass we had to lose elevation. Our immediate goal was Tully Hole, far below us in the Cascade Valley. We took the quick and fun way down—using our ice axes as brakes to control our speed, we glissaded down the slope by sliding on our fannies. We howled with care-free delight as we raced downward. Soon we arrived at the junction of Fish and Cascade Creeks. While standing on the edge of the creek, I remembered the ordeal that Orland Bartholomew had experienced here.

Bart was crossing the river on a snow bridge when it collapsed, sending him plunging into the icy water. He struggled to pull himself out. Time mattered; if he didn't get warm fast, hypothermia would kill him. His hands were so numb he could barely gather a pile of twigs. He needed a windbreak to get a fire going. Bart pulled his wet tent out from his drenched pack, crawled inside and started a small fire in his frying pan. To avoid burning his shelter, he dumped the fire outside onto a mound of dry kindling. Next he built a lean-to from tree branches. From this improvised structure, he periodically added fuel to the campfire to dry his gear. Only his down coat, which also served as his sleeping bag, remained damp for the rest of his trip.

Ken and I didn't have any trouble crossing the river here. We strapped our climbing skins, canvas strips with artificial mohair, onto the bottom of our skis to help us ascend up the steep slope on the other side of Cascade Valley. Just below Silver Pass we were surprised to see five pairs of ski tracks. They led up towards the gap at 10,700 feet. Later as we approached the top, a sickening feeling rose up from my gut. *Something terrible is going to happen on this trip,* I heard my inner voice warn.

I felt it deeply. Yet I had no idea what might actually happen or when and where it might occur. I only had a firm sense that something dreadful lay ahead during our trip. The awful notion persisted off and on throughout the day. I didn't know how to acknowledge or respond to this perceived premonition. Since I couldn't decipher if it was intuition or just fear, I tried to dismiss it. I told myself that Ken would think I was crazy. It just wasn't logical to abandon our trip based on a gut feeling. In hindsight, I wished I had listened to it. There is wisdom in paying attention to the inner knowing of a gut feeling.

As we skied upwards I was occasionally distracted by the magnificent views. The peaks of Mount Ritter, Banner and Isaac Walton dominated the skyline in the distance. Climbing up to Silver Pass turned out to be a cinch. The small cornice that draped over most of the ridgeline was easily avoided by ascending the pass on the other end. We had lunch on the summit. It was the perfect place to commemorate John Muir's birthday. Here on April 21st, we celebrated his legacy of wild places with a piece of chocolate. We had only been on the trail for seven days and already we had traveled nearly a third of the route.

Ideal snow conditions made for excellent skiing conditions on the south side of the pass. We enjoyed a long downhill run before glissading a short but steep section to Silver Pass Creek. By the time we reached the bottom our spirits were soaring.

Soon the ski tracks that we had been following changed from five sets to four. Instead of skiing, the fifth person walked. He post-holed through the snow by sinking deeply with each step. We wondered why he wasn't skiing. Was he hurt or was there another problem? Farther on we came upon the group's campsite. Their fire pit was filled with partially burnt trash and charcoaled tree limbs. We were disgusted with their litter but happy that the skiers' tracks headed west and out of the mountains.

Like us, these winter campers were drawn to the open water near Pocket Meadow. In some places along the river there was no snow at all. We were delighted to camp on dry, bare ground. The night was luxuriously warm. In the surrounding forest we found the carcass and loose quills of a porcupine. Coyote tracks told the rest of the story.

In the morning Ken went down to Mono Creek to fill our water bottles. As he approached the bank, he slipped on an icy rock and fell in the creek. His leather boots and his wool socks were drenched. It was a minor inconvenience but in different conditions, it could have been a disaster with serious consequences.

The spring snowpack was melting rapidly. It was turning the North Fork of Mono Creek into a wide, raging river. The fast-moving water was treacherous. It gurgled, roared and rushed all over the bottom of the valley. It was critical for us to find the bridge over this stream. Without even a search, Ken led us right to the wooden bridge indicated on the map. I was always impressed with his backcountry navigation skills. Ken was an expert at getting around in the mountains. With a map and compass, he consistently located the correct route even if we were in a dense forest with a thick fog.

Variable snow conditions were a greater test. To cope with the softening snow, we departed from our campsite early each morning. This allowed us to minimize skiing on the unforgiving mash-potato snow that developed in the afternoons. If we started too early though, the snow would be hard-packed and icy.

Slippery snow was a problem when we ascended the north side of Bear Ridge. The incline was very steep—too steep to ascend with skis cloaked in climbing skins and too icy to walk unaided with just boots and poles. Ken led the way. He kicked steps into the frozen snow with his now wet and not so sturdy ski boots. He created a line of toe dents that went straight up the slope for 2,500 feet. Soon our calf muscles ached from the toil.

While climbing upwards, the shoulder strap on Ken's pack suddenly tore apart and pulled the weight of his rucksack away from his back. He could barely keep his balance; he teetered back and forth on precarious and slippery footholds. I kicked steps into the snow until I reached his side. Then I delicately removed a large safety pin from the exterior of his pack and pinned the torn strap together. I wasn't sure how long it would hold, but it secured the strap until we could repair it. Kicking into the hard slope also took a toll on our insulated overboots. By the end of the day they were tattered and starting to fall apart.

The dicey ascent consumed our attention and forced us to proceed at a snail's pace. For three grueling hours we kicked, panted and pulled ourselves upwards. As we climbed Bear Ridge, junipers, western white pines and lodgepole pines gave way to firs and mountain hemlocks. Later while skiing through the forest near Bear Creek, we were serenaded by the cries of coyotes and the drumming of grouse.

Throughout the day we crossed one slope after another laden with avalanche debris: hunks of frozen snow, four to eighteen inches high. It was slow and tedious to ski between them. We were grateful that the mountains had shed their loads long before our arrival. After traversing the expansive Marie Lakes Basin, we climbed up to Selden Pass. The view of Seven Gables Peak dominating the horizon uplifted us. Steep snowy gullies separated sharp rocky ridges that pointed towards the summit. As our day unfolded, clouds gathered in the afternoon sky. Their shadows softened the intense light radiating from the sun and snow.

We skied onward until dusk. Although we had traveled eighteen miles that day, we still didn't reach our goal of Blaney Meadows. Instead, we camped up high in a small clump of trees near Sallie Keyes Lake. After dinner we congratulated ourselves. Thus far, we had traveled ninety-nine miles on skis. Before sleeping we were graced with a good omen. A bright silver star streaked across the jet-black sky between two silhouetted peaks. My only wish was for a safe and happy trip.

That night the temperature dropped to 12 degrees. Our tent was frosty in the morning and the snow was still rock-hard when we departed from camp. Without metal edges on our narrow skis, it was impossible to glide across the super-frozen landscape. Instead we walked up a steep slope just south of the lake. Ken was ahead of me carrying his skis in his hand when he slipped suddenly on the icy snow.

"*No!*" he bellowed.

His grip loosened. The skis fell out from his hand and slid down the slope like quick lightening. They whizzed down the white mountainside and disappeared into the dense forest hundreds of feet below us. We were worried; what if we didn't find them here in the middle of nowhere?

Once in the trees, we began a frenzied search. A few minutes later, I spotted something yellow in the snow. It was the tip of one of Ken's Epoke skis. The second ski was still missing. Farther down, we found it lodged against a tree trunk. We had learned our lesson; before continuing our descent, we lashed our skis to the sides of our packs.

Snow conditions were always in flux. They varied with the time of day, altitude and slope exposure. By the time we reached the valley floor, the snowpack was wet and patchy. Conditions were imperfect for any mode of travel. On this day we walked more than we skied; it was easier than taking our skis off and on every hundred yards.

Farther on we encountered bare ground. For the first time, the John Muir Trail was actually visible beneath our feet. For a short distance we no longer traced an invisible trail buried under a white mantle. Spring had arrived at the lower elevations. The air was thick with the rich scent of recently unveiled soil.

The trail became damp, then soggy, then water-logged. Water from melting snow pooled between the pines making it impossible to keep our boots dry. Sporadic snow drifts lingered in the shade. Each time we encountered a drift, we sank up to our knees. Then up ahead we saw something poking above the snow. It was a wooden trail sign. It was the first one we had seen on our journey.

Up ahead we got our first glimpse into the lower portion of Piute Canyon. The steep and narrow gorge was the only passageway to our second supply cache. A cornice on Piute Pass had prevented us from depositing our food barrel in Hutchinson Meadow a few weeks earlier. Now it was about twenty-five miles out of our way. A shorter but dicey alternative was to travel roughly sixteen miles through the gorge and rejoin the John Muir Trail on the other side of Alpine Col. Both detours were lengthy and still required us to traverse Piute Canyon at least once.

We were at a crucial decision point. Discouraged by the existing snow conditions and abrupt terrain, we sat on the large wooden bridge over Piute Creek. The river raged below us, engorged with spring runoff. Meltwater from previous rain storms had flowed over the bridge a few weeks earlier leaving a striation of dirt, seven feet high, in the snow along the riverbank. We ate lunch on the bridge and then consulted the map and then with each other.

"What do you think we should do?" Ken asked.

I paused for a long time. I wasn't sure if we could continue our rapid pace. Snow conditions were unpredictable and the topography above us was very steep. There was a risk of running out of supplies if we skipped our second cache. On the other hand, existing snow conditions could make Piute Canyon downright dangerous and the cornice on the pass was also problematic.

"I don't like the looks of the gorge from here. It just doesn't feel right to me," I responded.

"Do you think we could travel greater distances for a few days to make our food last until we reach our third cache?" Ken asked.

"I don't know. It seems like the safest choice is to continue without our second food barrel. Let's skip it and retrieve it next fall."

Now we were committed. Long arduous days lay ahead on a limited food supply. Before leaving the Sierra National Forest, we took our picture next to an oversized, wooden backcountry sign. Then we skied into Kings Canyon National Park. A few miles later we were astonished to encounter two skiers. The men were skiing northwest en route to Florence Lake. Recently they had crossed Jigsaw, Bishop and Muir Passes, the same passes that separated us from our third cache. We exchanged valuable information on route and avalanche conditions before going our separate ways.

Farther on a torrent of snow had covered an entire mountainside with broken trees and hunks of snow. It was both fatiguing and irksome to pick our way across the slope on skis. We encountered more and more old avalanche debris as we continued along another branch of the San Joaquin River. The piled-up snow created dense and solid snow bridges. This allowed us to safely cross back and forth across the large river.

We skied well into the evening until we reached Evolution Creek. I went to sleep, eager for the next day's excursion through the Evolution Basin.

4

GLIDING THROUGH EVOLUTION

Our dwindling food supply motivated us to ski even greater distances over the next few days. We were up by 4:30 a.m. to maximize our use of daylight. A dusting of snow had fallen during the night making for a gelid morning. Even while skiing, I wore long underwear, wool pants, and a turtleneck and fleece coat to keep warm.

The sublime landscape came to life when the sun finally peeked through the clouds. We paused at Evolution Creek to marvel at the hoarfrost sparkling on the surface of the snow, the shimmering sunlight reflected in the water, and the icicles hanging over the riverbank. As the day progressed, clouds evaporated into an azure sky giving us the gift of warm sunshine and the curse of softening snow.

A thousand foot climb brought us past Hermit Peak and into the mountain sanctuary of the Evolution Basin. The landscape was surreal—white meadows and frozen lakes rimmed with grey monolithic peaks. The scenery here exceeded my wildest dreams. It evoked an inner response of *Oh, my God!* It was as beautiful and inspiring as any church or temple. Not surprisingly, John Muir once referred to this mountain range as a "cathedral of worship."

Muir inspired many mountain lovers, including Theodore Solomons who explored and mapped much of the High Sierra. He was the visionary behind the creation of the John Muir Trail. In 1895 Solomons named the peaks in the Evolution Basin. Here the mountains are as magnificent as the theories, scientists, and philosophers for whom they were named: Darwin who developed the theory of evolution; Mendel the father of genetics; Huxley a brilliant philosopher and writer, nominated multiple times for a Nobel Prize in Literature; and Spencer the scientist who first used the term "survival of the fittest."

Soon our peace was shattered near Sapphire Lake. A loud popping sound broke the silence like a shotgun fired in the middle of the night. An instant later, snow slid rapidly down a large rock face. I reacted almost simultaneously. As I turned toward the source of the noise, adrenaline rushed through my blood stream. My blood pressure spiked at the sight of a relatively small avalanche crashing down the mountainside just above and beyond where we had eaten a snack a few minutes earlier. The threat of avalanches continued to increase throughout the day as the sun rose higher into the sky.

After enjoying a steady and gentle climb past Wanda Lake, named after one of John Muir's daughters, we skied toward Muir Pass. There was a sense of timeless simplicity on the 12,000-foot plateau. A cobalt sky contrasted with the bright snow-covered ground. Solitude prevailed in the vast white space above treeline. Except for the swooshing of skis gliding across the snow, the beating of my heart, and the inhaling and exhaling of air, it was utterly quiet. The deep silence penetrated into the depths of my being. I felt like I had merged with the landscape, as if there were no distinction between myself and the surrounding terrain. We were simply one.

Without a single tree in sight there was no shade to be found. Ironically in this frozen landscape, heat exhaustion was a greater concern than hypothermia. We sweated profusely under our heavy loads as we skied up towards a circular stone shelter on Muir Pass. The charming structure stood out like a lonely sentinel in the middle of the white tableland.

After reading the metal plaque dedicated to John Muir next to the doorway, we went inside. There we found several hand-written notes. One read: *March 11–1982, four feet of snow in the last 36 hours. Got to get out of here—God, be with us. May we make it out alive.* Another read: *April 17—skiing the Muir Trail, left from Mammoth, hope to make Whitney in six days; then return to do the Yosemite to Mammoth stretch due to avalanche hazards.*

The notes were alarming. With the Sierra snowpack now at 225 percent above normal, we had more reason to be concerned about avalanches than usual. The risk would have been even greater if we had started our trip a month earlier as originally planned. Now we felt blessed by the obstacles that had delayed our departure. Le Conte Canyon poses a variety of risks for winter travelers. This was equally true for Orland Bartholomew during the winter of 1929.

Bart frequently slipped on steep slushy snow as he traversed up the eight-mile gorge. In other places the snowpack collapsed beneath his feet. Each time this happened he was afraid of breaking a ski or possibly a bone. These snow conditions slowed him down, taxed his energy and increased his exposure to avalanches. His anxiety increased each time he heard the thunderous echoes of snow slides hurtling down nearby mountainsides.

We too worried about what lay ahead. Now it was our turn to pass though the steep glacially carved valley. Here, our psyches seemed to reflect the landscape around us. The expansive plateau north of Muir Pass was like traveling through an open world where anything was possible. But Le Conte Canyon was imposing and confining. Its rugged topography made us fearful. With trepidation, we descended into the headwaters of the South Fork of the Kings River.

For the next two and half hours we skied several thousand feet down through the gorge. Conditions were nearly perfect. Below the pass, an ultra-thin, delicate film of ice known as *firnspeigel* floated slightly above the snowpack like gossamer. It was radiantly bright. Covering the entire slope, it reflected the sun like a giant frail mirror. The gauzy yet luminous layer of snow was not only beautiful to look at, it was easy for our skinny skis to cut through. For the moment, we were joyful and carefree. We delighted in carving thin lines and graceful curves into the snowpack.

Dramatic cliffs lined both sides of the valley past Helen Lake, named for John Muir's other daughter. We traversed a series of steep slopes covered with a deep mantle of snow. Black Giant Peak loomed above and behind us like a menacing monster. Its dark, metamorphic rock gave the mountain an ominous appearance.

Later in the day we unknowingly skied across a hidden convex slab of granite. Meltwater leaking from under the snow had lubricated the interface of stone and snow. One moment the snowpack was intact and a second later a fracture line tore across the slope. Alarmed and wide-eyed, we watched the snow peel apart. A slide was imminent. There was no time to hesitate. We quickly escaped into the safe haven of a nearby gully lined with trees.

Relief didn't last long. Farther down the canyon we heard a deafening *crack, pop* and *boom!* We paused for a split second, looking around to determine if we needed to ski like hell or if we could relax and watch the show. Farther up the valley, the avalanche ripped down the side of Langille Peak. The slide appeared insignificant only because it was far away and high on the mountainside.

Travel down the rest of the canyon was slow and annoying. Great care was required to cross slopes punctuated with broken branches and old lumps of avalanched snow. Our skis warped and bent as they bridged the gap between the blocks of ice. Sometimes it was better to remove our skis and just walk.

Avalanches and rock fall were reminders that the mountains were in a constant state of flux. We felt insignificant, like tiny specks in a larger universe. We were awed by the dreamy white landscape and humbled at the same time.

While skiing merrily along in an open glade of subalpine trees, I was suddenly jerked from behind. The next moment I was lying flat on my back, draped over my backpack, looking straight up into the sky. Bewildered, I got up and looked around. I could only move by going uphill. Tracing my ski tracks, I discovered the problem. The frayed edges of the red avalanche cord that trailed behind me, had wrapped around the branch of a small tree. Like a leash, it stopped me right in my tracks. I uncoiled the line from the snagged branch and then skied onward.

In theory, avalanche cords float to the snow's surface during a snow slide to help locate a victim buried beneath the snow. We hoped we would never test their effectiveness; the likelihood of surviving an avalanche was slim to none.

It was dusk when we reached the ranger cabin at the bottom of the gorge. For a moment, I daydreamed about working here during the summer. The scenery was even grander than the backcountry patrol cabin that I had staffed a few years earlier in Glacier National Park. Both places had their unique attributes. While the Sierras were crowded with hikers, grizzly bears and isolation prevailed in Glacier.

That night we camped on a triangular piece of land just above the confluence of Dusy Creek and the Kings River. The streams were bloated with snowmelt. This water, the lifeblood of Earth, was also part of my vitality and sustenance. Besides carving deep canyons as it raced downhill, it refreshed me with the cool rush of negative ions. The water's gurgling intonation calmed my nerves and lulled us to sleep after thirteen hours of skiing.

Author near Dusy Basin (left), Citadel Peak (right)

The next day we pushed onward at the crack of dawn. Using climbing skins we ascended a steep glacial bench that led us to upper Dusy Basin. Here we took a long break. I stared with disbelief at the scene before me. Never before had I experienced such profound beauty. Across the valley countless granite walls rose straight out of a sea of snow and into the crystal blue sky. From here, the backcountry of Kings Canyon National Park is a labyrinth of alpine canyons. Each hanging valley was enticing. During our break I fantasized about wandering aimlessly from one gorge to the next.

I felt as if I had arrived at the top of the world. The uplifting scenery gave us the urge to sing and dance, but instead we filled the big mountain spaces with shouts of joy and laughter. The echoes bounced back and forth across the valley. It was a moment of pure ecstasy.

Soon we skied on. The jagged crest of the Palisade Range dominated the skyline just east of us. Higher into Dusy Basin we spotted an orange tent in the distance. We were now close to Bishop Pass, an easy access point for winter campers to explore the High Sierra. Here, coyote tracks were rampant in the snow. Rosy Finches, small alpine birds, flitted about looking for hapless insects chilled by the snow. To our surprise, ants were crawling at 12,000 feet on the warm exposed rocks.

From Bishop Pass we had our first view of Jigsaw Pass. For a long time we stared at the two low points along the serrated ridge of the Inconsolable Range, a subrange just north of the Palisades. Which of the steep snow-filled gullies was the actual pass? It was critical for us to ascend the correct couloir so we could reach our third cache of food on the other side. With his map in hand, Ken pondered the question until the puzzle was solved.

Then we proceeded a short distance to the base of Jigsaw Pass. Before our ascent, we tied our skis onto the sides of our backpacks. Armed with ice axes and using our hands and knees, we scaled up the steep chute for 700 feet. Caution was needed to avoid catching the tips of our skis on the rocky gendarmes rising up on either side of us. It was difficult to climb up rocks and snow while wearing ski boots with protruding tips. In a few places, I could barely move up and over the ledges with my heavy backpack. At one place Ken helped me surmount a tricky section by giving me a small boost from behind.

The east side of the pass was gentle by comparison. Skiing down was easy until we arrived beneath the peaks of the Palisades. Here an expanse of thousands of "sun cups," each the size of a cereal bowl, covered our route. This uneven snow surface tends to form late in the season when the snow melts at different rates. Sun cups are dreadful to ski across. Our skis never touched their soft interiors and their hard, icy edges made it impossible to steer. As we glided across the cups' outer rims, our skis vibrated like jackhammers. By the end of the day, our bodies were jarred and nerve wracked from these small but continuous tremors.

As we lost elevation, the snow continued to change. Sun cups gave way to a large open field. Long blades of golden grass and short willows poked above the thinning white mantle. Traversing the slope was difficult. Chunks of ice from an old avalanche dotted the incline. Lower down, the snow was rotten, slushy and wet. Only the views made up for the difficult skiing conditions. We often stopped just to admire the silhouette of Temple Crag against the sapphire sky.

Farther down we encountered a lone telemark skier from Los Angeles. While chatting, he noticed our dried, cracked and bloody lips. He spontaneously dug into his day pack and generously offered us his spare chapstick. We were touched by his small act of kindness. The warm bright days required more chapstick than we had anticipated. My slightly soggy boots had also given me a minor case of trench foot.

Near Glacier Camp we took our skis off and hiked through intermittent snow and patches of dried grass. Our campsite at Big Pine Creek was a welcome reprieve from the wintry world high above us. Now that we were below 8,000 feet, the air was pungent. Our tent was surrounded by wild roses with pink blossoms, birch trees, and wild onions sprouting up through the soil. We spread our gear out to dry in the warm sunshine and walked around with bare feet.

Historic Glacier Lodge was a short walk away. Eager for a change in our cuisine, we bought a few treats at their tiny store. Over the next few days we savored the delicacies of bread, tuna, milk, juice and chocolate.

In the morning we stopped at Glacier Lodge to use their telephone. Before the trip, we had dropped our food cache here because the owners had assured us that we could use their phone upon our arrival. Nevertheless, the desk clerk informed us that their radio-phone was reserved only for life-threatening emergencies. Her proclamation was an unexpected blow and left us with no recourse; the proprietors were gone.

Now we were desperate for a phone to confirm our up-coming summer employment with the National Park Service. The next morning Ken hitchhiked to Big Pine, the closest town in the Owens Valley, to find a pay phone. Getting a ride down to Highway 395 was unlikely in April. Nonetheless, he walked down the road and disappeared for the rest of the day.

I spent most of the day around camp. The warm sunlight was perfect for lounging, washing and drying clothes, and repairing our tattered gear. Using fishing line for thread, I sewed our frayed over-booties and the shoulder strap on Ken's backpack. I also re-glued the ever-loosening metal plates that held our ski boots in their bindings. At two o'clock that afternoon I checked into Glacier Lodge.

With the exception of dark wooden beams that crisscrossed beneath the cathedral ceiling, the inn's old-world charm had lost its luster. Inside the air was stale and musty. The once elegant décor was now faded and outdated. The restaurant's threadbare upholstery matched the dusty velvet-like maroon and gold wallpaper. Instead of pictures of the Sierras, the walls displayed copies of paintings from the Alps.

I headed up the stairs and moved into our room. Shortly afterwards, Ken appeared. A fisherman had given him a ride to and from Big Pine.

"Guess who called our families to offers us jobs?" Ken asked.

"Who?"

"Mount Rainier National Park. They want me to return this summer. They also called your mom. She accepted a job on your behalf to work at the Paradise Visitor Center at Mount Rainier," he added with glee.

I was elated. Who wouldn't want to work in Paradise? Besides answering visitor questions, the job entailed leading nature walks beneath the glaciated peak in a subalpine meadow carpeted with wildflowers. The location was more appealing than returning to the desert at Colorado National Monument where I had worked the previous year. Now that my dream job was lined up for the summer and our expedition was going smoothly, my life seemed perfect.

Once our conversation ended, Ken and I went downstairs to pick up our supplies. After talking with the innkeepers, the couple retrieved our white plastic drum from their storage area. We felt smug to have skipped our second food cache without going hungry. Now with our third food barrel in hand, we had sufficient stock for the last leg of our journey. Before dinner we reorganized our things for the next day's departure.

Classical music played quietly in the background as we dined on a sumptuous meal. Compared to the freeze-dried food we had been eating, trout, fresh vegetables and ice cream were delicacies. Ken and I felt like outsiders, both literally and figuratively. We had grown used to living alone in the wilderness. Now we were in a fancy hotel. We could barely stand the noisy chatter coming from a large group at an adjacent table. They had come from Bishop to celebrate a special occasion over an evening meal.

Our stay at Glacier Lodge was pricey, but it enabled us to store our cache here. Since we were the only overnight guests, we were completely doted on by the owners. The next morning they treated us with hot tea, pancakes and country-style potatoes. We gladly indulged in the abundance of carbohydrates—we were skinny and needed the calories to climb back into the mountains.

We departed from the inn at mid-morning. Melting water rushed downhill in rivulets beneath the snow. It was too patchy and soggy to ski. Instead, we hopped from rock to rock and bush to bush, hoping to keep our boots reasonably dry. Eventually we encountered a gully with enough consistent snow for skiing.

We stopped in the afternoon at Brainard Lake so we could be positioned for crossing South Fork Pass early the next morning. Our 3,000-foot climb brought us back into the high country where everything was still frozen. The exertion made us thirsty. I pulled our empty bottles out from my pack while Ken unstrapped his ice ax from the outside of his rucksack. With the blade of his ax, he sliced through the ice. With each strike on the lake's frozen surface, small crystalline chips flew into the air and glinted in the sunlight. The repetitive sound of *chop-chop-chop* echoed off the nearby pinnacles. Slowly a hole appeared in the blue ice.

We dipped our bottles in and quenched our thirst.

A large rocky island rose out of the frozen lake, beckoning us to make camp on its dry surface. For the remainder of the day we reveled in relaxation, enveloped by the luxurious warmth of sunshine from above and radiant heat from the rock below us.

The Palisades were an imposing fortress with a sinuous and precipitous wall embellished by jagged stony pillars. I longed for a glimpse of this magical kingdom in summer when the riches of gleaming alpine glaciers and turquoise lakes were no longer hidden from view. For now, I focused my eyes on Norman Clyde Peak towering above us and Mount Alice on the distant horizon. The latter peak made me think of my mother who shares the same name.

While lying idle, we listened to the sounds of the promise of spring. The earth was coming alive; bird songs filled the air and melting water trickled below us. More jarring was the rumble of rocks falling from the peaks when the sun loosened their frozen joints

I iced my ailing knee with a snowball while Ken pranced about the rocks with bottled-up energy. It was still early afternoon. We had nothing to do. We couldn't ski any farther because we had to be strategically placed for the next day's climb. Once Ken settled down, we conversed about the future.

"What would you think about ending our trip on the west side of the Sierras?" he asked.

His question caught me off-guard. Wasn't skiing the John Muir Trail enough for this trip?

He continued, "We could climb Mount Whitney and then ski the High Route over Milestone Pass. Then we could finish our trip at Lodgepole on the west side of Sequoia National Park."

"Let's see how our energy and food resources are then. We can make a decision at that point." I answered.

Then I changed the subject. Talking about spending the summer at Mount Rainier was more appealing. I was excited about working in the same national park as Ken. But it wasn't to be. Instead, I spent the summer lying in my mother's bed under her loving-care.

5

BEYOND THE PALISADES

A warm raging wind blew throughout the night. It roared down from the Sierra Crest through the back window of our tent, over our sleeping bags, and out our partially opened tent door. Shortly after sunrise we skied into the headwind towards South Fork Pass. I was filled with apprehension; our guidebook described the route as a steep strenuous climb that required a rope.

To my relief, our ascent was uneventful. It was too steep to ski, but a rope was unnecessary. The snow's texture was ideal. We surmounted the couloir with the aid of ice axes and spiked metal crampons strapped onto our boots. After reaching the summit we glissaded down the other side.

Once the terrain was suitable for skiing, we etched elegant S-shaped curves across a broad white valley. The tempo changed when Palisade Lake came into view below us. The snow had turned into an icy sheet. Ken was skiing ahead of me when a loud echo rose up from below.

"No, no, noooooooo!"

I looked down to see what was happening—Ken was on his belly, sliding helplessly down the slippery incline. One of his skis was airborne. Hoping to control his rapid descent, he dug his ski poles into the hard snow. The momentum pulled the poles out from his hands and sent them tumbling downward. In a desperate attempt to stop himself, he dug his fingers and elbows into the slope. Ken slid for several hundred feet. He finally came to a stop near a small cluster of short trees. He appeared unhurt.

We yelled back and forth to each other but our words were undecipherable. Only echoes bounced off the peaks. To understand each other, we took turns waiting for each reverberation to subside before answering. I moved cautiously, side-stepping downwards. After retrieving Ken's poles, I continued towards him. Then I glissaded down the slope with my ice ax to reach him.

Ken was completely undaunted by his long uncontrolled slide. He had already found his missing ski lodged against a stunted subalpine tree. While searching for it, he spooked a gigantic wild dog out of the grove. It was probably just a coyote; wolves no longer roam the Sierras. They were thought to be extinct even during Orland Bartholomew's winter odyssey back in 1929. Nevertheless, Bart had reason to believe otherwise; he spotted wolf tracks on the north side of Mather Pass and he heard their distinctive howls elsewhere on his trip.

Shortly after Ken repaired his ski binding with a pair of pliers, we heard male voices in the distance. Two men were skiing down towards us from Mather Pass. I was a bit jealous that they were traveling on wide skis with metal edges. They informed us that they were skiing the John Muir Trail but in the opposite direction. We also learned that they were friends with Lisa, the desk clerk back at Tamarack Lodge in Mammoth Lakes. They also worked as seasonal rangers. When we introduced ourselves, Ken immediately recognized the name of one of the skiers: John Dollie Mollie was a legend in National Park Service circles. As a climbing ranger at Mount Rainier he had played an important role in many epic search and rescues on the mountain. His buddy worked at North Cascades National Park.

This was the perfect place for the unlikely encounter of adventurous rangers. Mather Pass, looming just above us, was named for Stephen Mather, the first director of the National Park Service. For a brief moment in the vast, rugged and wintry backcountry of Kings Canyon National Park, we weren't alone. In the middle of nowhere our paths crossed with two strangers with similar life experiences. After a few minutes of camaraderie we parted ways.

The stiff climb up to Mather Pass made us hot and sweaty. The 14,000-foot summits of the Palisade Range were now far behind us. Ahead of us, the wind-swept mountains were streaked with geologic veins pigmented in gold, maroon and green.

After lunch we took our picture at the top of Mather Pass in the same place where Bart had made his self-portrait fifty-three years earlier. Our descent was gratifying. A long glissade brought us to Upper Basin. From there, we strapped on our skis for a mellow ski run down to another branch of the Kings River.

Our rhythmic movement gained momentum through the day. Again, it was too early to stop when we reached the campsite on our itinerary. The endless expanse of white terrain was mesmerizing as we glided onward. As long as there was daylight, we just kept on skiing.

Near Lake Marjorie, the reflecting sunlight lit up our ski tracks. They resembled silver filaments woven into a white blanket. Now that we were farther south, the snowpack was slightly thinner, more stable and less prone to avalanches.

Author on Pinchot Pass

By early evening we had crossed our third 12,000-foot pass for the day. The view from Pinchot Pass was stunning. Clouds hovered in the distant valleys and around Mount Clarence King, named for the famous geologic explorer. Our rapid pace ended on the far side of the pass. Snow conditions became variable again. Late afternoon shadows had transformed the snow into a slippery, frozen crust. Elsewhere in the sunlight, rotten snow prevailed. It frequently collapsed beneath our feet, plunging us into a hip-deep hole. Each time we sank downward we cursed the warm rocks concealed by the snowpack.

As evening approached our frustration gave way to enchantment. Across the valley ribbons of thin, pink-tinted clouds were suspended in the sky. Below us, Woods Creek was enveloped in a localized fog. We skied onward hoping to find open water. Time was of the essence. Blue shadows crept slowly across the canyon signaling the coming of twilight.

We stopped for the night as soon as we reached the first open creek. While lying on his belly, Ken carefully inched his way across a snow bridge. He dipped our plastic bottles tied onto his ski pole with a bandana, into the water and waited patiently for the liquid to trickle inside.

Just before dark we set up our tent in a small grove of subalpine trees. After a full day above treeline the forest was a welcoming haven. It was comforting to be surrounded by something other than sterile snow. The trees emitted a sweet tranquilizing aroma and their green branches protected our camp from the cold breeze like a mother embracing her child. Completely exhausted, we gobbled up our dinner and fell into a deep sleep.

Grey skies the next morning offered a break from the usual brightness. The canyon leading up to Rae Lakes was filled with patchy snow making it easier to walk then ski. Progress was slow. We traversed the gorge by stepping on rocks and balancing precariously on the thin branches of manzanita bushes. Occasionally as we stepped from one branch to another, a stem would bounce back and smack us in the face. Nonetheless, we delighted in their crimson-colored bark. It was the only vivid color in our mostly white world.

The surrounding summits were partially obscured by fog. Swirling clouds presented only fleeting glimpses of Mount Clarence King, Mount Gould and Fin Dome. Below us, red and black specks decorated the snow. Even at 10,000 feet, lady bugs were everywhere now that it was spring. Before slurping down a handful of slush to quench our thirst, we always checked for bugs.

The broad stone monolith of Painted Lady towered over our tent that night. Its sheer face was ornamented with veins of brilliantly colored minerals. After dinner we calculated our mileage: we had skied 175 miles. Coyotes sang in the distance as dusk faded into darkness.

The next day we discovered an easy passage up Glen Pass. The ascent was very steep, but the effort was minimal because someone before us had created a narrow staircase by kicking toe indents all the way to the 12,000-foot summit. Compared to Orland Bartholomew's climb up Glen Pass, our ascent was uneventful.

Bart was absorbed in following the tracks of a wolverine that led up and over the divide. These fierce creatures were scarce in the Sierras even in 1929. Drawing from his expertise as a naturalist and his trapping and surveying experience, Bart was convinced that the footprints belonged to a wolverine. As he continued towards Glen Pass he also encountered wolf tracks. He was familiar with them from his previous trips in Alaska.

Bart stopped to rest 300 feet below the top. He had a foreboding feeling about the slope above him. It was covered with fresh snow. A few minutes later a cracking sound broke the quietude. A torrent of snow had released near the summit and was racing towards him. A second later Bart was dragged down the mountainside. Death seemed imminent. He swam frantically through the snow to keep from being buried alive. Luckily, he was cast aside from the snow slide. In a dazed state, Bart watched the avalanche continue downslope without him. Miraculously, he was uninjured. The only casualty was a strap torn from his ski pole. After the incident, he resumed his northbound journey.

Ken and I were fortunate to have great snow conditions on both sides of Glen Pass. After descending into a steep-walled glacial cirque, we turned the corner and traversed into the basin above Charlotte Lake. A smooth ski run took us all the way down to Bullfrog Lake.

Over the course of many ski trips, I had developed a strong heart-connection to Bullfrog Lake. Each visit rekindled a special memory. The first time I camped here in the winter, I woke up in the middle of the night with an urge to pee. First, I had to psyche myself up. It took some moxie to wiggle out of my toasty, down-filled cocoon and out into the wintry air, but lying awake with a full bladder was even worse.

Soon the silent night gave way to the sound of zippers. First, unzipping my sleeping bag and then the tent. I donned a down coat over my long underwear and pulled nylon stuff sacks over my down booties to keep them dry. Then I re-zipped everything to keep the frigid air from invading our shelter. Next I scurried outside. To avoid sinking I conducted my business behind our tent on a compacted platform of snow.

Entranced by what I experienced, I quickly fell under the spell of nighttime in the wilderness. It was unfathomably quiet in the dark night. I actually heard the "sounds of silence." It was a vast, deep stillness full of faint murmurs echoing within the quietude. It's something that can't really be described. It was such a wonderful experience that over the ensuing years, I learned how to intentionally tune into this peacefulness. It can be found both inside and outside of oneself. This stillness has to be listened for, but it's always present even in the chaos of everyday life.

Standing under a jet-black canopy illuminated only by the constellations, was awe-inspiring. The sublime beauty of a greater universe touched me. I felt connected to something bigger; the cosmos dwelled both inside and beyond myself. It was as if nothing and everything existed simultaneously.

For a moment, I was enraptured by these memories of winter camping at Bullfrog Lake. A few seconds later our situation brought me back to our present reality. We still had many miles to go to position ourselves to cross Forester Pass. We rested at Bullfrog Lake only long enough to claim our last cache of food. We easily located the twisted old tree that held our plastic barrel of supplies. Ken climbed into the branches, unlashed the drum and lowered it to me. Everything appeared in order. We transferred the food and fuel into our packs. Then we sealed the empty drum with duct tape and strapped it back into the tree. Ken would return the next autumn to retrieve it along with the abandoned cache near Piute Pass.

Just before leaving I filled our water bottles at the lake's outlet. I cursed when I realized that the strap on my ski pole had fallen off. It disappeared into the water and under the ice before I could retrieve it.

Another typical afternoon unfolded. The incline between Bullfrog Lake and Vidette Meadows was steep and slushy. One moment we were on top of the snow and the next moment the snow collapsed beneath our weight. Soon more avalanche debris confronted us. Our skis bent slightly whenever we made the transition between the large chunks of frozen snow. I often worried about cracking a ski—and then it happened.

"Oh, shit!" Ken yelled.

His ski had just broken. It was unusable. Ken pulled his rucksack off and rummaged through it to find his repair kit. We had an emergency ski tip with us, but it was useless for this situation. The ski's fracture was too far from the tip; it was just above the binding. A paper-thin layer of fiberglass on the underside of the ski was the only thing that held it together.

Now we needed to be creative and resourceful—we still had forty miles left to complete our journey. Right on the spot we performed emergency surgery on the ski. Using his ice ax, Ken split apart the two pieces of our metal pot grippers. These became splints. We put them over the ski's fracture line and wrapped them with white medical tape. As a final touch, we used paraffin wax on the bottom of the ski to make the tape slick enough to slide across the snow. To our amazement, it worked. The ski was now serviceable, though not ideal.

We now pondered which pieces of our equipment would go next. Already we had loose bails on some of our ski bindings, a loose boot plate requiring frequent repairs with epoxy glue, and two pairs of overboots now beyond use. Our cookware and fuel containers were severely dented, our avalanche cords were extremely frayed, and our thermometer and one headlamp were cracked. We were missing one ski pole strap, and the shoulder strap on Ken's backpack was sewn together with fishing line. To top it off, we had soggy ski boots.

Ken with his ski. The repair site is visible above the arrow

We persevered nonetheless. We continued downstream to our camping spot near Bubb's Creek. As we crawled into our shelter, the evening light tinted nearby Center Peak with pink alpenglow.

6

CROSSING THE GREAT DIVIDE

Forester Pass weighed heavily on my mind throughout the night. Separating the major watersheds of the Kings and Kern River Valleys, it was the last and most challenging pass on the John Muir Trail. We had seen both sides of the divide on previous ski trips, but we weren't sure if current snow conditions would allow us to bypass the rocky band on its south side to reach the valley below. These cliffs had also been problematic during the trail's construction—dynamite was required to blast through the escarpment.

If Forester Pass proved impassable there were less desirable alternatives. We could retrace our steps up to Bubb's Creek, go east into Center Basin, and then over Junction Pass. Besides adding mileage, this route involved crossing another highpoint, Shepherd Pass, to access the Kern Plateau.

We could also cross the divide over Harrison Pass, a shorter but unfamiliar route farther west. This was the pass that Orland Bartholomew crossed by chopping his way through a cornice. For this reason Harrison Pass lacked appeal. It didn't seem like a realistic option.

The morning was still cold when we departed. With the sun hidden behind the clouds, the north side of the divide was cloaked in shadow. We skied upwards into a stiff wind interspersed with strong gusts. We ascended through the snowy terrain by using climbing skins on the bottom of our skinny skis.

The approach to Forester Pass was long, steady and steep. With the exception of a few black-rocked peaks on either side of us, everything was white. Before pushing to the top, we stopped to refuel ourselves with peanut M&M's and water mixed with powdered electrolytes.

Our timing was spot-on. The snow wasn't too soft or too frozen. This made the ascent easier than expected. A few old ski tracks traversing the slope towards the summit helped too. The wind had scoured around the once compressed tracks, leaving slightly elevated lines on the snow's surface. These narrow ledges of wind-beaten snow enabled us to dig the edges of our skis deeper into the incline as we climbed uphill.

Near the summit, the wind shifted direction. The change caught our attention because it didn't conform to the prevailing weather patterns. Instead a steady wind blew from the east, gathering dark cumulous clouds over the Sierra Crest.

A small grey sign sticking out above the snow greeted us on the summit. Its peeling red letters inscribed in metal read: "Forester Pass, 13,200 feet. Entering Sequoia National Park." Here we stood on the boundary between Kings Canyon and Sequoia National Parks. There were no entrance fees or crowds. Our national park experience was just how we wanted it—wild, scenic and full of solitude.

The views were breathtaking. With the exception of Mount Whitney, the mountains in the distance looked like snowy dwarfs. In just one or two more days we would complete our journey. That was our plan anyway. While atop the highest pass, I marveled at how acclimatized I was to the altitude and how I had reached the pinnacle of my strength and fitness.

A curious blue bird graced us with a brief visit just after we sat down for a break. He didn't beg for food, but he looked at us a long time before flying onward. Perhaps he sensed that something wasn't right with our food. I nearly gagged when I took my first bite of lunch. Our crackers, cheese, dried fruit and nuts all tasted like gasoline. For a few minutes we were baffled by the odd taste. Then we realized what had happened. Some of our food had absorbed vaporized gas fumes from the cylinder of fuel that had been stored in our food cache. Fortunately, our other provisions were uncontaminated.

Orland Bartholomew had a similar problem on his trip—his food was inadvertently tainted by the perfumed scents in his soap. In his journal he described eating "hot cakes de lilac."

After lunch we continued onward. The south side of the pass was crowned by an old cornice. We were relieved to discover that most of it had already melted away. We scrambled easily around it, entered the steep couloir and descended straight down the chute by plunging our feet and ice axes into the snow. The bottom of the gully brought us to the vast white tableland of the Kern Plateau.

Summit and south side of Forester Pass

It was easy cruising from here; skiing was fast and effortless with good snow and gentle terrain. We quickly zipped down to the trees just above Tyndall Creek. Since it was still early afternoon we skied onward, once again passing another campsite scheduled on our itinerary.

The 12,000-foot notch between Tyndall and Tawny Points brought us into the Wright Lakes Basin. We were surrounded by views of Mounts Trojan, Hale and Young. The snow quickly changed with the loss of elevation. Once we were in the Wallace Creek drainage we were devoured again by a series of rotten snow pits. Our frustration was tempered only by the beauty of perfectly spaced groves of foxtail pines. Their amber-colored limbs and twisted trunks were sculpted by cold winter winds and the passage of time. Sap beneath the weathered bark released an aroma reminiscent of root beer in the warm afternoon sunlight.

We continued along the flanks of Mount Young towards Crabtree Meadows. Towering 4,000 feet above us was Mount Whitney—the culminating prize of our winter journey.

Mount Whitney had also beckoned Orland Bartholomew. By the late 1920s no one had made a successful winter ascent of the peak. Bart confirmed this by researching Sierra Club records and asking the famous Sierra mountaineer, Norman Clyde. Bart was determined to be the first. He attempted Mount Whitney several times during his trip only to be turned around by winter storms.

Like us, he planned to ascend the mountain via a maze of gullies on the west face. When the weather finally cooperated, it took him five exhausting hours to climb his way up to the top. He was shaking from low blood sugar when he reached the highest point. Despite his accomplishment, Bart spent only twenty minutes on the summit; lingering at over 14,000 feet could be fatal on a short and cold January day.

Since daylight was fading he was anxious to get down the mountain quickly. Before leaving the western edge of the mountaintop, he lashed his skis together to create a crude sled. He lay face up on his new toboggan and hung his heels over the tail-end of his skis, hoping to control his momentum by digging his heels into the snow.

During his wild descent he held onto his bindings for dear life. Bart's speed was soon out of control. He quickly realized this ride could be his last. His prospects were looking grim; he prayed to regain control of his homemade sled. In desperation, he leaned the ski edges into the mountainside and shot off into the adjacent chute. Shortly afterwards he came to a stop. Bart was relieved to be alive. He prudently put on his ice creepers and walked the rest of the way down the mountain.

Over fifty years later Ken and I skied into Crabtree Meadows. At last we had arrived at the final campsite designated on our itinerary. As we watched the last rays of evening light fade from the west side of Mount Whitney, we searched for the trail register near the ranger station. We were eager to sign our names along with the other wild-spirited souls who had passed this way during the winter. We never did locate it; the register was completely buried in snow. Then we put up our tent on a patch of dry ground beneath an old and gnarled pine tree. After dinner I noticed a dim light glowing across the meadow.

"Hey Ken, there's a light on over there!"

"I'm sure it's coming from the backcountry ranger cabin. Let's go see who's there," Ken insisted.

Using our headlamps to navigate through the darkness, we followed the scent of pine smoke swirling out from the cabin's wood stove. Just outside the door, we heard the voices of two males inside. Not knowing what to expect, we knocked on the door. The voices quieted momentarily in disbelief. Footsteps followed. The door opened. Standing before us were two very surprised Sequoia National Park rangers who were on a backcountry patrol. They invited us inside. The warmth of a heated cabin, the hissing of a kerosene lantern, and a steaming cup of hot tea were seductive.

Our interaction felt slightly awkward though. Perhaps it was us; we were no longer accustomed to socializing. Or maybe our exchange was clumsy because I sensed the rangers were skeptical that we had actually traversed the John Muir Trail on skinny cross-country skis. Nevertheless, our interface served as a useful transition back to civilization.

Each of us commented on the extraordinary amount of avalanche debris on the mountain slopes this year. All four of us agreed that traveling through the wintry backcountry was probably safer than driving on Highway 395 in the Owens Valley. The rangers warned us that a storm was forecasted sometime over the next few days. They advised us to consider going down the north face of Mount Whitney if the weather deteriorated during our climb.

By 10 p.m. we were back in our tent and snuggled into our sleeping bags. In hindsight, this had not been the best way to spend our last evening on the John Muir Trail. It was a mistake to get lured into a late night with a hot caffeinated beverage the evening before the biggest day of the trip. Nonetheless, we felt pleased about our day. We had not only crossed the Great Divide, we had covered another seventeen miles.

In the last seventeen days we had skied over 200 miles. Our grand journey had taken us through a mystical landscape. Instead of riding the wind on a magic carpet, our skis glided across pure white snow and transported us into a world where mountains touched the heavens and rocks and snow crashed down to the earth, where sculpted trees were on display and animals roamed freely across the land. Along the way, the snow and sky had been a kaleidoscope of ever-changing color and light—bright whites, brilliant blues and soft pastels.

As we drifted off to sleep we thought our adventure was coming to a conclusion. Perhaps it was really just the beginning. Traveling deep into the wilderness had been an inward exploration as much as it had been an outward journey. The trip had been a catalyst for self-discovery. It revealed our strengths, weaknesses, hopes and fears—all of which prepared us for what was still to come.

7

A MOUNTAIN OF REGRET

The big day was finally upon us; our plan was to climb Mount Whitney, descend to Whitney Portal and finish our expedition. Ken and I slept later than we intended. While we were packing up our campsite the rangers stopped by to wish us well before continuing their backcountry patrol up towards Tyndall Creek.

Shortly afterwards, we began our ascent up the peak. Mount Whitney rose high above us under partly cloudy skies. I gazed up at the mountain with excitement and awe—I was eager to climb it.

The west side of the mountain was riddled with a maze of chutes, each filled with talus and snow. Since some of the slope was blown free of snow, we strapped our skis to our backpacks and hiked up through the labyrinth of couloirs. The gullies were bordered by imposing stone spires with icicles that resembled daggers draping over their sides.

Our ascent was straightforward until we encountered an impassable barrier of rocks. We turned around and hiked down a few hundred feet until we a found a passage between the gendarmes. Then we traversed into another chute and resumed our ascent. Our route required only a few easy climbing moves to get through a short band of rocks. Otherwise the ascent was uneventful.

On the way up we paused occasionally to enjoy the scenic vistas and catch our breath. We could measure our upward progress by how high we were in relation to the surrounding peaks. In the distance, clouds were building into thunderheads with misty trailers. They were far away and didn't overly concern us. After a few hours the gully widened into a broad bowl that led towards the summit plateau. Soon the slope angle lessened and we stood on top of the peak.

We were so high that I felt we could touch the sky. I expected the mountain's top to be small, but instead a large and flat field of rocks stretched out across the summit. The peak was ornamented with a single stone shelter. It had been constructed in 1909 by astronomers with the Smithsonian Institution. They had used the tiny building as a home and office. From here, they researched high-altitude phenomena and conducted stereoscopic studies hoping to determine if water existed on Mars.

Author on the summit of Mount Whitney at 14,505'

Our only interest in the lone cabin was to find shelter from the wind for a bite to eat. We were out of luck. A pearly white block of ice, over two feet thick, covered the floor. We grabbed a quick snack and drank our last drops of water out in the open. We took a few victory photos and then looked over the precipice of the sheer eastern face. We both felt a great sense of accomplishment—we had finally reached the culminating point in our journey.

By now, the clouds had partially descended onto the summit. Farther south they enveloped the long ridge leading towards the Ramparts—our intended route down the mountain along the summer trail. Soon thunder boomed in the distance. It moved rapidly in our direction, closer and closer. The metal pipe protruding from the shelter's roof started making a loud, eerie buzzing sound. Simultaneously I felt static on my head. My hair was standing upright. When Ken touched his head he experienced a strong shock. A split-second later a bright flash of lightening lit up the nearby clouds. The summit of the highest peak in the continental United States was the worst place we could be in a lightning storm. While the flashes of light and booms of thunder continued around us, it started to snow.

Ken and I exchanged glances. Both of our faces expressed fear and concern. We quickly discussed our options. To descend from the peak via our planned route would require traversing the elongated summit ridge directly into the storm. Since the exposure time would be lengthy, it seemed a poor choice.

Then we recalled our encounter with the rangers the night before. Their suggestion, if the weather deteriorated, was to descend from the summit via the north face. Going down in this direction would be a quick escape with less exposure to the storm, but vigilance would be necessary to get down safely. Throughout our descent we would have to constantly evaluate the texture and color of the snow to avoid any patches of ice.

We quickly traversed back and forth along the northern edge of the summit looking for the best place to go down. The westernmost side of the north face was blocked by a long wave of overhanging snow. It was too risky to descend near or below this cornice. The eastern end of the north face was interspersed with cliffs, snow and ice. In the middle of the slope were a few long, steep, snow-filled couloirs. They appeared to go straight down the mountain.

"Here—we can go down this way!" Ken blurted into the wind.

I looked over the edge with both curiosity and trepidation.

"My God, it's so steep!" I exclaimed. "Can we really descend this way?"

Ken assured me we could. We needed to go soon; the weather was rapidly deteriorating. Thunder continued to explode all around us. The threat of being hit by lightning seemed imminent.

With his skis and poles strapped to the sides of his pack, Ken turned towards me so that his back faced the abyss. He looked briefly into my eyes before he stepped over the edge and into the top of the couloir. Then without a word, he kicked steps into the snow with his light-weight ski boots and made a tiny platform to stand on. Next he adjusted his ice ax in full self-arrest position—hanging vertically from his ice tool while his feet dangled against the steep snowy slope. Ken leaned into the mountainside with his ice ax and then began his descent.

All appeared to be well, but I still felt hesitant. Now it was my turn. I took a deep breath, faced inwards towards the summit, stepped over the edge, and slid the toes of my boots into the pre-cut steps. I planted my ice ax's pick firmly into the snow. Then, with my right hand grasped over the top of the ax's black metal blade and my left hand on the blue fiberglass shaft, I started a hanging glissade. I was grateful that we had practiced this maneuver many times before in the snow-filled gullies on San Jacinto Peak and San Gorgonio Mountain in Southern California.

I hung onto this tool for dear life. My ice ax was my life link—it was the only thing that connected me to the mountain and kept me from becoming one with space. The teeth on the ax's metal tip bit only a half inch into the slope. It held my entire body weight, my full backpack, skis and poles. My descent route was slightly to the right of Ken's path. A few feet can make all the difference in the world. So can a moment in time.

Ken was below me making steady but slow progress. Then he changed his posture. He went from a vertical hanging position to a sitting glissade. After only a few seconds, from the corner of my eye, I saw something blue moving fast—Ken was sliding uncontrollably, hurling down the mountain. Then he disappeared from sight. His ice ax must have bounced off a patch of pure ice, leaving him without a way to hold onto the mountainside.

Adrenaline shot through me. I gripped my ice ax tighter. Thoughts flashed through my mind—*Oh my God, what if he's dead when I get down the mountain?* I tried to concentrate, but one thought raced after another. Intensely focused, I kicked small steps into the snow to stop my descent. Then I tilted the tip of my ax deeper into the snow for a firmer hold.

"Ken, Ken. Ken, are you OK? Ken!" I yelled into space.

My voice only dissipated into the void below. No sounds or echoes returned. A heavy feeling came over me. I was scared and feeling all alone. I was deeply worried; I didn't know if Ken was alive or dead. I only knew that I would have to get down safely on my own. Then my inner voice took over. It started to coach me. *Stay calm, stay calm. Keep your mind on what you are doing. You have to make it down safely to help Ken.*

I could only see right in front of my nose where my ice ax penetrated the icy skin of the mountain. If I looked between my feet, I saw the steep white slope dropping away beneath me. There was no room for error. If Ken were still alive he would need my help. The only way I could safely get to him was to continue descending at a slow and steady pace. If I hurried, I would fall with an uncertain outcome. It was an agonizingly long descent. As I continued downward, I stopped periodically. Hanging on to my ice ax, I kicked my toes into the slope, yelled, and then listened.

"Ken, Ken! Are you OK?"

No response ever came. I could only hear the wind and the beating of my adrenaline-filled heart. Then I gingerly resumed my descent. I controlled my speed by adjusting how deep the blade of my ax penetrated into the snow. This was done by maintaining a perfect equilibrium between pulling the shaft of the ice ax up and away from the mountainside with my left hand while simultaneously tipping the pick and pushing the blade into the snow with my right hand.

Fear was my only companion. I was afraid that the outward pull of my weight, backpack, and skis would throw me off balance and send me plummeting into the void. I was also distressed about what had happened to Ken. Periodically my inner voice would remind me—*don't hurry, just take your time. Concentrate. You can do this.*

I continued down the mountain hanging from my ice ax in a full self-arrest position. Over and over again, I stopped, kicked toe holds into the snow, clenched on to my ax, and yelled to Ken below. Not once did I hear his voice. My severely limited view of the slope below revealed nothing about Ken's fate.

Concentration was critical as I moved downward. I didn't dare look around or take my eyes off what I was doing. Without landmarks, I wasn't able to gauge how far down the mountain I had already come. I watched and listened to my ax's metal blade slicing a thin line through the hardened snow. It was the only mark of progress that assured me that I was actually moving downward. The descent dragged on for what felt like eternity.

Eventually, the angle of the slope eased-up. Broken rocks now dotted the white couloir. At last, I could support myself with my own two feet. From a rocky perch, I looked down slope towards the base of the peak.

The silhouette of a small figure moved slowly about—it was Ken. He waved his arms above his head, crossing them back and forth to show me that he was alive. Tremendous relief swept over me. As the tension in my body released, warm and comforting feelings flowed through my veins.

After a while, it appeared that Ken was climbing up towards me. He wasn't carrying any of his gear. Instead, he had left his backpack where he landed in the snow beneath a band of cliffs. I didn't know if this was a conscious decision. Perhaps he was in a hurry to reach me, or maybe his rapid and mostly airborne descent had left him dazed.

While Ken ascended, I continued to climb down the mountain. It was slippery. Rocky ledges and broken slabs of granite punctuated the snowy slope. Eventually I grew tired. I stopped for a short break. It felt incredibly good just to sit down and rest. I was both physically and emotionally exhausted. Now that I was on predominately rocky terrain, I strapped my ice ax onto my pack. The thunder and lightning were long gone, but snow was falling intermittently and dark fluffy clouds hung over the surrounding peaks.

After a long wait, Ken and I were reunited. He appeared fine. At the time, I wasn't aware of how far down the slope he had fallen. I knew it was a quite a distance, but I wasn't familiar with the terrain below me nor could I see where he had landed. For the moment, I was just happy he was alive.

As it turned out, he not only bounced on firm wind-packed snow, he flew over low-angled rocks and then a band of cliffs. His final landing was in soft snow at the base of the wall. It was truly amazing, if not miraculous, that he had survived an 800-foot fall down the mountainside.

After hugging each other we traversed westward towards easier terrain. En route Ken complained that his feet were cold. The loss of sensation in his toes had compromised his ability to walk. We stopped as soon as we found a small ledge flat enough for both of us to sit on. By now, Ken was nearly hypothermic. I took off his boots and wet socks. His feet were bluish-white and felt like blocks of ice. I knew what had to be done: I unzipped my coat, lifted up the layers of my sweaters and slipped his frigid, numb feet under my clothes and into my bare arm pits. A shock of cold went through me. I tried not to make a big deal out of it. It was the best way to restore warmth and function to his feet.

As we sat on the ledge facing each other, rocking back and forth with Ken's feet in my arm pits, I noticed tears welling up in his brown eyes.

"My back is really hurting me," he divulged with a choked up voice.

Then he started shaking with emotion. Until now, he had appeared uninjured and even unnerved from his fall. Except for the lengthening shadows, time seemed to stand still. Ken held my hands and looked intensely at me as tears ran down his cold red cheeks.

"It will be so good to grow old with you. Will you marry me?"

"Yes," I replied without hesitation.

A marriage proposal should be one of the most romantic occasions in life. Instead, this moment was a brief and joyous interlude in a period of uncertain desperation. It was difficult to entertain any idea of what our future together would look like. Tomorrow would only exist if we got off this damn mountain.

The afternoon was giving way to early evening. It had already been a very long day. It had taken us five hours to come down 1,300 feet. Descending just a few more hundred feet would deliver us to less hazardous terrain, or so we thought.

Once Ken's feet warmed up, we down climbed a short distance over low-angled rocks mixed with snow. We had hoped to traverse farther towards the east, but we changed our minds when plummeting temperatures and falling snow glazed a thin layer of ice on the rocky slabs between where we were and where we wanted to go. Our view of the terrain below us was becoming limited; daylight was fading and clouds now hugged the mountainside. So instead we continued down until we found ourselves above a band of relatively low-angled cliffs.

"Wait here—I'll climb down to my backpack and get the rope," Ken said while looking up at me.

Then with relative ease, he descended a short but steep section of rocks. This brought him to a long sloping ledge above a rocky wall. He avoided the cliffs below by traversing eastward across a shelf to easier ground. Ken was now out of my view as he hiked down through a talus field and then headed west back to the base of the cliffs where he could reclaim his abandoned backpack.

In the flash of a split-second, I decided to just down climb the rocks that Ken had. After all, I was strong and fit. But I failed to consider that Ken had down climbed without a load while I carried over a third of my weight in my backpack. My shorter stature also meant that I couldn't reach the same holds that Ken had used.

It's often the descent that's most problematic to mountaineers. After a long and rigorous ascent to high altitude, blood sugar declines, exhaustion and poor judgment set in, and the clock ticks inevitably toward darkness.

Standing atop that precipice was the critical edge between solid ground and space, and time and fate. As I looked downward in the decreasing light, I realized that my skis and poles were now a hazard. If they snagged on the rocks while down climbing, I would surely fall. I reached above my head and pulled each ski and pole up and out from the side straps on my backpack. Then I launched them, one at time, down the mountainside.

I pulled off my mittens and shoved them into the outer pockets of my coat. While my hands grasped onto the cold granite, I looked for a few small protrusions in the rock face below. Then I cautiously lowered my feet and hands, one step at time, onto each minuscule hold.

Climbing down was more difficult than I anticipated. I was wearing old-style ankle-high leather ski boots with fairly smooth soles. The tips of the boots had one inch protrusions that fit into our three-pin ski bindings. With each succeeding move down, I carefully selected which small bumps in the rock would be my next set of hand and footholds.

I descended into a shallow chimney, an indented section of rock with vertical walls jutting out on either side of me. On my right was a rounded buttress. On my left was a rocky corner with a sidewall that stuck two feet outward. A small crack separated the left sidewall from the granite face in front of me. Climbing down just twenty feet would bring me to the rocky ramp that Ken had traversed to evade the cliffs below.

During our descent the peak was mostly covered in snow
Summer image of the north face of Mount Whitney
Photo credit: with permission, Dirk Summers

Soon I ran out of reachable holds for both my hands and feet. I counter-balanced my legs by partially stemming across the shallow chimney. My left foot pressed against the rocky corner while my right leg pushed onto a foothold on the right-sided buttress. It didn't matter that I had done this kind of move countless times before on rock climbing trips. I was exhausted and cold, and the light was waning. I could barely keep the front tips of my ski boots on the meager footholds. Soon my right leg trembled violently with muscle fatigue.

Out of desperation, I gripped harder onto the granite with my cold bare hands. I couldn't go up. I couldn't go down. I couldn't reach the next foot or handholds below me. There was no place I could go and I couldn't hang on forever. My body was stuck, spread-eagle across the shallow chimney.

I wondered where Ken was with that rope. Now I regretted my decision. I was gripped with fear. I hung on to the rock as tightly as I could. My whole body was shaking from the sustained effort. I couldn't find a position that would allow even a moment of rest. I was afraid of falling. I wasn't ready to die; I had too much to look forward to, including marrying Ken. With each passing second, I grew weaker. I couldn't hang on much longer. Then I heard my inner voice plead loudly, *God! Don't let me fall!*

In an instant, my world went dark. I heard a single loud *THUMP!* It was the sound of my head pounding on the rocks. I plummeted into the space below, past the ledge and over the cliffs. I saw and felt nothing. Sound was my only sensory stimulation. I heard my body and backpack banging on the granite as I bounced off and on the rocks before I went unconscious.

Below, Ken watched in horror. As my dark silhouette tumbled towards him, my ice ax scraped against the stone sending orange and yellow sparks into the twilight sky.

8

MIND OVER MOUNTAIN

My fall came to an abrupt end. After I regained consciousness, I could feel that I was severely injured, but I didn't comprehend what had happened. When I opened my eyes, Ken was removing my backpack from my body. Suddenly I was moving again; Ken grabbed my hand and pulled me upright. I didn't realize where I was or what was going on, I only understood that Ken was frantically dragging me horizontally across the snow with my legs partially buckling beneath my feet. I had no choice but to surrender to the new momentum.

"Are you OK? Are you OK?" he asked.

I don't remember how or if I answered his question. I was dizzy and disoriented. Ken led the way as we continued across the incline at 13,200 feet. With his help, I stumbled along, collapsing several times in just 200 yards. Ken stopped next to a rocky rib where a deep apron of snow had drifted in below it. The space was sloping slightly, but it was the only safe place where we could pitch our narrow tent. Ken was in a hurry; darkness would soon be upon us.

Before setting up our shelter, Ken vigorously stomped the snow with his feet and then packed it down with his avalanche shovel. While I lay on the snow, I noticed that his skis weren't on his pack. Presumably, his skis and poles had broken during his fall earlier in the day. They were now scattered somewhere on the mountainside.

I felt light-headed, dazed and incapacitated. My head was throbbing. I reached up and gently wiped the blood away from my eyes. Despite my injuries, I was awed by the sight across the valley. As the sun set to the west, long shafts of golden light filtered through the dark clouds over Mount Russell. *This is a beautiful place to die*, I thought while lying helplessly in the cold snow.

Despite wanting to live, I was surprised that I now felt calm and even accepting of the probability of dying right here. Perhaps I was too numb or weak to feel or think otherwise. As the light faded from the peak, I wondered if the light of my own life would be extinguished next. I gazed at Mount Russell with such intensity that the image became burned into my memory forever. Soon the gap in the clouds disappeared and the scene became grey and gloomy again.

Once the tent was set up, Ken mumbled for me to get inside and rest. I could barely crawl in; my body was disabled and wracked with pain. Ken unzipped his sleeping bag and draped it over me. Then he disappeared into the fading light to retrieve my backpack at the base of the cliffs.

All was quiet as the twilight sky turned black. Now alone, I felt weak and vulnerable. Ken's absence dragged on. It seemed like I waited forever. Blood oozed out from the upper left side of my head. It glued my hair into a thick mass and trickled down my face. I reached up with my left hand and applied pressure to slow the flow, but I couldn't determine the extent of my head injury.

When Ken returned he blew up my Therm-a-Rest mattress and helped me into my down-filled sleeping bag. Warmth slowly returned to my chilled body. While lying there I assessed what was going on inside me. The pain in my back was excruciating. More pressing was the rapid swelling in my left buttock. It was half-numb from nerve damage yet it had just enough sensation for me to feel the wetness of blood and that it hurt like hell.

Blood was everywhere. It soaked through my pants and overflowed into my sleeping bag. To slow the bleeding, Ken applied pressure with our spare clothes. Even more blood was flowing internally, under my skin, deep into muscle and tissue.

We desperately needed food and water. Later while lying on his side, Ken reached outside the tent and placed a six-inch square of closed-cell foam atop the snow and under our cooking stove. He warmed up our white-gas stove by priming it. Next he protected the flickering flames by surrounding it with a small aluminum windscreen. From the tent door, he scooped snow into our cooking pot to melt some drinking water. Our stove barely puttered along. The wind was racing and snow was falling again. After melting a small amount of snow, a gust extinguished the flames. Despite repeated efforts, Ken couldn't get the stove going again. It was too difficult to deal with; we went to bed without food or water.

I felt overwhelmed by exhaustion, the weather and my injuries. I desperately needed some rest. Besides feeling weak and dizzy, my breathing had become very shallow.

"Ken, would you stay awake all night? I feel like I might stop breathing in my sleep," I asked with a soft, concerned voice.

Ken assured me that he would monitor my breathing. If necessary, he would resuscitate me. I wondered if I would slip into a coma during the night and never wake up again. The air was filled with uncertainty.

"I love you. We're going to be OK," I uttered, hoping to conceal my doubt about the future.

Then I closed my eyes and tried to relax. The tent was filled with silence. My mind was quiet too—I was too weak for any internal chatter. I couldn't even think enough to worry about what might come next.

I was still conscious when I felt something very unusual. A presence came over me. It was dark and heavy yet insubstantial like a shadow. It seemed to be shaped like a body. It was suspended horizontally just a centimeter above my own frame. I felt it most strongly above my face, as if it was about to kiss me. It was as close as anything can get without actually making tactile contact.

It was Death. I knew it without any doubt. I sensed it hovering above my body similar to the way that a fog sits above a lake on a cold morning. This strange presence had a masculine energetic quality. It was powerful yet somewhat peaceful. It seemed that if I just accepted it, I could merge into it and become one with it, but if I fought it laden with fear, I would experience it as something oppressive. Pure exhaustion kept me from reacting. Death would either take me or leave me.

This thick and heavy presence gradually dissipated. I clearly remember that once it left and before I surrendered to sleep, I made this vow: *If I live until morning I will live all of my most important dreams.* Shortly after making my promise, I fell asleep.

I was surprised to be alive when I woke up at 1 a.m. Death had not taken me, at least not yet. Ken was exhausted but awake. We were both parched. Again he tried to melt snow for drinking water. Soon our small stove roared to life. Frozen snow crystals gradually transformed into enough liquid to partially hydrate ourselves.

I was miserable the next morning. My head and back pulsated with pain. I was so stiff I could hardly turn over. The left side of my buttock was swollen three times larger than the right side. The puffiness made it impossible to zip up my pants. I could still feel the blood seeping under my skin. I was grateful to be alive, but now we had to focus on surviving.

Outside the sun was hidden in swirling clouds. Wind blew down the mountainside and snow fell from the steely sky. The wind continued to be a menace; we could only melt enough snow for a small amount of drinking water. Ken ate a light breakfast, but I had no appetite.

After his meal we made a plan to manage our temporary confinement. We would use snow on the uphill side of the tent for melting water for cooking and drinking. Snow on the downhill side was reserved for food scraps and urine tossed outside.

I was jealous that Ken could crawl out of the tent to piss, even if just near the entrance. I had to urinate, but I couldn't crawl out of the tent or squat to pee in a bottle. I needed a bed pan. The only thing we had flat enough for the job was the stainless steel lid to our cooking pot. Ken adjusted the newly appointed bed pan while I lay in the tent trying to pee. The task proved impossible. My bladder would not relax, release and empty itself. Ken massaged my lower abdomen, but still nothing came. Each time I pushed to void, my head throbbed in pain. It felt like my brains might pop out of the gash on my scalp. Each effort to pee failed to deliver even a trickle; nerves leading to my bladder had been damaged.

Thankfully, I wasn't menstruating. My period had just ended a few days earlier. It would have been unmanageable; my injuries were severe and the weather kept us trapped inside our tiny tent.

Ken needed a rest after staying up all night to make sure I was still breathing. He slept off and on throughout the day. I was also tired from the strain of our descent. I tried to relax, but I couldn't get comfortable. Fist-sized rocks poked through the snow beneath my sleeping pad. Lying flat on my back, directly on my injuries, increased my pain. I could only lie on one of my sides for limited periods of time. The best option was to lie on my stomach, but this became unbearable as fluid mounted inside my bladder. My injuries made each movement difficult. Whenever I tossed and turned, I moved slowly and cautiously. Besides minimizing pain, I wanted to keep my broken bones stable.

Later in the day Ken asked, "What do you think we should do?"

We were in no position to make a move yet, but a plan was needed.

"I could hike out to get help," he offered.

Initially this seemed like the logical thing to do. After all, we were only about seven miles from the trailhead at Whitney Portal. Of course, it wasn't as simple as that. The terrain between here and there was extremely rugged.

I bombarded him with things to consider. "Are you sure you could make it out in one day? It's a long way to go in deep snow without skis. What if no one is at the trailhead when you get there? After all, it's still winter in these mountains."

"You're right. I don't know if I could really make it out in a single day. But I'm willing to try. You would need the tent to lie here exposed on the side of Mount Whitney."

There were other factors to consider. I was too weak to collect and melt snow for water. I couldn't cook for myself and I couldn't urinate.

We carefully weighed our options. Would it be better to stay together with all of our equipment in one place or to separate so that Ken could go for help? Or should we abandon our gear and travel light and fast? This idea was appealing. Neither of us wanted to carry a load on our broken backs, but without our gear we could die if we didn't make it to the road in one day. We decided it was best to carry our equipment with us and to remain together to increase our odds of survival.

Getting from our remote campsite to civilization would not be easy. We would have to traverse rocky and snowy terrain over a mountain pass, drop 4,800 feet into a deep canyon choked with snow, and navigate through exposed ledges and melting creeks. Before attempting this feat, we would have to wait for the snowstorm to subside. In the meantime, we rested and waited.

As I lay in the tent, I often thought of my family. I sent my mother all the mental vibrations I could muster hoping that she would somehow sense that we needed help. It was to no avail. Oddly, several weeks later I learned that Ken's grandmother had called my mother because she was worried about us. Our loved ones then rechecked our itinerary. There was no reason to initiate a search; we were a full week ahead of schedule.

I also fantasized about a helicopter flying rescuers to Arctic Lakes below us. I wished for nothing more than to be scooped out of this cold hell and off the mountainside. Cell phones and emergency locator beacons didn't exist; the only way to get help was to evacuate ourselves.

Time was not on our side. We desperately needed medical care. My soft-framed Lowe backpack had saved my life. It protected my core during my fall. Still, my injuries were severe. I had a head injury, many damaged nerves, a dysfunctional bladder and my left buttock was bleeding both internally and externally. Medically, my body was in a state of severe shock from the loss of blood. Pain spiked through my body with the slightest movement making me certain that I had multiple fractures in my lumbar spine and pelvis. Besides these broken bones, hospital x-rays would later reveal that my sacrum was also displaced and fragmented in several places, and that my tailbone had shattered into smithereens.

At the time, Ken estimated that I had fallen between sixty and eighty feet. Decades later when I measured the distance on Google Earth, I discovered that I had actually bounced down the rocks for over 150 feet.

Ken was remarkably intact after his lengthy fall. His knees and elbows were abraded and thin pink skin was visible beneath his ripped clothes. Inexplicably, he had sustained only a few compression hairline fractures in his lower back.

Lying in the tent hour after hour for an indefinite time felt like an imprisonment. With nowhere to go, I slowly retreated into my mind. I didn't like everything I discovered. As the day wore on I became irritable every time Ken moaned and groaned with pain. I understood his injuries were painful but mine were life-threatening. Sometimes I wished he would just shut up. Instead I kept silent. In the scheme of things how bad could whining be? After all, our survival depended on mutual cooperation and support.

I soon realized that without any control over my physical situation, the only way to stay alive was to rely on the power of my mind. I had survived the first night after my fall—now I needed to get out of these mountains alive. My vow to pursue my life's dreams kept me going.

Our own inner resources are our greatest gift. The mind is amazing. It influences every cell in our body, the moods and actions of those around us, and it has the ability to change ourselves and the world. In fact, I am certain that it was my mind that kept me alive.

It was here on the side of Mount Whitney that I first glimpsed how powerful the mind can be. The phrase "mind over matter" took on a new meaning. In my case, it was "mind over mountain." Out of nowhere, a mantra naturally arose in my mind. Instead of giving it a voice, I kept it to myself. I didn't want to feed any fears that Ken might have. I repeated this mantra in my mind, over and over, hour after hour, day after day. *I am going to live, I am going to live, I am going to live, I am going to live.* I said it until I believed it was possible. The mantra didn't stop unless I was sleeping fitfully or talking to Ken.

Ken developed his own mantra which rang out through the silence every few hours—*we are going to make it, we are going to make it.* I wasn't sure if he was trying to reassure me or convince himself. At the time, it didn't matter.

That night the wind worked against us again. Several times it blew out the flames of our camp stove. Cooking inside our tent was not an option; if the tent didn't burn down, the build-up of carbon monoxide would kill us. We melted just enough snow to make a lukewarm powdered onion soup. Then, while fumbling around in painful positions, I spilled half the soup onto the floor of the tent. I felt utterly discouraged. We gave up on eating and went to sleep.

Another day dawned. It was still snowing outside. My stomach gnawed and growled for food, but I didn't have much of an appetite. I was only able to eat a few bites of an energy bar.

Ken started blaming himself for my accident. It didn't help. In fact, it upset me. We needed to stay focused on our survival. The slope above us was our most immediate concern. We were at the mercy of the mountain. It was becoming loaded with snow. I wondered if the snow would slide down, peel us off the mountainside and bury us alive in an avalanche.

Our tent sagged under the accumulating snow. Ken periodically crawled out and shoveled the snow off the uphill side of the tent—otherwise it would have collapsed. The subdued lighting, confined space and my life-threatening injuries made the interior of the tent feel like being inside a coffin.

Our primary sensory stimulations were pain, sound and smell. The walls of our tent flapped incessantly when the wind howled. When it subsided, I heard snowflakes falling softly as I drifted in and out of a light sleep. Our sleeping bags crinkled whenever one of us tossed and turned. The tent reeked of blood, urine, sweaty, unwashed bodies, and spoiled food that had been spilled on the floor.

I desperately needed to pee. Throughout the day I tried to relieve myself. I perched on my knees over the lid of our cooking pot, bent forward and contracted my abdomen, hoping to push out some urine. I did this over and over, until a few drops were released. More often than not, I was unsuccessful. I gave up whenever the strain from pushing made the laceration on my head feel like it was going to explode. Afterwards, I rested; the effort was exhausting. By the end of the day, after a lot of straining and discomfort, I managed to excrete three ounces of urine. At first, I felt victorious. Then I noticed the dark color that comes from stagnation and dehydration. It fueled my fears—I wondered if my urine could become toxic to my already weakened body.

During the day, we retreated inward. We passed the hours shifting positions, trying to rest, and melting snow for drinking and cooking food. Our energy had completely drained away. It was impossible to get sufficient sleep; our bodies were riddled with pain and our minds worried about escaping from the mountains. I continued to rely on my inner mantra—*I am going to live, I am going to live, I am going to live*......

Out of desperation, I prayed periodically. I am not sure to whom I prayed. I prayed for relief, I prayed for help, and I prayed for any improvement to our intolerable situation. I wondered what thoughts were going through Ken's mind. We rarely talked. Our discussions were limited to the logistics of getting out alive.

By early evening we were both feeling a bit stronger. The weather also appeared to be breaking up. We were hopeful that we might be able to evacuate the next morning. We could not lie on this mountain forever. We had to get medical attention soon, but how would we pull it off?

9

BETWEEN HOPE AND FEAR

After three dreadful nights, we were graced with clear weather. Since our journey would be long, unpredictable, and over rugged terrain, we started very early in the day. Every action was painstakingly slow. I was dizzy and my head throbbed each time I moved. It took us two and a half hours just to eat our breakfast and pack up our camping gear. Now we would have to walk out; our skis and poles were littered across the mountain, and possibly broken too.

Finally we were on our way. Ken hoisted my backpack up from the ground and loaded the thirty-five pounds onto my broken back and pelvis.

"Whoa! God—that hurts!"

My pack felt incredibly heavy. It was too laden for my injuries, but there was no other choice. I had to grin and bear it. I was also eager to escape from this nightmare.

Joy filled my heart as we left our tiny camp on the mountainside. As a symbolic gesture of carrying on with my life, I didn't look back. Nevertheless, Whitney's shadow had become part of me. The mountain and I were now inseparable; my injuries and near-death experience here would shape the rest of my life.

As we proceeded onward, my mantra was replaced with the

momentum of physical movement. I no longer repeated to myself, *I am going to live, I am going to live, I am going to live.* Instead I focused on moving forward, one step at a time.

The rarified air gave the sky a blue-black color. After the days I'd spent in our tent, the light reflecting off the snow seemed unbearably bright. I had trouble focusing. Besides feeling dizzy, my vision was blurry without my prescription eyeglasses. My gold-rimmed spectacles had been ripped off my face during my fall. In desperation, we stopped and searched through our packs until we found our dark glacier goggles.

Here the terrain angled away at about 30 degrees. I used my 70-mm ice ax in my right hand as a cane for support. I grasped it at the head and leaned into the uphill slope as I stumbled forward. The snow was interspersed with jumbles of rock and patches of sandy soil.

I was weak, dizzy and panting to catch my breath. I walked only a hundred yards from our campsite before I had to lie down on the ground to rest. Inside, I wondered how on Earth I was going to get out of these mountains alive. The task seemed impossible. Then I remembered my vow to live my dreams and forced myself to get up. I moved forward again, inching my way across the landscape. It was going to be a very long journey.

En route, I rested frequently. When we came to a large semi-flat boulder, I actually sat down. It felt good to sit for a change. Despite my shattered pelvis and spine, the position was a novelty for my body. It was a temporary improvement from lying for days on broken bones.

We stopped occasionally to take off our boots and warm our feet. My toes felt slightly numb and my feet were cold to touch. During our ordeal in the tent I was so preoccupied with survival that I didn't notice my waxy white toes. They must have been frost-nipped while kicking steps into the snow during my decent from the summit.

We traversed along the north side of Mount Whitney at just over 13,000 feet. The Whitney-Russell Col was about a half a mile ahead. This gap between the north side of Mount Whitney and Mount Russell would lead us over the Sierra Crest, through the mountains and down to the town of Lone Pine where we could get medical help.

For us, this pass was a psychological marker as much as it was the physical boundary between two drainages. From the top of the divide we could see the dry brown desert in the Owens Valley. It stretched out far below us, appearing tantalizingly close and very inviting. It gave me hope.

The east side of the col was steep. A carefully controlled descent was needed to avoid slamming into the rocks at the base of the pass nearly 500 feet below us. My injuries dictated my position. I leaned against the slope with the right side of my body. Then I used my ice ax, elbows, and the toes of my boots to dig into the snow. At times, I even dug my bare fingers into the softened snow to reduce my speed.

As we approached Iceberg Lake the terrain eased up. Keeler Needle's sheer face towered above us. My jaw dropped wide-open in awe—I could hardly take my eyes off this magnificent blade of rock. It rose straight up for over a thousand feet and resembled the kind of pinnacle that one might imagine could connect Earth to Heaven.

Iceberg Lake appeared to be mostly frozen. Nonetheless, as a precaution we walked on rocks that had melted out along its shore. It was the easiest walking we would have on our trek out. I stopped frequently to take in the incredible beauty of our surroundings. While pausing, I made a wish to camp here in the future, set my strong intention and left it to fate.

Just south of the lake we descended into a glacial trough filled with deep snow. It was a nightmare. The late morning sunshine had turned the snow to mush. Without skis, we sank up to our thighs. The weight of a full backpack bearing down on my fractured spine and pelvis increased the torment. After each step, I carefully extricated one leg from the snowpack and put the next leg forward before helplessly plunging into the snow again. It was unbearable. I squinted my eyes, clenched my teeth and groaned in silence with each movement.

My despair increased the deeper I sank and the farther we traveled. I was terrified that my damaged bones might suddenly shift, sever my spinal cord, and leave me paralyzed and half-buried in the snow. For more than a half a mile, we plummeted up to three feet into the snow and pulled ourselves out again and again, step after step. It was a humbling and painful ordeal.

The mountains above me seemed even more immense in my

weakened state. I felt insignificant, like a drop of water in the ocean. I often lifted my eyes towards the sky and prayed for the endurance, strength and patience to get out alive. Throughout the day my emotions wavered between hope and fear.

Later Ken had a stroke of genius. He stopped, whipped off his backpack and took out our purple 7-mm climbing rope. While I waited in the shadows of Thor Peak, he stacked our two backpacks on top of each other. Then he lashed them together. Ken wrapped the remainder of the rope around his waist. He dragged the packs six feet behind him like a mule hauling a sled. The combined weight and surface area of our backpacks created a partially packed runway for me to walk on. This also freed me of my heavy load. Now with each step I sank only five inches into the snowpack.

The slope steepened just above Clyde Meadows. Soon our makeshift sled raced ahead of Ken, pulling him forward and pushing him into the snow. Another plan was needed. We donned our packs again and like desperate dogs, crawled on our hands and knees across the snowpack. We floundered less with our weight more evenly distributed, but this technique only worked for this particular slope. Farther below, we alternated between walking on firmer snow and sinking or post-holing wherever the snow had softened.

Lower down, Boy Scout Lake presented other challenges. Spring had arrived here. It was impossible to keep our boots dry. We carefully navigated around the lake basin through the tall yellow-green willows, rotten snow and muddy swamps. Before heading into the steep gorge below, we sat down on a large dry rock at the edge of the meadow and took a break from the intense exertion. Snacks, warm sunshine and chirping birds cheered my spirit.

Shortly afterwards, we descended into a box canyon along the North Fork of Lone Pine Creek. Travel became difficult, tedious and frustrating. We frequently had to bushwhack through the willows, and traverse back and forth across the stream to find the safest route down the valley.

Crossing the riverbed over and over was downright dicey. Besides being steep, the creek was lined with slippery stones and the stream itself was choked with chunks of snow and ice. Occasionally we found shreds of faded red survey tape that marked the unofficial climber's trail, but they were few and far between. Otherwise the route was completely obliterated by snow and running water.

Then the canyon narrowed. Unstable snow banks lined the rushing stream on one side and steep cliffs rose up on the other side. We were hemmed in, trapped on a series of ledges above the creek. Each of the stony shelves was two to four feet apart. I was nervous about being on rocky terrain again. The day was growing long and I, weary and weak. We wasted a lot of time and energy route-finding and scrambling over and down these rocky benches.

Soon we were forced to a halt. The next ledge was ten feet below us. The drop off was more than we could safely down climb. We didn't have rock climbing hardware with us. Instead we were equipped for climbing steep snowy slopes, with crampons, ice axes, ice screws, and snow stakes and anchors inside our packs. The only option to get down to the ledge beneath us was to be lowered.

I took a deep breath, closed my eyes for a moment to compose myself and stepped over the precipice. Hanging in space with a rope around my broken pelvis was torturous. Once my feet landed on the rocky ramp, Ken tied the rope to our packs and lowered them, one at a time, towards to me. I wasn't sure how Ken planned to get down.

Then he spoke up. "Jeaner, Can you catch my feet as I lower myself?"

This is not what I expected.

"Uh, I am not sure. I guess I could try."

"You can do it," he encouraged me.

I stood on my tiptoes and held my arms above my head with the palms facing the sky. Ken faced away from me and then squatted down. He held onto the lip of the ledge next to his feet and then slipped his legs over the edge. His feet dangled in space just a few inches beyond my reach.

Next Ken carefully slid down the granite face, intentionally skidding off small, stony protrusions on the wall to slow his speed. Soon the heels of his boots were cradled in my hands. I felt his body weight thrust down through my spine like a plunger—pushing the pain from my head down to my toes. It hurt like hell. My eyes nearly bulged out from their sockets as I tried to maintain my composure. Then I guided his feet down to the ledge that I was standing on.

Late afternoon slipped into evening. A pale yellow sky gave way to darkening shades of blue. Mountain shadows crept across the desert floor far below us. Then lights twinkled in the distant town of Lone Pine. The city lights were alluring. My goal was clearly visible, yet we were disheartened by our slow progress. As the hours passed, I realized we would have another night out before reaching help. I was overcome with sadness and uncertain if I could make it.

Soon it was too dark to wear my prescription glacier goggles. Without my spectacles, I traveled onward with blurry, near-sighted vision. Our dim headlamps lit the way. Ken was intensely focused. He traced the faint mountaineer's trail which randomly appeared and disappeared between the bushes while I followed the dark figure ahead of me.

A few hours later, a nearly full moon rose on the horizon. Its silver light gradually illuminated the canyon walls. Travel became easier. We were now below the snow line and the added moonlight improved visibility.

The moonlight nearly vanished when we later descended into a forest—it was almost pitch-dark under the canopy of new spring leaves. Here, I started having trouble keeping my balance. Exhaustion exaggerated my dizziness. Several times I lost my equilibrium and fell to the ground.

At 9:30 p.m., I declared myself incapable of going any farther. Ken insisted that we continue. We needed a suitable place to camp. Thirty minutes later we found a place flat enough for sleeping. We were so debilitated we didn't even set up the tent. Instead we laid it on the ground, put our bags inside, crawled into the giant sack and fell into a deep sleep.

I could barely move the next morning. I was stiff and sore. I had to crawl on my hands and knees across the ground to get out of my sleeping bag. My bladder felt like it was going to rupture. I was desperate for a catheter. Ken insisted that I drink a powdered protein shake before we headed down the trail. I forced it down; I needed the energy to walk

Dizzy and feeble, I walked down the trail like a staggering drunk. I concentrated on every step as I swayed on my unsteady legs. I was always on the verge of collapsing, barely able to keep myself upright. Periodically I reminded myself not to give up; I had dreams worth living for.

Occasionally Ken looked back and encouraged me. "You got to keep going, Jeaner. You got to keep going."

Summer image of our approximate escape route
from the Whitney-Russell Col to Whitney Portal Trailhead
Mount Whitney in late afternoon, with clouds
Photo credit: istock.com/pleum

Thankfully, our escape was almost over. I couldn't go much longer without medical care. Despite my determination, my life force was rapidly vanishing. Finally, I gave in—I lay down in the dirt right in the middle of the trail. After a brief rest, I remembered my aspiration to see the Himalayas. This rallied me onward. I crawled onto my hands and knees, leaned onto a rock, stood up and wobbled down the path.

"Stay here and rest. I'll come back to get you," Ken said with a concerned look on his face.

Wearing his pack on his back, Ken put my rucksack onto his chest and disappeared out of sight with an eighty pound load. I closed my eyes. I waited and hoped that he wouldn't be gone too long. After about thirty minutes he returned. He scooped me up into his arms while I wrapped my arms around his neck and held on as tight as I could. By now, I was so feeble I hardly felt any pain as we bobbed down the trail.

Then I heard the sounds of hope; a car rumbled in the distance, doors opened and slammed shut and faint voices rose up through the forest. Since it was May 5th, still early in the season, I felt encouraged that others were nearby.

Suddenly the trail ended. Black asphalt stretched across the parking lot beneath the trees. Despite my love for wilderness, the sight of man's mark on the landscape could not have cheered me more. Ken carried me to the edge of the parking lot and laid me on the ground. He retrieved the backpacks that he had stashed in the bushes and put them next to me.

"I'll be right back. I am going to find help."

He dashed through the parking lot looking for someone who could take us to the hospital. A sense of relief swept over me. I was too weak and light-headed to lift my head up and look around. I lay motionless under a small tree, next to a bush. I felt dull and lifeless. I reached up and touched my left buttock. It was swollen, black and purple, and full of dead tissue.

For the first time in five days, I finally let myself cry. I would have died if I had indulged my sorrows or allowed myself to feel the full extent of my physical and emotional pain any sooner. Now, confident that I would survive, I finally released my feelings.

Ken flagged down the first car he saw. When he asked the occupants to take us to the hospital, they declined. I was shocked when he relayed this to me. How could anyone refuse? Ken looked like he had been through an ordeal. Wasn't it obvious that we needed help?

Ken waited for another car. The next vehicle was filled with three passengers and their household belongings. Ken waived them down and pleaded for a ride. After parking the car, the man dashed over to the roadside to see me. I was covered with dirt and blood, and was white as a ghost. My braided brown hair was matted by blood. The stranger gently stroked my head and then muttered encouraging words to comfort me.

His family was moving from Utah to their new home in California. Since it was a pleasant spring day, they had taken a scenic drive up the road to Whitney Portal. After a brief conversation with his wife, the man quickly unloaded all their belongings right there in the parking lot. His wife graciously agreed to wait at the trailhead until her husband returned. Holding a baby wrapped in a warm blanket, she sauntered around the parking lot while the driver hoisted our equipment into the back seat of his car. Then the stranger came to my rescue. He gently picked me up, carried me to his vehicle, and carefully placed me on top of Ken's lap in the front passenger seat.

Gratitude welled up inside me, as did my pain. Our driver took it slow and steady through the winding curves en route to Highway 395. It was a long thirteen mile drive. Every crack and bump in the road caused me to clench my jaw and shudder.

I felt an enormous relief when we finally reached the tiny hospital in Lone Pine. Ken took our packs inside while the saintly stranger cradled me in his arms and carried me though the door. He didn't care that I was wearing dirty, stinky and blood-stained clothes. I looked up into the eyes of our driver and paused for a long time. I didn't know what to say. With a choked voice and tears streaming down my face, I tried to express my appreciation for his kindness. He carried me inside, put me onto the nearest gurney and left me in the care of doctors.

The wilderness felt far behind us now. We were quickly overwhelmed by the rush of staff inside the emergency room. Our world was suddenly noisy, sterile and safe.

I screamed in desperation, "Catheterize me, please, catheterize me!"

No one seemed to care that I had hardly peed in the last five days or that my bladder felt like it was going to explode. I had to wait; procedures had to be followed.

I was embarrassed when a nurse cut off my stained and dirty grey wool knickers. Fortunately, I couldn't see her expression when she discovered my black, blue and purple pelvis. Despite my discomfort, I still recalled the advice my mother had given me when I was a child:

Always change your underwear every day, just in case you're in an accident. Her instructions were unrealistic for backcountry travel in the wintertime. It had been a very long time since I had changed my underwear.

With my clothes removed, I was poked and prodded and examined and x-rayed. I lay motionless on the gurney while everyone around me moved in a dizzying blur. Oddly, I felt utterly alone.

The initial physical exam showed minor frost damage on my toes, a head concussion, nerve damage to my bladder and thighs, and a hematoma covering my entire left buttock, with large areas of gangrene.

X-rays revealed a long list of broken bones. Along my spine I had fractured T-12, L1, L2 and L5. My sacrum, the cornerstone for supporting the spine and pelvis, was displaced and broken in three pieces. My tailbone was completely shattered and pushed inward. My sacroiliac joints had rotated and widened. The medical report also listed probable fractures of the pubic bone and right hip. I never understood why those fractures weren't investigated any further.

Soon five pints of blood products were delivered intravenously along with periodic shots of morphine and antibiotics. I felt doped up and isolated.

The next day a surgeon sliced a six-inch swath across my left buttock. He removed blood clots, dead black tissue and subcutaneous fat. He also found a one-inch bone fragment that had come from some unidentified location in my body. Since I would be in bed for many months it would be a long time before I discovered how important butt tissue is for walking and sitting.

Despite insisting otherwise, Ken and I were placed in separate rooms because we were unmarried. We were put in adjacent rooms so that we could see each other only through the doorway.

Ken had been valiant in assisting me to safety but became emotionally distant after we had arrived to the hospital. Clearly something had changed between us. He rarely said a word from the other room and never came to visit me or initiate any interaction between us. He would wave at me from the other side of the doorway only after I waved first. I thought his behavior was odd, but I was so drowsy from painkillers I didn't give it much thought. A few days later Ken's mom picked him up and drove him home.

I was lethargic, listless and remorseful during my stay at the hospital in Lone Pine. I could barely function physically and emotionally. Yet I needed to tend to some unfinished business. First, I called my mother to tell her I was in the hospital. I didn't want to worry her so I told her I was fine, but Dr. Christenson told her otherwise. Regretfully, I also had to call Mount Rainier National Park to inform them that I would not be able to work that summer. Lastly, overcome with guilt, I also called the Inyo National Forest office to apologize for leaving my skis on the mountain.

While recovering in bed I made the last entry in our trip journal. I forced myself to recall and record our ascent and escape from Mount Whitney before it faded from my memory.

Not long after my surgery, one of the doctors told me that he didn't think it would be possible for me to hike again. For a brief moment, I was devastated. Then I decided to prove him wrong. My inner spirit was too strong to be denied. It was even larger than the mountains from which I had emerged. I was determined to roam freely again. Mount Whitney had taught me that the mind is even stronger than matter.

A week later, slower than a slug, I emerged from my bed. I hobbled unsteadily down the short hallway wearing a half-opened hospital gown. Behind me I toted a wheeled metal pole with bags of IV fluids and blood transfusions. Looking around, I noticed that the other patients were all elderly. That's when I realized that the hospital was primarily a geriatric facility. Perhaps that explained why the residents seemed so shocked to see me.

As I inched my way down the hall, doctors and nurses were aghast. Yet they were also amazed by my determination. Soon smiles crept across their faces. As I strolled slowly back to my room, everyone cheered me on. These were only baby steps, but they marked a new beginning.

10

THE SHADOW OF WHITNEY

Nine days later I was stable enough to be transferred. My concerned mother arrived in Lone Pine with a borrowed station wagon and convinced the staff at Southern Inyo Hospital to let her take me to a better facility. I was loaded into the rear of the vehicle and then covered with blankets. An IV bag mixed with morphine was hung on a hook by the back window so that I would be oblivious and pain-free for the entire journey. The long drive must have been torturous for my mother. She endured five hours of silence while her disabled, unconscious daughter lay out of sight behind her.

I was confused and disoriented when I woke up. Men dressed in scrub suits leaned over me in a parking lot. They transferred me onto a gurney, wheeled me past a sign with large red letters and took me into the emergency room at Scripps Memorial Hospital in San Diego.

Attentive nurses watched over me. At all hours they entered my room to administer more IV fluids, pills and medical advice. I dozed in and out of sleep for seven more days before I was finally sent home.

New challenges awaited me. It was too painful to sleep with Ken on our futon on the floor. I couldn't lower myself to the ground, and the bed was too hard for my broken bones. Instead I moved into the spare bedroom with a softer twin bed. That angered Ken. His response left me bewildered. Couldn't he understand that comfort supported healing?

A few weeks after I returned to San Diego, Ken departed for his summer job at Mount Rainier National Park. Sadness filled my heart when he drove away. My dream had been crushed. We wouldn't spend the summer together at Mount Rainier nor would I lead nature walks from the Paradise Visitor Center. Instead, unable to live alone, I moved in with my mother.

It was the summer from hell. My life was dreary. I spent four months in bed dulled by painkillers. For the first few weeks I wore a horribly uncomfortable white medical corset. Once it was removed, I lay as straight as I could. This was the advice I had been given to heal.

I read books, watched television and slept a lot. I was astounded by how much physical energy is needed to heal the body. I required inordinate amounts of rest. I was also weak and thin. I weighed less than a hundred pounds. To bulk up, I frequently indulged in chocolate brownies with vanilla ice cream.

As a young adult I was humiliated to be living with my mother. She graciously shared her king-size bed with me. It must have been difficult for her too. She was single and outgoing. That summer she gave up dating and entertaining—activities that ordinarily brought her a great deal of joy. Now her weekends and evenings were devoted to assisting her helpless daughter.

Each time I needed to get out of bed, I maneuvered slowly and carefully. With a foggy mind I waddled across the wooden floor to the bathroom. One day while trying to empty my catheter bag, I inadvertently tilted the plastic pouch and spilled urine all over the floor. I cried out loud. I was filled with shame and embarrassment. My mother came to the rescue. She cleaned up my mess and helped me back into bed. I felt like a child. I desperately wanted my independence, but it would be many months before I would be able to take care of myself.

In the meantime, medications lessened the physical pain. These drugs also numbed my mind and emotions. During brief periods of lucidity, I searched for answers. I reflected deeply about life and suffering. Watching the news reminded me that I was not alone; every day all over the world, people endure a great deal of misery.

My mother, a psychologist, wanted to help me find peace. One day she came home with the 1981 bestseller by Rabbi Harold Kushner, *When Bad Things Happen to Good People*. The author made a case for people as victims of random events. For a short while I believed it. I accepted the notion because I needed to make sense out of my situation. With time, the book's logic no longer worked for me. I continued to search for understanding and dreamed of new adventures—the kind I had vowed to live for.

First, I had to heal. My mother took me to the best plastic surgeon in the area. He took out the drain tubes that had been put in my buttock after the gangrene was removed in Lone Pine. During a follow-up appointment he gave me two options. I could leave my buttock to heal as it was or have reconstructive surgery. Unfortunately, I was young and stupefied from painkillers. I didn't understand that plastic surgery could be partially reconstructive, so I elected to live with an ugly butt that few would ever see.

Over the ensuing weeks I received out-patient treatment at the hospital. Several days a week I was strapped into a full-body harness. Then I was lowered into a special chest-deep hot tub to clean the deep wound on my buttock. Before redressing my butt, nurses gently applied an antibiotic cream imbedded with silver minerals.

Physical therapy followed. I was given only a few ineffective sessions. I am not sure why, but I was left to regain strength and movement on my own. Decades later, I am still dealing with the consequences of scar tissue and insufficient early rehabilitation.

All summer my mother and I consulted with specialists. A pattern soon emerged. Despite each doctor's area of expertise, the nature of each interaction was predictable. Every physician was amazed that I was alive and none could fathom why I wasn't paralyzed. Criticism came next. I endured the disapproving words of countless doctors who reproached me about the ski trip. Their words hurt me and weakened their ability to be trusted by their patient.

My urologist was the exception. He understood that people in crisis need more than medical attention They also need loving support, patience and sometimes forgiveness. Dr. Ambrose McLaughlin connected with his patients on a personal level. He expressed his passion for mountains through sharing his own stories with me about his treks and climbs in the Peruvian Andes. He was the only doctor who had the courage and integrity to talk honestly with me about how my injuries might affect my future. His medical expertise and gentle bed-side manner also helped me to cope with a dysfunctional bladder.

By summer's end I could take incremental strolls near my mother's home. I increased my endurance one block at a time. My mind became clearer as medications became a thing of the past. Still, I worried about the mounting medical bills. I had virtually no savings and couldn't work. Then my mother informed me that I had been covered under my father's health insurance for most of the summer. I was relieved that I wouldn't be in debt for the rest of my life. The highest expenses were incurred just before the coverage expired on my twenty-third birthday. My father paid the majority of the remaining bills without ever mentioning it.

When Ken returned home in the fall we moved back into his grandmother's empty house in San Diego. Now that I was mobile Ken insisted that I not tell others what had happened on Mount Whitney. Nor did he want anyone to know about our amazing adventure. He made it a taboo topic even between the two of us. I didn't understand why. He refused to explain why this was important to him. I often wondered if he felt guilty, embarrassed, or ashamed. Not talking about it was his way of not dealing with it, and perhaps even denying what had happened. I shouldn't have been surprised. Ken had responded the same way after his father died during his childhood.

The shadow of Mount Whitney was now visible in our relationship, like a narrow crack splitting the stony face of a mountain. At first, it was just a dark crevice shaded from the sunlight of open-hearted communication. It was the place where neither of us dared to probe. By not healing this fracture between us we unconsciously let it erode into a deep chasm.

It wasn't until I agreed to do a presentation for the San Diego Chapter of the Sierra Club that I learned how vehemently Ken felt about keeping our incident quiet. While arranging slides for the presentation, he reminded me not to bring up the accident. He expected me to simply conclude the show by talking about our victory climb up Mount Whitney. I thought this was ludicrous. It was also dishonest. What could be so wrong with admitting that we had made some mistakes? After all, it's human nature to make poor choices once in a while. Reluctantly, I honored Ken's request. Over three hundred people came to the event in Balboa Park. They were all unknowing witnesses to my deceit. I disliked myself for not revealing the whole story.

I respected Ken's wish with only a few exceptions. I secretly confided in my college professor Bob O'Brien. We had a lot in common. We shared a love of geography, mountains and national parks. As a young man, Bob had worked as a seasonal ranger at Mount Rainier. Coincidently, shortly after my ordeal on Mount Whitney, he broke his back in a climbing accident on Mont Blanc in France. After he had recovered, I visited him at his office. Our friendship deepened after I shared my story with him. It also opened Bob emotionally so that he had someone he could talk to about his own tragedy with his son in the Alps. Discussing our ensuing struggles bonded us for life.

Bob was also the person who inspired my dream to see the Himalayas. Even after I graduated from college, he invited me to come to his classroom whenever he taught about Nepal's cultural and physical geography. Bob's lectures were always interesting, but it was really the images of the peaks that lured me back to his classroom. Of all the places that Bob had traveled, Nepal had touched his heart the most. It was as if he had given me the torch to carry on his love for the Himalayas.

Bob and I never lost contact even after I moved away. Each time I returned to San Diego for family visits, we got together for a hike or a meal. Bob played a crucial role in my life. He inspired dreams, counseled me on careers, listened to my struggles and believed in me. He was a friend, mentor and fatherly figure.

During the first year after my accident, I slowly regained physical strength. Then I became active again. With the exception of my bladder, it was almost as if nothing had happened. For the next two years Ken and I returned to the mountains each spring for short trans-Sierra ski trips. During the summers we worked as park rangers. Ken returned to his job at Mount Rainier while I went back to Glacier National Park. Ken was offered a permanent job at Rocky Mountain National Park in 1985. We got married shortly after we moved to Colorado.

By 1986 I felt that I was finally strong enough to pursue my dearest-held dream—to trek in the Himalayas. My struggle to stay alive on Mount Whitney had been fueled by this ambition. I needed to honor the vow I had made to myself when Death visited me. Since Ken had no desire to go to Nepal, I invited my friend Maura. I didn't actually know her very well. Nevertheless, I felt that we would be compatible travelers.

Maura and I met while working as seasonal rangers in Glacier National Park. She had been a backcountry and law enforcement ranger while I provided educational programs. She was a fit, accomplished climber with exceptional leadership skills. Maura had a formidable presence. She was ambitious, strong willed and confident. Even though she was straight to the point whenever she spoke, she had a great sense of humor. Her face was framed with shiny jet-black hair that draped down to her shoulders. Her sharply pointed nose was off-set by deep, piercing blue eyes.

I was elated when she accepted my offer. We planned to depart in October of 1986. In the meantime, I needed to acquire funds for the trip. My savings were limited. Both of us were traveling on a tight budget due to the seasonal nature of our incomes. To raise more money, I sold my Volkswagen Bug. Next I pawned the diamond ring that I had won in a bingo game as a teenager. I borrowed money to cover the remaining expenses. That first trip to the Himalayas was the best investment I ever made. The journey changed the direction of my entire life.

A few months before our departure, my bladder became an obstacle. It was increasingly difficult for me to urinate. No matter how hard I bared down I could barely pee. Something had to be done. I flew back to San Diego to consult with my urologist. I didn't like his plan. He suggested that I self-catheterize every time I needed to relieve myself. I was horrified, but out of desperation I was willing to give it a try. Not only was it uncomfortable, it was socially awkward. I spent a long time in the bathroom at work, at home and when out in public places.

It was even more difficult to catheterize myself on weekends. I hated everything about it. The medical supplies had to be kept sterile even though I was outside. While hiking I disappeared for a long time to find a private location to do my business. Worse yet was having to pee while climbing up a cliff. Being female didn't help. I would stop on a ledge, tie myself into protective climbing hardware, and remove the climbing harness around my pelvis before relieving myself. I trusted that this procedure might help the few nerves still working in my bladder to relax enough for less forceful urination.

As the summer progressed I wondered how I would manage to catheterize myself while in Nepal. I worried about getting severe infections on the trail in an undeveloped country. There had to be a way. I wasn't going to let my dream vanish. I tallied up the number of disposable catheters I would need for seven weeks and how many porters I would need to hire to carry them all! In hindsight this seems ridiculous, but at the time, going to the Himalayas was the single most important thing in my life.

Slowly my bladder improved. By autumn I could urinate on my own with less difficulty. Dr. McLaughlin's plan worked. To be safe, I packed a few reusable catheters in my luggage as emergency insurance.

PART II

A HARVEST OF DREAMS

One must remain in the vastness,
alert and lucid,
Letting one's gaze encompass
the infinity of the sky,
As though seated on the summit
of a mountain open
to all horizons.

Shabkar Tsogdruk Rangdrol,
Eighteenth century Tibetan yogi

11

TEARS OF PURE DELIGHT

A Korean Airlines jet carried Maura and me from Los Angeles to Anchorage. Our connecting ticket to Seoul included a sunset flight over the sea and multiple layovers. As we embarked over the Pacific Ocean, the twilight was mystical. Below us the Aleutian Islands peeked in and out of a rose-colored fog and the endless expanse of azure water slowly faded into the dark night.

By the time we reached Seoul, we were delirious with jet-lag. Utterly exhausted, we searched the airport for a suitable place to sleep. Upstairs we collapsed onto two tattered brown couches. Though filthy and threadbare, they were comfortable. Seven hours later we departed for Taipei. By now, we were beginning to question our sanity. Were our cheap air tickets worth the price of puddle-jumping between Asian countries just to save a few hundred dollars? Probably not. Our stop in Taiwan was also lengthy. There, we spent another five hours pacing through the airport before continuing to Thailand.

Bangkok sprawled across the landscape like a sea of corrugated cement. Congested roads crisscrossed the city. Buildings were marked with neon signs, laundry hanging from windows, and the sinuous roof-lines of Buddhist temples.

It wasn't the greenery that told us we were in the tropics; it was the hot steamy air. Our air-conditioned hotel offered the only respite from the heat. A few hours later, we were awakened by a cacophonous sound coming from outside. Maura and I leapt from our beds and pulled the curtains open. Flashes of white lightning tore across the midnight sky. Outside monsoonal rains fell in thick sheets.

The next day we flew to Nepal. During the last part of the flight, passengers suddenly jumped up from their seats and rushed over to the right side of the airplane. The Himalayas stretched beyond the windows from Bhutan through Nepal and on to India. They were cloaked in flowing robes of ice with sharp summits piercing the clouds.

Amidst the expanse of white jagged peaks, Mount Everest rose far above the other mountains. Extreme winds from the jet stream had blasted its black triangular summit free of snow. I smiled with the anticipation of standing at its feet. Soon the plane descended through a thick band of clouds before breaking out into the sunshine. Below us were steep chartreuse hills, terraced and dotted with earthen houses.

Now I am home, declared my inner voice.

This statement took me aback. How could that be? Curious, I asked myself where that thought came from. How could I feel that way? I had never been here before. The jet was still in the air; we weren't even on the ground yet. This thought was unexplainable. It was just an inner-knowing. I had come home; I was finally where I belonged.

Just before landing, a massive white dome came into view. It was other worldly. The imposing edifice was the stupa of Boudhanath, a sacred Buddhist structure filled with holy objects. Rising out of its arched roof was a tower composed of tiered layers of cement. The spire extended towards the sky like a mountain soaring up from the Earth. Large eyes, painted on all four of its sides, looked out across the landscape. They were the eyes of the Buddha.

Soon we landed on the tarmac, collected our luggage and emerged into the city. I expected Kathmandu to be the size of an over-grown village. Instead it was a cluster of three large cities. The Kathmandu Valley was dissected with narrow dirt streets meandering among red-bricked buildings. Roadways were jammed with pedestrians, rickshaws and cars.

Here, the divine intermingled with the profane. Sacred cows dodged honking cars while dining on heaps of rotting roadside garbage. Nearby pilgrims, beggars, and Indian salesmen jostled for sidewalk space. Hindu shrines were on every block. They came in all sizes and shapes. Stone statues were decorated with the devotions of marigold flowers strewn on their laps and vermillion powder smeared on their faces. Wafts of incense sweetened the polluted air. Kathmandu was the epitome of exotic. I loved it.

On our first day of sightseeing Maura and I took a taxi to Swayambhunath. The 2,000-year old temple was the crowning ornament on a steep hilltop. We first had to tromp up 365 stone steps to reach the top. Nirvana wasn't waiting for us at the summit. Monkeys were. Hundreds of them lived on the grounds explaining why this site is also known as the Monkey Temple. These primates were obnoxious and dangerous. Cooperating together like vicious gangs, they taunted hapless tourists for handouts of food and stole their cameras and bags. I found their aggressive behavior downright threatening, especially knowing that they were prone to rabies.

Gilded in gold and glittering in the late morning sunshine, the stupa was uplifting to behold. Buddhist and Hindu pilgrims were more numerous than monkeys. Devotees circumambulated the stupa with hopes that they might reach a higher state of being. They prayed to realize enlightenment, the symbolic meaning of the stupa. The faithful believed that aversion, delusion and unquenchable desires were the roots of mental anguish. These emotions give rise to a monkey-like mind with thoughts leaping from one to the next, in a state of perpetual distraction and dissatisfaction. Instead, the devout sought enlightenment. To abide in this state of lasting tranquility and joy, they first had to conquer the ego that ruled their minds.

I was curious about these worshippers. Their rituals, prayers and beliefs seemed radically different from my Catholic upbringing. As we strolled through the complex, I was intrigued by the unusual religious figures, sacred shapes and symbols. Colorful prayer flags, cooing pigeons and thick greenery growing on the hillside enhanced the area's charm.

Although we enjoyed visiting Swayambhunath and other tourist sites in the city, Maura and I were eager to get into the Himalayas. A few days after our arrival, we got together with Dwayne and Peter, whom we had met on the plane from Bangkok to Kathmandu. We decided to join together for our trek to Everest Base Camp and our climb up Island Peak. Since we were starting our hike at the same time and with the same itinerary, it made sense to share the costs of porters to carry our gear. We also thought that having two climbing teams would increase our safety.

Dwayne was from California. His tall frame was capped with light brown hair. He was sociable and sometimes cocky. Peter was just the opposite with dark curly locks, a short stature and a calm, laid-back personality. Since Peter was from Canada he often shared a refreshing perspective on the world around him.

Before leaving the city we tended to logistics for the trip. Supplies needed to be purchased and trekking permits secured from government offices. We scrambled to get everything done quickly. A Hindu holiday was about to shut down the country for ten days.

A few mornings later the four of us gathered at the bus station. Ramshackle buses were chaotically packed into the area. The parking lot was muddy and covered with pond-sized pools of water left from the monsoon. We wandered around until we found the two porters that we had hired the day before to carry our gear into the mountains. Together we boarded a crowded coach. Once inside, I was grateful for my short stature. The seats were designed for small-framed Asians.

Our vehicle made frequent stops all day. At each town more passengers crammed inside. When the bus was full, new riders piled onto the roof. The contraption was packed with people, luggage, caged chickens and burlap sacks full of rice. Whenever the bus stopped for a tea break, our foursome rotated turns riding on the roof. Sitting on top was advantageous. The breezy location kept us out of the reach of carsick passengers and their projectile vomit. From the top, we could also watch our duffle bags. Preventing thievery was paramount. Each time the bus stopped at a village the baggage was reshuffled as passengers clambered off and on the vehicle.

From our perch we enjoyed views of green terraced hillsides. Enormous rivers, frothy with mud and glacial silt, raged below us. The bus careened around countless curves and climbed up and down steep slopes. Our wild ride concluded in the dark twelve hours later. We were finally at the end of the road in the village of Jiri.

Both sides of the street were lined with dingy guest houses. We stumbled with exhaustion into the closest accommodation. The interior was dark and smoky. After a simple meal of rice and watery lentils, we were shown to the lodge's sleeping room, a large space lined with wooden platforms covered with thin, soiled mattresses. Maura and I grinned at each other with disgust. The place wasn't appealing, but it was the kind of lodging we would sleep in for the next six weeks. We laid out our bags and went to sleep.

Over the next ten days we trekked through the Solu Khumbu, the hill country leading towards Mount Everest. Each day Dwayne and Peter disappeared far ahead of us. At first, I managed to keep up with Maura but after a few days on the trail, I knew I couldn't match her pace for long. The rugged terrain was challenging on my knees. Each day we hiked several thousand feet up and down from one canyon into the next.

By the third day Maura and I nicknamed ourselves Gumby and Pokey. Like the cartoon character Gumby, Maura was lean, fast and nimble. I was Pokey because I consistently lagged behind the others. Nevertheless, I enjoyed going solo at my own speed. Maura and I often met for lunch at a tea house along our route. In the evenings our group of four reunited at a designated village. Dinners were always enjoyable. After our meal we sat around a hissing kerosene lantern and conversed with other trekkers about trail conditions and the rain.

The monsoon was lasting longer than usual. Trails were slippery and treacherous with water and mud flowing across the stone-stepped paths. At times it seemed as if we were hiking down a narrow river instead of a footpath.

The rain brought out the leeches. They lingered on the dense vegetation waiting for a hapless pedestrian. Their presence made us tenuous about peeing in the forest. One night Maura and I camped in our light-weight floorless tent rather than stay in the dismal lodge nearby. It was a poor decision. I urinated in the woods just before sleeping. Then in the middle of the night something squirmed between my legs. I grabbed my headlamp, dashed out of the tent and pulled down my pants. A leech was in my crotch. I felt violated. It was utterly disgusting. We didn't camp again until we reached the dry, higher elevations.

Our trek traversed through terraced fields interspersed with groves of forest. Waterfalls occasionally poured down the steep slopes. The villages were increasingly picturesque. Nepali culture was part of the terrain and our experience. Everything about the culture was foreign and fascinating. It was as if I had landed on another planet. The locals had different lifestyles, beliefs and values. These made me question my own world view. At first this was unsettling.

Life seemed very hard in Nepal. Families had nothing. They struggled to eke a living off the land. Their rural homes were made of mud or wooden planks. Chimneys were rare. From a distance, whole villages sometimes looked as if they were on fire. Smoke poured out from the gaps of homes while the woman cooked inside on an open fire pit. Trash littered the landscape and outhouses perched over rivers. Human waste dropped right into the water where it was carried downstream to the next village.

Higher into the mountains, hamlets were more prosperous. Many Sherpas worked as shopkeepers or porters. Others owned their own lodges. The Sherpas, an ethnic group that emigrated from Tibet hundreds of years ago, dominated the Everest region. They were Buddhists just like the more recent refugees from Tibet. Since the 1950s, many Tibetans had fled to Nepal for religious freedom. Some had suffered from the Chinese occupation of their homeland. Many had lost family members, been jailed, tortured or raped.

Despite the hardships that people from Nepal and Tibet had endured, they seemed remarkably happy. Their attitude towards life inspired me. They accepted their situation with greater ease than Westerners could. They had virtually nothing and yet they seemed content. These impressions set me on a life-long inquiry about the essence of happiness. I knew from experience that the American model for happiness was an illusion. Happiness is not about having more.

Our porters also had very little. They worked for only pennies a day as laborers who carried loads for trekkers. This was the going wage.

Nonetheless, they were thrilled to be employed. They were indispensable to us for transporting our excessive gear. We had brought a lot of equipment with us for high-altitude hiking, camping and mountaineering.

Since our two porters were hired in Kathmandu, they weren't prepared for high altitude weather or rocky trails. The men relied on sheets of plastic for rain coats and flip flops for footwear. Years of hiking in rugged terrain had toughened their feet. Their soles were covered with deep grooves and thick calluses.

After nearly ten days of trekking, our porters decided to return to the city. They declared their intentions when we reached the village of Namche Bazaar at 11,000 feet. Now we were in a predicament. It was nearly impossible to hire new porters here. We soon learned that low-elevation workers frequently quit as soon as they reached the mountains. This resulted in a severe shortage of employees at the higher elevations.

Our only option was to hire a big black yak, a hairy high-altitude beast related to the buffalo. Pasang Norbu, from whose family we rented the yak, spoke only a few words of English. We were suspicious when he told us that he was nineteen years old. He looked and acted like he was fifteen. We also had doubts about his ability to guide a yak.

The next morning Pasang carefully loaded our duffels onto his yak before bidding his mother farewell. At first he seemed a bit tenuous about herding the animal up the trail. He walked slowly behind the beast, shouting and whistling to keep him on track. Gradually Pasang grew accustomed to the yak and to our company.

The air became thin as we approached the hamlet of Tengboche. From a distance it looked like Shangri-La. It's the kind of place that one imagines in a dream, with a white and ochre-colored Tibetan monastery perched on the center of a long ridge with giant Himalayan peaks rising 17,000 feet higher than the settlement.

When we finally reached this tiny village we were dazzled by the setting. Besides the mountains that towered above us, the temple at Tengboche was alluring. Monks sat on the steps singing, chanting and praying in the sunshine. The monastery was encircled by a stone wall inscribed with hand-chiseled Tibetan prayers.

Shortly after our arrival, Maura and I walked quietly through the building's courtyard. Following the local custom, we stopped at the entrance door and removed our shoes. Filled with curiosity, we knocked on the door. After a short wait the door squeaked open. Standing behind it was a monk in his early twenties, dressed in maroon-robes and wearing a gentle smile. Although he seemed embarrassed by his limited English, he gestured for us to enter and then politely showed us around.

Silence pervaded the interior. We could appreciate the sensory feast inside only after our eyes adjusted to the darkness. The atmosphere was tranquil. Illuminated in the dim yellow candlelight was the focal point of the temple, a huge Buddha statue gilded in bronze, copper and gold. Its face was serene. Adorned with a subtle smile and eyes gazing gently downward, the Buddha appeared to possess the secret to happiness. Before the figure was an altar with neatly arranged offerings. Small bowls were filled with the liquid gold of saffron-infused water. Each miniature pool reflected the adjacent flames of flickering butter lamps.

The other walls of the shrine room were lined with intricately painted wooden cupboards. Their open shelves were stacked with prayer books. They were carefully wrapped in a rainbow of colorful brocade. In the center of the room, thinly cushioned benches were arranged in rows, each dotted with small piles of burgundy blankets.

A strong musty smell from burning candles made of rancid butter was mixed with the sweet, earthy aroma of juniper incense. The whole scene was intriguing. I left with an insatiable curiosity about what I had just seen and experienced; it was as if I had just glimpsed inside a treasure box full of mysterious items, each with an untold, fascinating story.

Outside, our companions Dwayne and Peter were nowhere in sight. They had gone to a nearby tea house as soon as we arrived. Instead of staying at a lodge, Maura and I decided to camp in the meadow below the monastery. We set up our triangular blue and grey tent in one of the most scenic campsites in the world. There were even views of Mount Everest from the outhouse!

The immense black wall of Lhotse dominated the skyline. It towered above us at nearly 28,000 feet. Poking above Lhotse's ridge was Mount Everest. From this viewpoint, we could only see its pyramid-shaped summit. In the foreground were the mountains of Kangtega and Ama

Dablam. Their names were familiar. For years I had stared at them on the map that hung on my bedroom wall. I had cherished the sight of that topographic map everyday; it reminded me to pursue my greatest dreams.

Although Ama Dablam is 7,000 feet lower than Mount Everest, many people think it is the most beautiful mountain on the planet. The peak's name is translated from the Sherpa language as the *Mother of Jewels*. The mountain is draped in wrinkled robes of ice with two long rocky arms descending on either side of its pointed summit. Each snow-covered crease rises thousands of feet up the mountain's flanks. The peak's shape, with its fluted white ridges, gives it the appearance of an angel spreading its wings.

These mountains were such a divine sight to behold that there was no other place in the world that I wanted to be. I felt like I belonged here; the Himalayas were the abode of my spirit.

Ama Dablam glowing in the moonlight

A cold night awaited us. After midnight Maura and I woke up intentionally to see the full moon illuminating the Himalayan giants. Our eyes nearly popped out of their sockets when we exited our frost-covered tent.

"Wow!" we exclaimed almost simultaneously.

We gawked at the peaks together for a few minutes. Then we wandered off in separate directions to enjoy the scenery in solitude. After about twenty minutes I saw Maura return to the tent. I was determined to stay out as long as I could. Despite shivering from the bone-chilling temperature of 10 degrees, I experienced ninety minutes of bliss while strolling around Tengboche in the dark.

Tengboche Monastery in the moonlight

Heavy frost covered the ground. The moonlight had transformed it into a field of shimmering diamonds. The highest peaks on Earth glowed like silver-white goddesses reaching for the sky. With steam coming from my breath, I walked to the hilltop to maximize the view. The soundscape was equally enchanting; glacial rivers rushed in the distance, yak bells chimed in the pastures below, and occasionally an avalanche rumbled down a mountainside.

I was mesmerized by a flag pole in the center of the meadow. Stamped with prayers in black ink, its vertical white cloth whipped back and forth in the breeze carrying blessings to the world's inhabitants. For a long time, I sat beneath the pole and stared at the mountains. I felt

Tengboche's strong spiritual energy permeate my soul. After years of yearning to see the Himalayas, I wondered if this was merely a dream; it was just too good to be true. I soaked in the beauty and silence until I couldn't endure the freezing temperatures any longer. When I crawled back into the tent, Maura was fast asleep.

The next day we left Tengboche and began our ascent into a long glacial valley. As we gained altitude the trees became shorter. Eventually the junipers completely disappeared; it was too cold for them to live up here. Still, the brown tundra vegetation excited me; growing next to the path were some of the same alpine plants found in the Rocky Mountains.

Shortly after reaching the tiny village of Periche, we got our first glimpse of Island Peak. Its 20,000-foot summit was dwarfed by larger mountains in the adjacent valley. Island Peak is one of the easiest ascents in the Himalayas. Our plan was to climb it after we returned from Everest Base Camp.

It hadn't occurred to me to question whether I was physically up for mountain climbing. Nonetheless, upon seeing Island Peak, doubt arose in my mind. I didn't know if my trepidation was just a shadow from the emotional ghost of Mount Whitney, a lack of confidence or intuition.

While I felt anxious about the climb, Maura and Dwayne expressed their disenchantment. Island Peak looked easier than they expected. I felt conflicted. I did not want to let Maura down. Climbing Island Peak was important to her. After a full day of thinking about it, I told Maura that the mountain was too much for me. Peter had also lost interest in the ascent. Maura responded with grace and compassion, and then made plans to climb the peak with Dwayne.

From Periche we headed up the valley that would eventually take us to the base of Mount Everest. En route we traversed a broad basin with short brown grass and a braided, meandering stream. The river was thick with grey glacial silt and sparkling bits of mica. Upstream the Khumbu Glacier was actively grinding rocks, adding minerals and pulverized stone into the waterway. When I dipped my hands into the icy river to filter some drinking water, my fingers quickly turned purple and numb.

Up ahead, the trail climbed steeply towards Lobuche. Our map indicated that it was a village, but it was actually just a compound of canvas tents serving as temporary guest houses.

I felt queasy as I dragged myself up the path to 16,000 feet. I wondered if I was nauseated from something I ate at a tea house. More worrisome was that I might be experiencing the early symptoms of acute mountain sickness.

Soon a sobering sight came into view. Up ahead neatly stacked piles of rocks, each from three to five feet tall, formed a line across a ridge. They were memorials to climbers who had lost their lives on Mount Everest and on other surrounding peaks. I walked off the trail to take a closer look. Names of the deceased were painted or chiseled onto the center stone of each monument. Written in multiple languages, they were a testimony to the lure of the Himalayas. People come from all over the globe to climb these mountains, behold the sight of them, and even worship them.

A solemn mood swept over me. The cairns alerted trekkers and climbers that these mountains could be deadly. The lack of oxygen, avalanches, and steep slopes could kill any of us. To me, the monuments were symbols of untold stories of tragedy and loss. My eyes became wet and my gut tightened as I strolled past the stone pillars. Before moving on I paused with gratitude. Despite the shadow that Mount Whitney had cast upon my life, I felt blessed that I had survived my own ordeal in the Sierras. I whispered a prayer for the unfortunate and then hiked on.

Even though it was only mid-afternoon, we stopped for the night at Lobuche. It was critical to limit our elevation gains to small increments each day. Sometimes we spent multiple nights at the same altitude. This was the best strategy for preventing altitude sickness. At 16,200 feet, Lobuche was a chilly place to linger; we needed warm clothing just to lounge in the afternoon sunshine.

As evening approached, trekkers gathered in anticipation of another entrancing Himalayan sunset. Blue shadows inched slowly across the glacial valley while the setting sun tinged the peaks in red alpine glow. The short moment of twilight awe was followed by a long and wickedly cold night.

There weren't many options for dinner. We were hesitant about eating at one of Lobuche's primitive lodges. The sanitation was questionable—heaps of trash and piles of human excrement littered our surroundings. Only the mountain views compensated for the stench. While dogs dined on waste outside, we ate at the local restaurant inside a large canvas tent.

Our meal was unappetizing, but we needed the calories. Lively conversations were common at dinner. Although Dwayne could be charming and engaging, Maura and I were sometimes annoyed by his egocentric behavior. His voice often dominated around the dinner table. That night he didn't have a chance. Instead fellow trekkers were more interested in Dr. Ben Levine. The doctor captivated everyone with his hair-raising tales of evacuating hikers with pulmonary edema. The American physician was taking a break from his work at a medical clinic in Periche so he could visit Everest Base Camp. That night, like most evenings, we shared a dialogue with mountain lovers from all over the world. Foreigners conversed until bedtime about politics, terrorism, dreams of peace, and the next best place to travel.

I returned to our tent filled with excitement for the coming day. Before going to sleep I wrote in my journal:

I'm not even at Kala Pattar yet, but the dream becomes clearer and clearer. I am here. I am alive, and at last I am seeing and experiencing what has been so important to me for so long. This is above anything I have experienced before. Being here is the greatest gift of all time.

The next morning we hiked into a surreal alpine world filled with icy brooks, rocky glacial debris and mounds of hummocky grass. I stopped frequently to catch my breath in the cold, thin air. The scenery became more spectacular with each step. A morainal ridge dropped steeply to the Khumbu Glacier on the right side of the trail. This river of ice flowed down from Mount Everest and its satellite peaks. Occasionally rocks tumbled off the moraine and onto the ice below. The Khumbu Glacier wasn't as white and pristine as the Alaskan glaciers that I had seen in my teens. Instead it was covered in dirt, rocks and rubble. It was heavily furrowed and pockmarked with ridges, holes and crevasses.

Sharp white peaks loomed above. They struck a deep chord in my soul. Tears of pure delight poured down my red, raw and wind-burned cheeks. Finally, I was approaching the valley of my dreams. It was a sanctuary of sorts—a bowl-shaped basin lined by a wall of immense mountains.

I felt privileged to be here. My supportive boss back at Rocky Mountain National Park had also dreamed of trekking in the Himalayas, but his wish would never be realized. He had fallen out of a tree in his twenties while doing raptor research. As a paraplegic, Michael Smithson, couldn't walk these trails. Along the way, I thought of him frequently and carried him in my heart.

After several miles we arrived at Gorak Shep. In the middle of an expansive sandy flat was a single tea house, its earthen walls topped with a canvas canopy. It provided hikers with meager food and shabby cots for sleeping. At nearly 17,000 feet it would be a bitter November night regardless of where we slept. Dwayne and Peter opted to sleep inside while Maura and I preferred to camp.

After setting up our tent, we headed up the trail towards Kala Pattar. Its summit offers quintessential views of Mount Everest. The trek appeared easy and straightforward with diverging trails that crisscrossed up a tall conical hill.

The altitude proved otherwise; it was a grueling hike. Gumby was far ahead of me. I stopped every few hundred feet to catch my breath. Higher up, I paused every thirty feet. The elevation gain made my mind dull and spacey. I felt giddy and slightly delirious too. The altitude made me feel like I had consumed too much wine on an empty stomach. I also had a headache. My body needed rest and hydration. I sat down on a large rock and drank a quart of Gatorade before continuing the ascent. By the time I neared the top, my exuberance had completely suppressed my headache. Soon I scrambled gleefully across the black rocks on the pinnacle of my greatest aspiration.

The light was dazzling up at 18,619 feet. It was painful to be without sunglasses for even a moment. The white peaks glistened in the afternoon sunshine and reflected the intense light off their heavy coats of monsoonal snow. The Himalayas contrasted sharply with the dark sky. At this altitude, daytime skies are the color of indigo ink bordering on black.

Mount Everest seemed close enough to touch. Rising into the jet stream at over 29,000 feet, its windblown summit was bulky, barren and less attractive than its neighboring peaks. By contrast, the adjacent mountain, Nuptse was striking. Its long ridgeline curves thousands of feet towards the sky, culminating into a narrow pointed summit.

The upper Khumbu Glacier was nestled between the two peaks. Glacial ice flowed down from an alpine cirque into a steep jumble of ice blocks the size of multi-storied buildings. Below us, at the bottom of the valley was Everest Base Camp. Colorful tents dotted the dirty, rubble-strewn ice. It didn't look particularly inviting.

Maura and I joined a handful of trekkers on the narrow summit of Kala Pattar. The scene reminded me of a small party. While waiting for the sunset, the group shared their stories of adventure. As evening approached the sun slipped behind the jagged horizon and left us in the shade. The air temperature plunged. Everyone reached into their packs; out came the winter clothes—down coats, wool hats, and mittens. After bundling up, a dozen cameras were poised to record the evening light.

Soon the sun painted a fiery palette on the mountains. Everest and Nuptse turned orange against a navy blue sky. Next, the peaks were tinted salmon, then rose, before turning a wintry grey. Exclamations of wonderment broke the silence. The roof of the world had beckoned all of us to this place. We each had our own reasons for being here.

I needed solitude to process my emotions. As I moved away from the group, I hoped that my glacier goggles were dark enough to hide my moist eyes. This very moment was a personal triumph—I was finally at the place and point in time that I had lived for when I had promised myself on Mount Whitney, that if I lived until morning, I would pursue my greatest dreams. For me, Everest symbolized being alive. The apex of the world had galvanized me to accomplish the impossible. In its enormous shadow, I sobbed with joy. I was overcome with gratitude for having escaped the Sierras with my life and now for living my life to the fullest in the Himalayas. I wanted nothing more than to feast my eyes on this view; to pay homage to that which is sacred, beautiful and inspiring.

I lingered on top longer than the other trekkers. I wanted to stay, but the fading light and frigid air drove me downward. I descended by the light of my headlamp. With each step, I left behind my own trail of tears. It had been the best day of my life.

Sunset on Mount Everest (left) and Nuptse (right)

At Gorak Shep I joined our group in a smoke-filled canvas tent for a flavorless meal of rice and lentils. After dinner Dr. Levine read aloud from *A Fine and Pleasant Misery* by Patrick McInnis. He even read my sister Debby's favorite short story, "The Big Trip." This yarn captures the essence of nearly every outdoor adventure—there is always some degree of despair in every important journey. For me, this adventure was no exception.

Later that night, I felt the altitude catch up to me. My head throbbed. Occasionally my skull felt like it was being hit with a baseball bat. My stomach twisted and turned and I hacked up thick phlegm. I wasn't sure if I had bronchitis or if this was my cold weather, exercise-induced asthma. I hoped it wasn't pulmonary edema. I was awake most of the night just trying to breathe. I lay on a partially filled backpack to prop my chest up.

To distract myself from discomfort, I listened to the soundscape of barking dogs, clanging yak bells, and the music of flowing streams and the swooshing of wind. The mountains felt alive. The Khumbu Glacier creaked and moaned each time it shifted, and ice popped off the nearby peaks sending massive avalanches roaring down the steep slopes.

I drifted in and out of sleep. Then I heard soft footsteps on the frozen ground outside our tent. I didn't think too much of it. It might have been another trekker peeing in the night. Later, I was awakened again. This time by a chewing and gurgling sound close to my ears. In my high-altitude delirium, I thought it was Maura. Were her lungs full of fluid from the altitude? Then I noticed that the bubbling sound was accompanied by irregular breathing. I turned to check on Maura. To my surprise, a dog had wrapped itself around my head to keep himself warm. He was breathing in my ear. I flung my arms at the animal to shoo him away.

"Get out of here!"

Maura woke up just as the critter skidded across the ground tarp and out our floorless tent. We burst into giggles and laughed until our bellies ached. Then I went outside to relieve myself.

Above me was the most brilliant night sky I had ever seen. Far from electric lights, high in the Himalayas, the starlit sky spoke of eternity. Ten thousand stars shimmered in the black canopy overhead. For a few minutes I merged with the universe, then the wintry air forced me back inside. Before crawling into my down sleeping bag, I checked our thermometer. It was zero degrees Fahrenheit.

Laughing children woke us up the next morning. After the first hour of sunlight it was still only 5 degrees. Nonetheless, they ran about with bare feet on the frozen compacted dirt. Swathed in clothes made of repurposed burlap sacks, the kids endured these harsh living conditions with jubilance. How could I not be moved by their fortitude?

12

GUMBY AND POKEY'S NIGHTMARE

An insatiable quest for adventure kept us moving. My mountain sickness waned as I lost altitude, but I still had a bad cough. At 14,800 feet the air felt thick and warm when we reached the village of Dingboche. We lazed in the sun for a full day, reading and washing. Each bucket of heated water was precious. It was time-consuming for the innkeepers to heat the liquid. And it was expensive too; the fuel had been carried for weeks on the backs of porters. It was worth every penny. This was our first semblance of a bath in several weeks.

We also washed our clothes. With a borrowed pail, we gathered water from the nearest river. The grey-colored liquid was laden with glacial silt and ground up bits of mica. My fingers quickly numbed from swishing my clothes in the bucket's soapy water. Afterwards, my clothes didn't look any cleaner. Minerals in the water had decorated my dark pants and long underwear with silver flecks that resembled shards of sequins. The shiny specks were also imbedded in my clean hair.

The next day we headed up the Imja Valley to the settlement of Chhukung at 16,000 feet. The hike was taxing. My worsening cough made breathing at altitude even more challenging, forcing me to walk slowly and stop frequently. Our map implied that there would be a village in Chhukung, but it was just a single tea house made of packed mud.

The lodge was more like an infirmary. Once inside we discovered that nearly all the guests were ill with chills, vomiting, headaches and diarrhea. My frequent bouts of coughing only added to the noise of sick foreigners getting up at all hours of the night to take care of themselves. Maura had problems too. She spent the evening picking shards of glass from her gums. They had been in her dinner.

Early the next morning Dwayne and Maura departed with Pasang and his yak for Island Peak Base Camp. They hoped to secure a desirable campsite. Sleeping high would help them acclimatize and position themselves to start their climb early the following day.

Pasang returned to Chhukung in the afternoon to earn some extra money. The lodge owners paid him to scout the alpine pastures for dried yak dung patties. These would be used as fuel for heating and cooking in the guest house. While Pasang roamed about, Peter and I relaxed at the primitive inn.

The following day Peter and I left Chhukung with Pasang and his yak. Our plan was to meet up with Maura and Dwayne at base camp. En route we traveled through the alluring Imja Valley. The basin was ringed by dazzling icy peaks beneath a lapis-colored sky. Some wore impressive pleats and gargoyles of snow. It seemed impossible that snow could cling so heavily to the steep mountainsides.

Island Peak loomed on the horizon. It's technically a spur from a larger ridge but isolated enough to be considered a mountain. The south face of Lhotse was more imposing. Its massive black wall bordered the valley for miles, towering more than 10,000 vertical feet above us.

We trudged on along a narrow path and onto a sandy plain. Over the millennia, glaciers had pulverized nearby rocks into fine particles resembling beige-colored talc. Each gust of wind forced us to halt. Blowing powder obstructed our view, trapping grit beneath our glacier goggles and burning our eyes.

By early afternoon we arrived at the base camp. Most of the tents were vacant since climbers were already high on the mountain. Our plan was to wait for Maura and Dwayne to return from the summit. Together we would celebrate their ascent.

Peter and I enjoyed yak cheese and sweet biscuits from India for lunch in the alpine pasture. Then we each wandered around separately to pass the time. Pasang ambled over the nearby hills to graze his yak. Peter quickly grew impatient. He soon disappeared to smoke the wild marijuana he had picked a few weeks earlier in the hill country. With a deep hacking cough, I didn't have much strength for anything. I couldn't have climbed the 20,305 foot mountain even if I had wanted to. I was content just to stroll around and gaze at the gorgeous mountain scenery.

After three and half hours of waiting, Peter was impaired and bored. He returned to base camp to announce that he was going back to Chhukung. I felt obligated to wait for my friend Maura. Hours passed. There was no sign of her and Dwayne. Each time I heard voices and saw tired climbers dragging into camp, I perked up. I hoped it would be them. To bide time, I chatted with the Sherpas at base camp. Despite coming from different cultures, we had a lot in common. One of them had even lived in Boulder, Colorado for a few years. We had also climbed many of the same peaks in the Rocky Mountains.

Slowly the sun slipped behind the horizon. Pasang and I were getting very concerned. We had waited five and half hours for our friends and there was still no sign of them. Base camp sits at over 17,000 feet beneath Island Peak. It wasn't a suitable place to spend a November night without winter camping gear. Since we planned to return to Chhukung that afternoon with our companions, we had left our sleeping bags at the lodge. I was in a quandary over what to do. Our yak driver also lacked warm clothes and a flashlight for the trek back. Then I saw two people approaching camp.

"Are you Jean?" the man asked.

"Yes," I responded hesitantly, wondering if something was wrong.

Speaking with heavy accents, the couple informed me that my friends had deviated from the standard ascent route.

"They won't get back to camp until later this evening. They will hike to Chhukung late tonight using their torches. They want you to take their camping gear back to the village."

I felt conflicted. Was this really what Maura wanted me to do? Was this information correct? I also wanted to believe that my friends were OK.

"Are you sure they want me to remove their camp?" I inquired again.

"Yes," the couple nodded in agreement.

As instructed, Pasang and I dismantled Dwayne and Maura's camp and loaded their gear on the yak. Nonetheless, I felt uneasy about hauling away their overnight equipment in these temperatures and at this altitude.

As we headed down the valley darkness fell upon us. The air temperature was freezing. My dim headlamp was our only source of light. It was barely adequate. Changing the batteries didn't help. The trail was faint and the terrain was difficult to negotiate. It crisscrossed over a glacier covered with stony rubble, then passed over moraines and along a river.

Periodically, I scouted the way up ahead while Pasang stayed with the yak in the dark. Often there were multiple narrow trails to choose from. Once I was reasonably certain I was following the right track, I retraced my steps back to Pasang. Then we continued together until the route became questionable again. We repeated this strategy all the way down the valley. It took hours.

The yak periodically froze in his tracks and refused to move forward until we soothed and coaxed him onward. The three of us trudged slowly beneath an ink-black sky. Sparkles glimmered above us. The Milky Way looked like an endless thick smear of silver glitter streaking across the universe.

At times I grinned and laughed out loud. Pasang seemed bewildered. Once he realized the humor of our situation, we giggled together. Before this night, our group had never really warmed up to Pasang. Trekking under the stars with a yak had bonded us. Our relationship changed when we depended on each other for our safety. It was the catalyst that bridged two cultures.

After a few hours, a faint yellow light appeared on the horizon. It was Peter. He used his flashlight to help guide us back to Chhukung.

"Where's Dwayne and Maura?" he inquired.

"I don't know."

"What do you mean?" He asked.

"I'm not really sure what's going on. A couple who climbed the peak told us that Maura and Dwayne were climbing a different route. They're planning on returning to the village later tonight."

"It's already late. Are they OK?"

"Peter, that's all I know. I am worried too." I responded irritably.

We headed back to the lodge together. An ice dam had formed over the stream near the tea house. The dam was slippery. We were uncertain if it could hold our weight. Either way we might get wet. The only choices were to brave crossing the ice dam and risk falling through, or to ford through the icy water. The yak didn't like either option. He spooked at the riverbank. Pasang took the animal downstream from the dam. He spent a few minutes stroking the beast and talking to him in the dark. Soon the yak moved through the frigid water and onto the stream bank on the other side. Peter and I cautiously crossed the bridge of ice instead.

By the time we arrived at the lodge we were hungry and chilled. Trekkers were already asleep. Peter woke up the owners. They graciously made hot drinks and prepared some late night snacks for us. After we were satiated, Pasang went to stay with the innkeeper's family. I laid Maura's and Dwayne's sleeping bags out on the spare cots so they could fall asleep shortly after their arrival.

The night was long. We were awake with worry. Thoughts raced through my tired mind. Where were they? What was taking them so long? Were they safe? As the night grew colder, I huddled deep into my sleeping bag. I felt wracked with guilt. Perhaps there had been a miscommunication. Maybe something terrible had happened on the mountain. I wondered if Maura was dead or alive. I was disturbed by the thought of making an overseas phone call to her mother when I returned to the city. How do you tell a parent that their child has disappeared or died?

Twice during the night, Peter and I trekked a short distance up the valley by headlamp. We carried a thermos of hot tea to support our companions. We waited in the dark, hoping to see bobbing lights coming down the trail towards us. They never appeared.

At first light there was still no sign of the climbers. After breakfast Peter and I headed up the trail to search again. At 8 a.m. we spotted our friends coming over the moraine. They were exhausted. Maura looked like a walking corpse. Her face was pale and her skin appeared dry and wrinkled like an old woman. She walked unsteadily down the path and required our help to make it across the partially frozen river.

Later that day Maura recounted their escapade on Island Peak. During their ascent they stopped to rest at 19,000 feet. The brisk morning temperature made it necessary to stop and warm their feet. Dwayne also had a headache. Hoping to reduce the build-up of fluid in his brain, he popped a tablet of Diamox. The high-altitude diuretic worked only briefly.

Next the pair were led astray by following a series of cairns, piles of stones that were supposed to mark the route. Soon they were on the wrong ridge. To get back on route they scrambled slowly across a gully of loose rocks. They roped up when they finally reached the glacier. More challenges awaited them. The summit was still over two hours away, wind swirled the snow around the icy ridge leading towards the top, and they both had symptoms of acute mountain sickness. Maura was fatigued and slightly dizzy. Dwayne felt nauseated. She recommended that they turn around, but Dwayne was determined to make the ascent.

The day was growing late. Blue afternoon shadows crept across the glacier. During their climb the pair crossed paths with two Australians descending from the summit. Maura asked them to relay the message to me at base camp.

Just above 20,000 feet, Dwayne started acting strange. He staggered and then collapsed onto his ice climbing tools. When Maura insisted that they stop and turn around, he untied himself from the rope and continued climbing without her. The altitude appeared to be affecting Dwayne's judgment. Dismayed and concerned, Maura moved slowly behind him. Now her only protection from falling was to focus intensely on her every move.

When they finally reached the summit Dwayne was jubilant, but Maura was worried about getting down safely. She knew something was amiss; her brain was foggy and she could no longer think clearly. After a short stay on the summit the pair started their long descent.

It was twilight by the time they reached the rock-filled gullies. They had only one headlamp between them; the other light had accidentally been left at camp during their pre-dawn departure. Exhausted and equipped with barely enough light, Maura and Dwayne staggered and stumbled down the mountainside until they reached 19,000 feet.

Up ahead several tents glowed in the darkness. When they arrived at the advance base camp, Dwayne invited himself inside one of the tents for hot tea while Maura collapsed outside, smack onto the dirt speckled with yak dung. She was taken aback when she regained consciousness; she heard Dwayne socializing with the occupants inside, apparently oblivious to her absence. She quickly picked herself up, dusted herself off and joined the group. The British climbers poured Maura a cup of hot tea, but she was so weak that she could hardly sip it. The climbers graciously offered Maura and Dwayne their extra tent, sans sleeping bags, as a shelter for the night.

Silence pervaded inside the borrowed haven. For a few minutes Maura and Dwayne enjoyed the psychological warmth of a candle burning inside an empty soup can. Then the flame flickered and died. The night was long and cold. Outside the temperature dropped to below zero degrees Fahrenheit. Despite the discord between the pair, they spent the night huddled together atop their coiled rope to insulate themselves from the frozen ground.

By comparison Peter and I had a less miserable night. Hearing Maura's tale made me feel smug that I had opted out of the climb. Our two friends rested all morning at the lodge in Chhukung. Later that afternoon we returned to our favorite tea house in Dingboche.

A celebration was in order. Our companions had not only survived their climb, they had also set a personal high altitude record. While debating which Nepali beer to order, Dwayne delighted us with a surprise. He pulled a bottle of Bordeaux wine out from his duffle bag. He had brought it all the way from France just for this occasion! Our party ended early that evening. At 14,000 feet, we quickly felt the effects of combining the previous day's exhaustion with wine and altitude.

The next morning we hiked to Periche to see Dr. Levine. He was back at the tiny clinic run by the Himalayan Rescue Association. I needed medical treatment; I was still hacking up thick green globs of phlegm. The physician diagnosed me with bronchitis. After giving me a bottle of antibiotics, we said our goodbyes. Afterwards our group left the village and hiked towards a small hanging valley.

It was early evening when we reached Dzongla, a high-altitude yak pasture. There was nothing here but a small stone enclosure used by herders. For us, it was a spectacular campsite. A glacial cirque with steep snow-covered arêtes surrounded us on three sides. In the other direction, Ama Dablam was partially shrouded in a veil of pink evening clouds. This valley captivated me. I rambled around in awe until it was nearly dark.

Author on Cho La Pass, Ama Dablam on left

"Maura, you've got to promise me something." I demanded when I returned to our tent.

"What's that?"

"I want you to scatter my ashes in this valley. I want my spirit to reside in Dzongla after I die."

"I guess that means I will be coming back here then." She replied.

"Yes, if I die first. There is something really special about this place." Maura nodded in agreement.

The next morning we trekked up to almost 18,000 feet. I was a little nervous about crossing the small glacier on Cho La Pass. It straddles a col separating two enormous valleys. Even though large crevasses didn't appear on the glacier's surface, there was a small possibility that a snow bridge might collapse over a hidden fissure in the ice. We took precautions. We roped up and carried our ice axes in hand. The locals looked at us as if we were crazy. Crossing the glacier was a necessary part of Sherpa life. Porters, wearing sneakers and flip-flops, ferried supplies back and forth across the glacier in baskets worn on their backs. One by one, we followed their packed trail across the snow.

After a long and steep descent we arrived at the edge of Ngozumpa Glacier. Crossing Nepal's longest glacier was less risky than traversing the higher alpine glaciers. Crevasses were already open and easy to identify. The challenge was linking a route around their long gaping holes.

We finally stumbled upon a single shelter at dusk. The owners rented out rooms whenever hapless travelers like us arrived. Our experience here was dreary; we slept on old, moldy straw mattresses in a tiny room filled with smoke. A few feet away, the innkeepers slept on the dirt floor next to a yak dung fire. Stomach cramps and diarrhea made the night all the more miserable for me.

The following day we hiked over to Gokyo. In contrast to the previous night, this tiny hamlet was inviting. We spent several days with a jovial family in their one-room home. The wife was a talented cook. She cooked tasty omelets and fluffy cinnamon rolls on a wood stove even at 16,000 feet. The couple and their small child often teased each other in the most loving way. Soon we were all friends with Di Di, the lady of the house. We spent several hours each day sitting outside in the sunshine together. Di Di kept us engaged in lively conversations and nearly constant laughter. Sherpa women call each other *Di Di,* meaning sister. I loved using this endearing expression. It connected strangers from different cultures on a deeper level.

During our last afternoon in the village, I hiked up the steep hill of Gokyo Ri. Below me, two turquoise lakes sparkled like jewels nestled against a brown glacial moraine. The village was a mere speck on the landscape. It was defined by yak pens made with piles of rocks taken from the nearby moraine. Buddhist prayer flags were strung between rocky cairns on the summit of Gokyo Ri. Some were faded and others had been whipped threadbare by the wind. Nearby, a Sherpa man lit a tiny fire between the stones and mumbled mantras. Wafts of juniper incense drifted towards the heavens. Something sacred was happening here. Intrigued, I paused to contemplate its possible meaning.

My tranquility ended when Dwayne joined me on top. He sat next to me and started to rant. He had lost his camera a few days earlier and despite backtracking to search for it, it was never found. Although my heart went out to him, I had grown weary of his company. I needed some space and time to myself. After a few minutes, I jumped up and ran down the hillside without him.

With only a few hours of daylight remaining, I hiked quickly upstream. The landscape was stark. Small glacial tarns filled with murky gray water dotted the terrain. The Ngozumpa Glacier on my right was mostly covered with stones. Up ahead, a cluster of white, icy pinnacles rose fifty feet right out of the dirty glacial ice. I headed straight for them.

Here, silence was my companion. The only sound besides my heavy breathing was an occasional clatter of rocks tumbling into glacial crevasses. The solitude was nourishing. I rested on a rock next to the faint trail. Two gigantic mountains, Cho Oyu and Gyachung Kang, loomed on the northern end of the valley with massive glaciers pouring down their flanks. These 8,000-meter peaks marked the border between Nepal and Tibet.

I shivered while resting here but it wasn't just from the cold. I was on a path that had been used by thousands of desperate souls. For decades Tibetan refugees had followed this very trail. They sought more than peace and a better life. They also wanted to practice their religion. These days, few refugees slip past the remote and rugged border. It's now heavily guarded farther upstream by Chinese soldiers.

After a few minutes the sun disappeared. Twilight tinted the peaks lavender and rose. In the gap between the mountains, I had a straight-shot view of Mount Everest in the setting sun. From this angle, I could see the classic climbing routes on the world's highest peak.

Suddenly Maura appeared out of nowhere. I was shocked to see her in this remote location. I got the impression that she was on her way back from hiking up to the Tibetan border. Instead, she was returning from an afternoon trek to Gyachung Kang Base Camp.

I wanted to linger, but the fading light forced us to descend. While trekking back to the lodge, I noticed that I was fit and strong again. My legs were taut and wiry. I felt like I could hike forever. I remembered this feeling from before. It was how I felt on the last few days of skiing the John Muir Trail before I was severely injured on Mount Whitney.

On this final night in Gokyo, I wrote in my journal by candlelight:

I was reluctant to leave this last view of Everest. Being here was like meeting a lover that I had dreamed about for years. And then, shortly after a wonderful encounter, time and circumstances forced us to part.

13

OVER THE BRINK

Our last night in the Everest region was at Namche Bazaar, a village of white-washed Tibetan-style buildings nestled into a dry hillside. The town was bustling. Foreign trekkers roamed the narrow streets shopping for trinkets and searching for vacancies at Sherpa-owned guest houses. After checking into our lodge, we paid Pasang for transporting our gear on his family's yak. A smile creased his young face when we handed him a wad of rupees. It wasn't possible for him to accompany us to Lukla; yaks are vulnerable to diseases from lower elevation animals.

After bidding Pasang farewell, our group scattered back towards the village shops. I walked alone down a terraced slope towards an alluring solitary, ivory-colored stupa, a Buddhist symbol for the mind of enlightenment. Garlands of prayer flags waved gracefully in the breeze. They resembled a load of colorful laundry strung on lines between four enormous wooden poles. It was the eyes that drew me in. They held me captive. Painted on each side of the stupa, the Buddha's eyes looked indiscriminately out towards the world. An upside down question mark was painted beneath the orbs. It stood for the Sanskrit number one, representing the inseparability of all phenomena. Thirteen small ledges tapered up the structure to an ornate golden top.

We had seen countless stupas on our trek. They were the center piece of Buddhist villages and were often found along high points near the trail. The stupa at Namche was particularly inviting. It was in the middle of town with a stupendous backdrop of snowy mountains. I could have contemplated here for hours, but since it was Maura's birthday and the last evening the four of us would share on the trail before leaving the Everest region, I forced myself to be sociable.

Stupa at Namche Bazaar

We gathered for dinner at the Khumbu Lodge. Unbeknownst to us, Dwayne had consulted with the restaurant's cook and arranged a special meal for the occasion. During our trek Maura and I had often craved enchiladas. With only limited ingredients to choose from, restaurant staff concocted a make-shift version—fried spring rolls stuffed with cheese and smothered with taco sauce. We shared our meal with climbers that Maura had met along the trail. The surprise dinner was followed by a bottle of rum and a specially made birthday cake.

Maura was hiking by day break the next morning. She traveled light and fast to the Lukla airstrip where flights were notorious for being overbooked. They had to be reconfirmed in person the day before departure. We were counting on Gumby to be at the head of the line.

The rest of us spent the early morning trying to find porters to carry our gear to Lukla. They gathered near the outdoor market waiting to be hired. The atmosphere was lively. Sherpas and lowland Nepalis bargained in broken English while foreigners became increasingly distraught. The price went up each time we attempted to negotiate a deal. Eventually, we employed three young men with thick dark hair.

The local custom for transporting heavy goods looked uncomfortable and awkward. Our duffle bags were suspended on the backs of our porters by a long and wide woven strap. One end of the tumpline was wrapped around our luggage while the other end encircled the porter's foreheads.

Soon we were on our way. Just as we approached the edge of the village, our workers suddenly stopped walking. They demanded a raise. We were dumbfounded and angry. Dwayne promptly fired our laborers on the spot.

Now desperate for porters, Dwayne approached a group of dark-skinned men in a nearby alleyway. They were smoking cigarettes, laughing and conversing. They weren't porters. Nonetheless, Dwayne waved to get their attention.

"Today, Lukla?" he exclaimed, full of hope as he pointed to our luggage.

Two men in the group looked interested in potential employment; they lifted their heads and raised their eyebrows. Dwayne offered them a fair wage for the day. Peter and I sighed in relief when they accepted. Soon our newly employed Sherpas had borrowed large woven baskets and a tumpline. Then they grabbed our duffels and tossed them into the baskets. For the rest of the day we each took turns hiking with the porters carrying our equipment. These men offered cheerful company and turned out to be our best porters during our entire trip.

White and grey clouds swirled around the peaks as we headed down an eroded trail. Fog completely shrouded the mountain views while snowflakes fell from the sky. The trail was steep. It dropped several thousand feet to the bottom of a deep valley. As we lost elevation the temperature gradually increased and the surrounding hillsides became cloaked in thick verdant vegetation.

Our route followed along the Dudh Kosi which translates to the Milk River. It churned violently. The water gushed downstream with enormous bubbles made of white froth and grey glacial silt. Rocks in the river forced the water upwards into large waves that curled backwards into the rushing torrent. The river sounded like thunder reverberating in the gorge.

It was unsettling each time the trail crossed a bridge. Each overpass was made of large hand-hewn logs. They were strapped together and cantilevered in three sections in order to span the width of the river. I was nervous and dizzy whenever I looked at the water moving rapidly beneath me. Instead, I focused on my feet, walking one step at a time across the bridge until I was on the other side.

At one point the trail traversed across the scar of a huge, recent landslide. A path only eight inches wide had been worn across the steep, hard-packed slope. The raging river was now several hundred feet below us. A single slip would end in the cataracts. Just after traversing the landslide I heard a yelp. I looked back. A porter was recovering his balance as loose items tumbled out from his basket and down the embankment. As I watched the belongings vanish into the river, I was glad they weren't ours.

At the end of the day, we hiked up a steep hillside and traversed a long, wide terrace. Lukla was visible on the horizon. Our party headed straight for the small mountain airstrip. A long line of impatient trekkers waited outside an aqua-colored shack. They were all hopeful of reconfirming their flights. Maura was sitting off to the side waiting for us.

"Good thing I went ahead and got here early," she informed us. "Flights are overbooked. The clouds have created a backlog. Hundreds of people have been waiting here for days to catch a plane back to Kathmandu," She informed us.

"What about us?" Peter asked.

"No problem, we're confirmed for a flight out tomorrow," Maura reassured us.

Before finding a guest house for the night, I strolled over to the short and narrow runway at the end of town. Mangled pieces of old aircraft littered the base of a hill. I was surprised that this was left in full view of tourists. The evidence of in-bound flights crashing upon arrival didn't exactly inspire confidence in the airline or its pilots.

God, help us if we survive this flight, I thought.

The sight of smashed metal parts took the enthusiasm of flying right out of me. I was already leery about flying through a narrow valley with towering Himalayan giants on either side of the plane. It was fortunate that flights were routinely cancelled whenever clouds obscured the view.

Nevertheless, I still wondered if it was really sensible to wait for the weather to clear. It could take a week to resolve the backlog of overbooked passengers. Perhaps we should just trek through the hill country back to Jiri and then take the bus to Kathmandu. The option of hiking ten more days wasn't attractive or realistic.

We spent a sleepless night at the Buddha Lodge. Travelers ranted loudly while drowning their frustrations with chang, a locally brewed Tibetan beer. Once the village was asleep, a concert of barking dogs sang through the wee hours of the night as I tossed and turned on my rock-hard bed.

The air was damp the next morning. A thick fog covered the airstrip. The mood in the village matched the weather. Everyone seemed depressed and exasperated. We all hoped the situation would soon change. We waited and waited. After a few hours, patches of blue peeked between the grey billowy clouds.

When the weather finally broke, there was a palpable tension among the trekkers. Foreigners scrambled with their luggage and lined up for the first flight out. Soon a faint baritone hum could be heard in the distance. It grew louder and closer. Mobs of people gathered behind a barbed wire fence to wait for the aircraft.

An airline official clad in a threadbare navy uniform called out the names of passengers who were being bumped from the first flight. Angry travelers shouted obscenities at the poor worker. Corruption was at play. Airline personnel had just accepted a few hundred rupees to let a small group of Kenyan dignitaries catch the first plane out of the mountains.

Meanwhile, porters moved another heap of luggage across the airstrip. Ours were among the pieces to be flown out. Once they were stacked by the jet, we carefully counted our baggage from a distance.

Then Peter spoke up. "Hey, where's the other duffle?"

A quick visual scan of the runway revealed that one of our bags was left on the sidelines. It contained our climbing gear. It didn't seem to matter that we had paid the excess baggage fee the day before. If the duffle didn't make it on the flight with us, it would never be recovered.

Soon the scene became chaotic. Nepali workers were removing the displaced passengers' luggage from the jet and loading the baggage belonging to the Kenyans. Foreigners stood nearby yelling and waving their arms at the flight officer. Everyone seemed confused about what was happening. Dwayne seized the moment. He quickly crawled under the barbed wire fence, walked across the runway to our abandoned bag, and carried it towards the plane. Without anyone noticing, he tossed the duffle into the bottom of the aircraft. He had just saved the day.

"Way to go!" We congratulated him when he returned.

Next the airline official read the names of those who would fly. We were on the list. There were only fourteen lucky passengers after the dignitaries boarded. Officials weren't actually checking who was who. As a result the flight was now first come, first serve. The crowd panicked when the gate was opened between the barbed wire fence and the airstrip. A horde of hopeful travelers pushed their way across the runway and towards the plane.

"Huddle together and push hard!" Maura instructed.

Using the power of four, we shoved our way through the throng, up the stairs, and into the quiet interior of the plane. As we walked down the short aisle, each of us sighed with relief. I sat down and buckled myself into a metal folding seat covered with cracked vinyl padding. A uniformed pilot and his assistant slammed the door shut. Then he returned to the cockpit to prepare for takeoff. Outside the window, airline staff forced disappointed hikers away from the runway.

A few minutes later the engine roared to life. Propellers twirled rapidly next to the wings. The pilot drove the plane forward before turning it around and pointing it downhill. The aircraft bounced between potholes as it taxied down the gravel airstrip. Brakes squeaked. The odor of burning rubber filled the air. My palms were sweaty and my heart was racing and pounding inside my chest.

"Shouldn't the brakes be released before take-off?" I asked Peter.

He shook his head. Then I realized the rumors were true. The brakes were on for a good reason—they moderated our speed as we approached the edge of a cliff. I was gripped with fear. I knew what was coming. The plane would get airborne by dropping right over the brink. We were hang-gliding in a nineteen passenger aircraft!

With a clenched jaw, I tightened my hold on the armrest. I closed my eyes just before we crossed the threshold between *terra firma* and space. For a split second the jet dropped. I felt my heart leap into my throat. There it was; that horrid sensation of falling. I felt like I was back on Mount Whitney again. Then the plane rose upwards. It made a quick left turn to avoid crashing into the escarpment on the other side of the valley. After the aircraft straightened its course, passengers cheered and applauded the pilot.

Thousands of feet below us, the Dudh Kosi River snaked its way through a vivid green canyon. I stared out the window for the entire flight. I did not want to leave these mountains. They held an even greater power over me than did the Sierras. Gradually the snow-covered peaks disappeared. Terraced hillsides announced that we would soon be landing in the congested valley of Kathmandu.

Our senses announced our arrival back to the city. Once again, we were immersed in dust and grime. The air was hot and polluted. Heaps of rotting garbage reeked in the streets. Maura and I went from shop to shop stocking up on supplies for our next mountain odyssey. Our frequent breaks included high-caloric meals. There was no guilt. We had lost considerable weight from weeks of high-altitude exertion and occasional diarrhea. That night, Dwayne and Peter joined us for a celebratory dinner. Afterwards we parted ways with the two men.

14

PILGRIMAGE TO THE SANCTUARY

Maura and I were happy to be on our own again. Our plan was to take a "vacation from our vacation." For this, we headed to the Annapurna Sanctuary, a high-altitude glacial cirque ringed by massive mountains plastered with glaciers. The Sanctuary is sacred. It's believed to be the abode of many important Hindu deities. We were excited about exploring this region of diverse cultures and semi-tropical vegetation before reaching the base of the world's tenth highest peak.

First, we had to travel to central Nepal. Before departing from Kathmandu, Maura and I traversed a maze of dirt alleyways early in the morning. We walked towards a tall white tower that dominated the skyline. The bus station was nearby. It was simply a large dirt parking lot where filthy, dented buses gathered to transport long-distance travelers.

Our immediate destination was Pokhara, a city five to seven hours farther west. We wandered aimlessly about the lot. Soon we became frustrated. It was nearly impossible to determine where each bus was headed. Some vehicles displayed their route in a long narrow window above the windshield. Since the names were written in Hindi script each destination board looked the same to us.

Whenever we inquired about the bus to Pokhara, we got the same response. Nepalis cocked their head from side to side and then pointed with uncertainty. We felt like we were going in circles. Eventually we located what we thought was the correct bus. Then Maura crawled up a ladder on the back of the vehicle. After I heaved our luggage up to her, she lashed our bags securely to the roof rack. Then we took our seats.

We were traveling light compared to the other passengers. Many toted old boxes, large burlap sacks of supplies and small caged animals. They piled their goods into the middle of the aisle or strapped them onto the roof. Finally we were ready for the next leg of our journey.

"Maura, where's our bus tickets?" I inquired.

She reached into her pant pockets. They were empty. Then she searched through her daypack.

"Shit. I can't find them!" she declared.

I searched through my clothes and belongings. Our bus tickets, purchased the day before, were nowhere to be found. Then our driver hopped into the bus. He looked somewhat official in his orange and green Nepali cap. He walked down the aisle collecting tickets from the passengers.

"What are we going to do?" I asked Maura.

A nervous look crossed her face as the man moved slowly in our direction.

"We'll just have to wing it!" she replied.

"That's not going to work. Without our tickets, we can't ride." I insisted.

Soon the man approached us. He reached his brown hand out towards us. In a halting voice he said, "Tiiiick – et."

Maura piped up, "We gave our tickets to the man outside the bus who was collecting them."

The driver looked puzzled.

"Tiiiick-et?" he asked again.

"We already gave our tickets," I insisted.

The driver asked several times. Each time we gave a similar answer. He was visibly irked. Then a commotion distracted him. A live chicken escaped from the arms of a woman sitting nearby. Several people moved quickly to capture the bird.

The bus driver continued down the aisle collecting tickets. Later he returned to us with a scrunched-up face. Maura and I both pointed out the window at the invisible and fabricated ticket collector. The driver threw his hands up in the air. He went to the front of the vehicle and plopped down into the driver's seat. Before departing, he lit some incense and placed it on a small Hindu shrine on top of the dashboard. Perhaps it would bring us good luck. Soon the bus engine sputtered. Everyone gagged on a cloud of diesel smoke while the last passengers climbed on board.

A European couple claimed the last seats at the front of the vehicle. Their presence made us hopeful that our bus might be bound for Pokhara. It was pointless to ask our neighbors where the bus was headed; they didn't speak any English. Besides we knew from experience that they would just nod their heads in an effort to please Westerners. We also didn't want to draw attention to ourselves since we hadn't been able to find our tickets. After a few miles, Maura became increasingly concerned about the vehicle's destination.

"What if this is the all-night bus to India?" she asked.

"Oh, my God, don't say that," I responded. "Surely we would know it if were on an overnight bus ride."

"We don't have an Indian visa," she continued. Maura had a worried look on her face. India was not on her bucket list.

"Wherever we are going, it will be a great adventure." I assured her.

We both sat back and hoped for the best. The fast moving bus careened between curves as it climbed up and down through hilly terrain. It wasn't long before Maura looked pale-green. She leapt up from her seat, crawled over the luggage in the aisle, and headed to a window seat at the back of the bus. For several hours she occasionally hurled vomit out the window and down the outside of the vehicle. I felt sorry for her. I also felt a tinge of guilt; I was enjoying the ride. I was entranced by the lovely scenery. We traveled through villages interspersed with rice fields and small plots of jungle vegetation.

Several hours later our bus made a lengthy stop at a major junction in the highway. Numerous passengers gathered their belongings and disembarked for southbound coaches to India. They were soon replaced by other travelers going our way. This boosted our confidence that we would eventually arrive at our intended destination.

After nearly five hours we arrived in Pokhara. Maura looked better the minute the bus came to a halt. We happily disembarked, retrieved our belongings from the rooftop and walked across the parking lot.

"Wasn't that a great trip?" I remarked.

Maura glared at me with disapproval. My remark was insensitive. For a moment I thought she was going to deck me for sharing my exuberance. From the bus station we caught a taxi to the tourist office. There, a laid-back officer in an army uniform issued us our trekking permits. The whole process was quick and straightforward. There wasn't the abundance of forms, hassles, and bureaucratic red tape that we had encountered in Kathmandu.

Wearing backpacks, we walked to the outskirts of town and along the shoreline of Phewa Lake. The setting was inspiring. Behind us was a backdrop of serrated Himalayan peaks poking up through the smog.

The town was a delightful mix of Western residents, Indian immigrants and Nepalis. The expats included hippies and drug addicts left from the sixties. Some were Krishna devotees who chanted songs on the roadside. Other expats were European businessmen who operated bakeries and cappuccino shops to serve the hordes of tourists. En route to our guest house we fended off an onslaught of in-your-face salesmen.

"Hello, want boiled egg?"

"Hello, chewing gum!"

The children swathed in rags were merciless and annoying. They followed us everywhere we walked.

"Give me rupees, give me money, give me candy, balloons, pens. Give me......., give me," they each demanded in succession.

It was the silent beggars, blind and limbless, that tugged at our hearts. Most of them worked for pimps. Some had been kidnapped, maimed and disabled to make them more successful at their forced employment. It was difficult to accept that people could inflict such horrors upon one another, particularly helpless children.

The walk to our hotel seemed endless.

"Taxi, Ma'am?"

"Boat ride, Ma'am?"

"Need hotel? Follow me, Ma'am!"

We followed no one. We forged our way through alleyways blaring with music. Tunes varied from Beatle songs to devotional Hindu ragas. We passed restaurants advertising enchiladas, brownies and samosas. Solitude was available only behind the closed door of our guest house.

The next day we headed out of the city on foot. Since we had stored our mountaineering gear and other non-essentials at our lodge in Kathmandu, we were able to travel light, carrying our own backpacks instead of hiring porters. Our journey to Annapurna Sanctuary started with a long traverse through a dry river bed. We choked on the dust stirred up by jeeps carrying trekkers to the end of the road. Eventually, a stone stair-cased trail led into the hills. We passed through charming villages belonging to the Gurung and Tamang tribes. Their packed earthen homes were painted ochre and black and topped with thatched roofs.

For two weeks we yielded the trail to pack mules instead of yaks. The animals traveled in groups of eight or more. Each one had a regal appearance, dressed in red, white and black headdresses, topped with long stiff fibers resembling a large paintbrush. The mules were decked with necklaces made from tiny silver bells which jingled with every step.

Day after day we hiked up the lushly vegetated Modi Khola River Valley. Our route took us through terraced fields and forests of rhododendron. Farther upstream, a narrow trail traversed through dense groves of tall bamboo. The semi-tropical terrain was hot and steamy. Sweat ran from my arm pits down to my wrists. The silver droplets then fell from my fingertips to the ground.

Farther upstream the gorge was so deep that we couldn't see the peaks that towered far above us. Along the way we climbed up countless steps of stone. I could hike faster now. I felt like superwoman, bounding up and down the hills with unstoppable strength and enthusiasm. It was hard to believe that less than four years earlier I was barely alive. I wasn't fully healed though; I still had to bear down to pee since the nerve damage associated with my bladder was permanent. But at least I no longer had to catheterize myself.

As we ascended farther up the canyon, enormous peaks cloaked in ice appeared. A few miles before reaching the high country, our journey was interrupted by the weather. Sheets of heavy rain fell from slate-colored skies. The storm forced us to stay at a lone lodge between the village of Dovan and Machapuchare Base Camp.

Trekkers lay awake all night from the noise and rhythm of raindrops. They pinged in rapid succession on the inn's corrugated metal roof. By morning, the terrain sparkled with a fresh coat of snow. Before breakfast the local residents shared the bad news with their guests—the trail above and beyond our lodge was now treacherous with snow and ice. There was a serious threat of avalanches sweeping over the route leading to the Sanctuary.

We were stuck in that crudely built shack for days. It was made of deteriorating narrow wooden planks separated by wide spaces. To make matters worse this dismal inn had poor sanitation. Maura had stomach cramps and diarrhea for several days. Periodically, other desperate guests ran outside to relieve themselves in the bushes. The dampness also gave rise to a chorus of hacking coughs. Our quarters became increasingly cramped; unhappy hikers arriving from down-canyon were forced to stop here until trail conditions became safe.

After spending two days inside, Maura confided that she was deficient in protein. I didn't understand what this meant, but she pressed upon me that she had experienced this before and that it was serious.

I took her word for it, but how could I help? I couldn't exactly run to a store. Then Maura noticed that a group of trekkers on a trip organized by a travel company had abundant supplies. They were camping adjacent to the inn where we stayed.

"Just grab a jar of their peanut butter," Maura suggested.

The idea of stealing went against me. If she hadn't been so ill, I would have rejected the notion. Instead, I waited patiently for an opportune moment. When it arrived, I sneaked into the group's mess tent, grabbed the prize, and ran back to our guest house. That night Maura hid under her sleeping bag delighting in each unscrupulous spoonful of peanut butter. The additional protein seemed to make a difference. My friend seemed better the next day.

Our moods finally lifted when the clouds dissipated. On our last night at the lodge I stood outside with a group of hikers. Together we watched the mist, backlit by the moonlight, rise up along the steep canyon walls. As the clouds cleared and stars peeked through the black sky, I listened with intrigue to trekkers sharing their tales of traveling in Tibet. Their conversation made me daydream about spending my life wandering in the Himalayas. I wanted to explore every mountain valley, east to west, from Bhutan to Pakistan, and north to south, from Tibet to India. I couldn't imagine anything more enjoyable than being a Himalayan pilgrim. It seemed an odd ambition for a young Western woman, yet I honestly couldn't think of anything more appealing.

The next morning, I was the first person on the trail to the Sanctuary. I was eager to see this huge glacial cirque surrounded by massive Himalayan peaks. Sunlight quickly melted the snow on the lower sections of the trail. From the guest house I climbed 3,000 feet up a very steep path. As I gained altitude my hands became numb with cold.

Black cliffs rose high above me on one side. Machapuchare jutted straight up from the other side of the valley to nearly 23,000 feet. Its name means fish tail in Nepali because the peak's summit splits into twin towers. The mountain is revered as an abode of Shiva, one of the principal Hindu deities.

Maura planned to catch up with me later that afternoon. I proceeded alone up the trail, reveling in the precipitous terrain around me. I was brimming with excitement as I passed through the Gates of the Sanctuary, the only gap in the peaks that provided access to the valley. Soon the view opened up into an amphitheater ringed with frosty white mountains. Directly ahead was Annapurna South and Annapurna 1. Both summits were just under 27,000 feet.

I headed straight for a primitive structure made of woven bamboo mats. I wanted to secure a sleeping spot inside before the other trekkers arrived. Shortly afterwards I was approached by a man who had been stranded at the guest house with us during the storm.

"Your friend is feeling sick," he informed me. "She won't be coming to the Sanctuary. She asked me to give you this."

He handed me a folded piece of paper. A short note was scrawled inside in Maura's handwriting. The message didn't offer any details other than that I was to meet her at the village of Chhormoro in a few days. I was disappointed that Maura wouldn't be joining me—it didn't seem right to be in this spectacular landscape without her.

I spent the afternoon walking over morainal debris covered with hummocky piles of brown grass. Then I sat in silence atop a large boulder. I listened to the sound of chirping birds and water babbling in brooks that flowed under the rocky rubble. Occasionally, rocks and ice broke off the mountains and crashed down the cliffs. Despite the chilly late November breeze, I was mesmerized by the surroundings.

The view of Annapurna made me recall the story of its first ascent in 1950. French mountaineer Maurice Hertzog had lost his gloves near the summit. On the descent he spent the night with his buddies in a glacial crevasse for shelter. They barely survived. The group had only one sleeping bag to drape over four climbers. They lived to tell the tale but suffered terrible frostbite. Later, while still in the mountains, emergency surgery was necessary to remove the gangrene that had consumed their digits. Hertzog lost all of his toes and a few of his fingers.

I no longer read epic accounts of Himalayan climbers as I once had. After my accident I couldn't bring myself to read climbing literature, nor could I watch survival movies. My personal epic to stay alive in the mountains was just too raw to be relived over and over again through someone else's story. While my own loss and struggles were less dramatic than those of famous climbers, they still took a toll on me, both physically and emotionally.

It didn't help that mountain rescues and fatalities were frequent where I worked in Rocky Mountain National Park. With each sad report, I always felt my heart crack wide open to an unknown suffering soul. My fall on Mount Whitney had made me kin to mountaineers, both past and present. We were forever bonded by tragic experiences with our beloved peaks.

On this first journey to Nepal, I discovered the power of the Himalayas. These mountains filled me with the immeasurable joy of being alive. I drank in the scenery of Annapurna Sanctuary until it was time for dinner at the guest house.

After dark, I returned outside to intoxicate myself with the overwhelming beauty. A full moon was already high in the night sky. It bathed the peaks in stunning silver light. Annapurna was aptly named the Goddess of Abundance. In this glacial cirque she bestowed a gift; a wealth more lasting than riches. She offered a sanctuary for the human spirit. Here, I was utterly at peace. For a moment I felt whole again. Before returning to the bamboo shack, I touched my heart and bowed to the divine peaks with gratitude.

The mountains warmed my soul, but my body was now thoroughly chilled. I curled into a ball inside Ken's sleeping bag. I shivered all night. I regretted that while packing for this trip he had talked me into taking his lighter-weight down sleeping bag. His intention was good, but the bag was inappropriate for high altitude cold. Winter was fast approaching.

A few days later I arrived in Chhormoro. There, I searched each tea house until I found Maura. She looked like a new person. She was happy, well-hydrated and fed. A physician had given her some antibiotics for dysentery a few days earlier. I realized then how selfless she had been; she had given me the last of her antibiotics when I was ill in the Everest region.

Our trip was almost over. By now, the challenges that we had faced during our journey were wearing on us. Maura and I were tired and impatient. We were weary of roosters waking us up before dawn and leery of meals served on wet dirty plates. I winced in pain as I hiked down the stone lined trail. The weight of my pack had rubbed me raw, leaving seeping wounds on my back and hips. We descended steep terraced slopes with crops turning from green to autumn gold.

Maura turned to me and bluntly declared, "You're hooked on the Himalayas!"

"I love it here," I admitted. "I've realized my dream now, but I can't just keep coming back, you know."

"Why not?" she probed.

"I don't earn enough money for frequent flights overseas. Besides, I am married," I replied.

"Oh, no, I am certain you'll be back," she asserted. "This place has really changed you. You won't be able to stay away."

Her words made me uncomfortable. I wasn't ready to ponder my self-imposed limitations. As we walked down the trail, Maura persistently spouted her opinions until I changed the subject.

We had spent nearly two months wandering through these rugged mountains. The surroundings were surreal and inspiring. Despite discomfort and illness, the trip had been the happiest time in my twenty-six years of life. Maura was right. I had no idea just how significant this dream had been. It shaped the rest of my life, though differently than Mount Whitney had. I would find my way back here. The Himalayas had stolen my heart.

15

INTO THE WIND

The Rockies were under snow by the time we left Asia. Maura returned to her home near the Tetons in Wyoming while I went to Colorado. As the months passed, I felt sluggish and down. I had picked up a parasite in Nepal. It plagued me for six months with intermittent diarrhea before I could get it properly diagnosed.

However, it wasn't just the giardia that ailed me. I was feeling depressed. There seemed to be a big void in my life, yet I wasn't sure why. A few months later I realized that it was because I had accomplished my most important goal in life while I was still in my twenties. Now I wondered if there was anything greater that could feed my soul and keep me going.

Eventually I relaxed into the uncertainty. New dreams would arise with the passage of time. Meanwhile, I read voraciously about the Himalayas, Eastern culture and philosophy. I wanted to understand the world that had spoken so deeply to me.

Over the next few years, Ken and I skied in the backcountry and occasionally climbed frozen waterfalls during our free time. Christmas holidays were spent climbing on warm south-facing rocks in Joshua Tree National Park. In the spring and fall, we took vacations to climb in Yosemite. Whenever I wasn't in the mood to climb, Ken bribed me with an offer to take me out for dinner. As an introvert, Ken depended on me, his one and only climbing partner.

Ken was driven. He climbed incessantly. On summer evenings he scooped me up in the car the minute I got home from work. I had already put in a long ten-hour day working at nearly 12,000 feet at the Alpine Visitor Center, the highest visitor center in the National Park System. While driving to the nearest cliffs we wolfed down a snack and then climbed until dark. We repeated this pattern several nights a week, summer after summer. It was utterly exhausting.

I felt like I had to keep up with Ken even though I didn't share the intensity of his passion. Scaling rocks at the limits of my ability kept me in a state of perpetual anxiety. I had believed that continuing to climb after my accident would help me get past the fear of falling. To climb again was to ride the proverbial horse after one's fall. Instead, it retraumatized me over and over. It might have helped if I could have talked to Ken about how our tragedy on Mount Whitney had affected me. Nonetheless, despite the challenges that we had while climbing, we still enjoyed each other's company. Our love for mountains kept us together.

Two years after my trip to Nepal we embarked on a journey that could be meaningful for both of us. On Thanksgiving Day of 1988 we flew from Denver to Punta Arenas, Chile, near the tip of South America. Ken had big dreams. He wanted to study the spires of Patagonia for a future climbing expedition. I had no such ambitions. I was content just to enjoy the wild, rugged mountain scenery.

Punta Arenas was bleak, dusty and wind-swept. A public bus with red, velveteen seats transported us northward on a sparsely traveled single-lane road. The motor coach was clean and comfortable, but video movies playing in Spanish at ear-splitting decibels made us miserable.

The road ended at Puerto Natales, a quaint seaside village next to a harbor filled with family-owned fishing boats. The town was orderly. Small shops lined the streets and white picket fences surrounded wooden houses. Except for a few soldiers bearing AK-47s, the village was peaceful and inviting. The armed men weren't threatening to us, so Ken and I split up to make preparations for the next leg of our journey.

Ken inquired around town for a driver to take us to Torres Del Paine National Park, a few hours to the north. My mission was to supplement our camping rations. Since I didn't speak a word of Spanish, it was challenging for me to purchase the items on our list. I couldn't just grab packages off the shelves and toss them into my basket. Instead a protective clerk stood behind the counter of each store. He guarded his goods much like a pharmacist does in America. I tested each worker's patience wherever I shopped. I pointed and pantomimed over and over, making the clerk engage with me in a game of "Guess What This Crazy Gringa Wants to Buy." Eventually I filled my bags with nearly everything that we needed.

Patagonia had a limited tourist infrastructure in 1988. Only a few unimproved trails connected the scarce and primitive shelters called *refugios*. Trail signs were rare and foot bridges were mostly non-existent.

The Cuernos with guanacos in the foreground

The region is notorious for its long-lasting and harsh weather. During a storm ferocious winds and torrential rains can force climbers and hikers to take shelter for days at a time. We were prepared. We carried an abundance of food and fuel for an arduous trek around Torres Del Paine.

The wind here seemed almost incessant. Up high, it whipped clouds around the peaks. Lower down, it stirred the surface water of lakes creating huge waves with white caps that reminded me of the ocean. One evening while filling our cooking pots on the shores of Sarmiento Lake, I barely escaped getting drenched by an incoming wave. I felt smug until a wall of wind-carried spray slammed into me just outside a refugio.

Besides the ever-present wind, water was everywhere. It fell from the sky in torrents as either rain or snow. Meltwater from alpine glaciers drained into rivers of churning white liquid and pooled into enormous lakes at the base of each valley. Depending on a lake's proximity to a glacier and the amount of sediment suspended in the water, each lake was tinted grey, turquoise or azure.

Massive stone towers dominated the horizon before us. They looked like something right out of a fairy tale. Known as the *Cuernos*, Spanish for horns, these pinnacles were slightly twisted and culminated in black, sharply curved summits. Atop a dark crumbly base of rocks, the central flank of each spire was made of light-colored granite. The mountains' surreal appearance was even more enchanting when they glistened in the rain or reflected the sunlight off their steep glacially polished walls.

Huge condors circled in the sky above us as we trekked towards the base of the Ascencio Valley. Here at another refugio we met Sue, a stranded woman from England. She had been waiting several days for hikers to appear so they could help her ford the raging stream. The next day, the three of us stripped off our socks, boots and trousers at the edge of the river. The hip-deep water was fast and deep. Bracing ourselves together for strength, our threesome moved slowly and cautiously through the frigid current. My legs were blue and nearly numb by the time I reached the opposite shore of the stream.

Our new companion trekked with us halfway up the gorge. Ken and I continued upstream until the path terminated at a grey-colored lake. Higher up, the wind created a loud eerie howl as it raced between the three massive spires of the Cirque of the Towers. The scene inspired Ken and I to dance among the boulders and yelp with sheer delight.

A few days later we trekked down-valley through cow pastures bordering the national park. Soon the trail completely disappeared. Mud covered the grass and cows searched for a suitable place to graze. Ken and I crawled under barbed wire fences, across fields and through mossy forests. Progress was slow. At each stream we searched for fallen logs to provide safe passage across the waterways.

Once we were on the remote side of the park, the weight of our packs became unbearable. Unlike in Nepal, there were no porters in Patagonia. Instead we carried our own equipment and supplies. My backpack weighed only thirty to thirty-five pounds, but it was bearing down on my sacrum and uneven hips. Ken was angry because he shouldered most of the load; his pack weighed about sixty pounds.

On a lunch break, he expressed his resentment. "It's not fair that I have to carry the bulk of our gear."

"I don't see any other options. I can't put that much weight on my spine. It's too much pressure on my old fractures." I responded.

We continued up the trail. It started to rain. Ken was cranky. A quarter of a mile later, he stopped, pulled his pack off, and plopped it on the ground.

"You try carrying this heavy load and see how you like it!" he shouted.

He was serious. Ken glared at me with a clenched jaw and lips pressed tightly together. Tears welled up in my eyes as I dropped my pack onto the wet grass. I didn't want a fight. Since we hadn't seen a soul for days in this remote wilderness, discord between us would only make matters worse. Ken put his hefty rucksack, more than half my body weight, onto my back and then grinned at me with furrowed eyebrows.

"Carry it for a few miles and see how I feel!"

He grabbed my lighter backpack and stomped up the trail. I dragged far behind him. After hiking a half a mile my sacroiliac joints were screaming at me. It was the first time after my accident that I had any inkling that they might be a problem. I wondered how long my hundred and five pound frame could carry this weight. I wanted to collapse, curl up into a ball and cry. Instead I sobbed quietly as I trudged up the trail. After a few miles Ken and I swapped packs again. We hiked in silence with a palpable tension between us for most of the day.

Soon the weather changed. Clouds covered the peaks, the wind blew in horizontal sheets of rain, and we quickly became cold and clammy. Concerned about becoming snowbound on the remote side of the park, we pushed onwards towards the steep pass on the horizon.

A thin covering of snow had already accumulated on the summit. A brief window in the fog gave us a glimpse of Grey Glacier far below. Deep crevasses created a pattern of black zigzags across the white surface. The immense valley was filled with more ice than I had seen in either Alaska or Nepal. The glacier spread its tentacles into vast sinuous gorges further inland. There, it merged with the Patagonia Icecap, the largest body of ice outside of Antarctica.

Ice and mud covered the route down from Paine Pass making the descent tedious, slippery and treacherous. The faint trail was nearly impossible to follow. It was absurd to rely on our maps. Staff at the park's visitor center had given us a map with useless, hand-drawn scribbles. Before leaving America, I had arranged for a government office in Santiago to mail us the only topographic map available for the region. The map's poor resolution and large scale made it impossible to decipher important details. Since our maps were inadequate and snow was obliterating the route, we used common sense to find our way down to the glacier's edge.

Farther down we entered a dense forest of ghostly beech trees. Enveloped in a thick grey mist, the wind-beaten tree trunks and limbs resembled the bones of twisted skeletons. Wet fallen leaves and muddy soil covered the ground. We descended the steep slope like ground-dwelling monkeys; grabbing and swinging between tree trunks and branches. It was challenging to keep ourselves upright and at times, downright fun.

Occasionally we got off route. Each time the narrow trail disappeared under a thick mantle of fallen leaves, we navigated by following old-fashioned trail blazes that had been cut into random tree trunks. Marked trees were few and far between. We often had to backtrack as much as a quarter of a mile to find the blazes that we had missed. The route was easier to find once we were on the valley floor. Exhausted and cold, we staggered down the trail until we found a suitable place to camp.

Six inches of snow fell during the night covering our campsite and the track to Grey and Nordenskjold Lakes. Our feet became wet and chilled as we plodded through the snow in a dense fog next to Glacier Grey. A few hours later, the sun poked out from behind pewter-colored clouds, melted the snow and boosted our spirits.

The Frances Valley was our last destination in Torres Del Paine National Park. Without a bridge to cross the fast flowing river, the gorge was almost inaccessible. My legs turned purple while fording to the other side. The melt water drained directly from an upstream glacier. It was worth the effort. The trail took us into a vast cirque surrounded by sheer granite walls.

Later when we reached park headquarters, travelers with a rental car offered us a ride back to Puerto Natales. Once back in town, Ken's high school Spanish proved to be an asset. At each business he asked about hiring someone to drive us across the border into Argentina. Eventually we found two willing locals at a gas station.

Ken and I met up with our Chilean guides the next morning. Our driver's face revealed years of experience in the outback. His dark, leathery skin was deeply creased. While the younger man loaded our backpacks into a beat-up red mini-van, our chauffeur tossed in extra cans of food, water and fuel. He knew what was ahead—our isolated route was linked by a maze of poorly maintained dirt roads.

It was an adventurous eight-hour drive across the Chilean Pampas. The terrain was mostly flat, dry and barren. Our van crawled and bounced across heavily rutted roads at a snail's pace. Huge puffy clouds hung low in the sky above us. Guanacos, a species of wild llama, grazed on the stark landscape.

Soon our dull journey was punctuated with excitement. After a loud *pop,* our vehicle slid sideways and stopped. A tire was flat. Our chaperones were unfazed. They stopped, jacked up the van, and put the spare tire on while rattling away in Spanish.

We drove a few more hours. Then a second tire burst. Ken and I looked worriedly at each other. Our driver had brought only two spare tires. Vast distances separated us from any human settlement. Several days could pass before another car traveled this route. A mechanical problem or another flat could be disastrous.

The Chileans were undaunted. They quickly changed the second flat tire while we waited on the sidelines. The prospects of a third flat tire were improbable. Even so, Ken and I were edgy. Our vacation time was precious. We didn't like the prospect of being stranded in chilly weather with strangers in the middle of nowhere. We also had limited supplies of food and water.

Our third flat tire came shortly after crossing an unmanned border into Argentina. We were doomed. Our driver slapped his thigh and chuckled loudly with disbelief. He quickly jumped out of the van to assess the situation. His young friend stepped outside to help. They managed to patch the tire but it leaked slowly as we drove onward. Over the next few hours frequent stops were necessary to re-patch the leak. Our anxiety increased with each repair. It became increasingly uncertain whether we would make it to our destination before dark.

It was early summer in the Southern Hemisphere. The high latitude graced us with long hours of daylight. Our failing tire expired just as the town of Calafate appeared on the horizon. Ken and I were exasperated. We discussed paying our drivers, donning our backpacks, and walking to town to get help. But since our Chilean companions had done their best while being models of resourcefulness and perseverance, we stayed with them to the end.

Just as the van limped into the first gas station the engine hose blew. Attendants came running outside to help. They pushed the disintegrating vehicle into their garage. As a gesture of appreciation, we paid for their services and purchased several spare tires for our driver's van. The men refused our offers to put them up in a guest house for the night. Instead they valiantly drove through the night back to Puerto Natales, Chile.

We spent a miserable night in a small inn. At two in the morning we heard pots and pans banging beneath us. Then the room became unbearably hot. Unbeknownst to us, our second-floor quarters were above a bakery. The next morning we upgraded to a European-style lodge surrounded by rose gardens. Afterwards we took a day trip to Argentina's Glacier National Park.

A bus dropped us off at a magnificent viewpoint where the road ended. Here the Moreno Glacier, another arm of the Patagonian Icecap, flowed out between two mountains and into an enormous glacial lake. The glacier's snout was a wall of ice several hundred feet high. Its surface was riveted with crevasses the color of blue sea-glass. Every few minutes huge fractures ripped across the headwall. The ice exploded with a loud popping *crack, boom*. Chunks of ice, several stories high, broke off the glacier and crashed into the lake to become icebergs. Whenever this happened, a giant plume of water sprayed towards a crowd of sightseers. I wasn't the only one awed by the power of ice. Each time the icy towers burst apart, onlookers exclaimed in unison.

We were back in Calafate before evening. The next morning we took a bus to the northern edge of the park. We disembarked with a small group of hikers at the tiny hamlet of El Chaltén. The place could hardly be called a village. It was composed of a handful of wind-blasted, dilapidated wooden buildings.

Fierce winds and moisture-laden clouds hid the mountains as we walked up the trail. Gusts nearly blew me off my feet when I crested a glacial moraine en route to Cerro Torre Base Camp. We slept here for several days hoping to see the great pinnacle of Cerro Torre. The spire's narrow summit is topped with a massive hunk of ice perched precariously above its sheer face. As the days passed, our spirits fell with the deteriorating weather. Cerro Torre remained invisible.

Later, at Fitzroy Base Camp we set up our tent in a dense grove of beech trees. We were still sleeping in "the coffin," the tiny light-weight tent that had sheltered us on Mount Whitney.

The forest danced all night. Savage gales swayed the trees' long curved branches back and forth. With each movement, their flexible and leafy limbs nearly touched the ground before arching back in the opposite direction. I was awake most of the night; fascinated by the sound of teetering tree branches and fearful that they would snap, smash our tent, and injure us inside.

Several European climbers were camping nearby. One afternoon we dropped by to visit with them. A make-shift clothesline, drooping with soggy clothes, was strung about their campsite. It didn't seem probable that their garments would ever dry. Both the weather and the firewood were always damp. While we sat around a smoky campfire, the men entertained us with their tales. They had been stranded on the rocky towers in pelting rains and horrific winds for several days. Their stories made me wonder if Ken still wanted to climb in Patagonia.

The summit of Fitzroy, the highest of the peaks, remained elusive. Wind-driven clouds swirled around it for days. Only the base of the mountain, a formidable mass of sheer golden granite, was visible. While taking short hikes from camp, we kept our eye on the pinnacle. We were ever-hopeful that the veil of clouds would grant us a glimpse.

On our last evening at Fitzroy Base Camp, the clouds dissipated briefly. Fitzroy and its neighboring minarets were silhouetted in the setting sun. Beams of light radiated between the peaks like golden filaments illuminating the dark spaces between black needles of stone. The scene was a brief and magical interlude from the usual stormy weather.

After three weeks in Patagonia we returned home. The trip had been gratifying, but unlike the Himalayas, these mountains didn't touch my soul. Ken never talked about returning to Patagonia. Despite his technical climbing skills, his shyness kept him from finding climbing partners with similar ambitions, an endurance for severe weather, and a willingness to accept the slim prospects for success.

Nevertheless, Ken continued to increase his talents as a climber. My skills grew too, but I paid dearly for it. Over the next few years my body started breaking down. First, I developed severe tendonitis in both of my elbows. Occasionally my sacroiliac joints throbbed. Soon the scar tissue in my butt and thigh tugged at other muscles in disconcerting ways. These weren't enough to keep me from being active, though. For a while I managed to ignore everything but the tendonitis.

When I eventually gave up climbing on summer nights after work, Ken looked for alternative climbing partners. Soon he disappeared nearly every evening without me. He bouldered at the local crags until winter forced him into the climbing gym. More often than not, I dined at home alone.

I began to dread weekends. How pathetic is that? I wasn't just tired. Climbing also kept me in a state of emotional exhaustion—Mount Whitney's shadow manifested in my subconscious as an ever-present fear of falling. Nevertheless, I climbed on as best as I could with the hope of keeping our relationship alive.

Gradually I stopped rock climbing entirely. Ken resorted to sporadic climbing partners. He left me home alone for four to six weeks a year while he climbed in Yosemite.

Then one day, he informed me that he would only use his vacation days to go climbing. I was crushed—his declaration meant that our shared adventures were now over. Our marriage was in trouble. Without a common thread to bind us, we slowly drifted apart.

16

ADVENTURES IN GUIDING

It had been two years since I had talked with Maura. Then one day out of the blue, she called me.

"Hey, Pokey, you won't believe this. I just got a job working as a tour leader. I'll be guiding clients on trekking trips into the Himalayas in Nepal."

"That's fantastic!" I replied.

"This is what you should be doing. It's perrrr–fect for you!" she continued.

"Really?" I asked.

"You should break into this field," she emphasized. "It has your name all over it. Think about it."

"Wait, tell me more," I implored. "How did this come about?"

"It was just a fluke, really. I happened to be in San Francisco when the idea came to me. I thought, what the heck, I'll drop by the office of one of the international adventure travel companies and see what happens."

I couldn't believe her good fortune. On the other hand, it was just like Maura. If there is one valuable lesson she's taught me, it's to act like you know what you are doing. Her confidence and negotiation skills were exceptional. The National Park Service often met her demands whenever she accepted a new position before transferring to another park.

With her encouragement I sent my resume to adventure travel companies based in America. My cover letter stated that I would be in their area in September and that I wanted to set up an appointment to discuss possible employment. My real intention was to fly out for a meeting only if they expressed any interest. My plan worked. Soon three companies in the Bay Area contacted me for an interview.

Maura was supportive of my quest. She even met me in San Francisco. Two interviews fell flat. My prospects seemed more promising with Mountain Travel Adventure Company. My appointment with the Asia branch manager, a male named Jan, was delayed when I arrived. He was busy dealing with a crisis in Bhutan.

While waiting, the Africa branch manager spontaneously called me over for an interview. My skill set piqued his interest. I had leadership and customer service experience with the National Park Service. I was well-honed at resolving visitor problems. I was also adept in backcountry and international travel, and a certified Emergency Medical Technician.

He paused after our conversation, "There's only one problem."

"What's that?" I inquired.

"I wish you had already traveled to Africa. That would clinch the deal for both of us."

I didn't mention that Africa was low on my list of travel destinations. With a limited income I focused my explorations on where my heart was—Asia. An hour later the Asia branch manager had resolved the plight in Bhutan.

"Let's do the interview over lunch," he offered.

I hopped into the passenger seat of his blue Honda. To my relief, fine dining wasn't on his agenda. I wasn't likely to make a positive impression at a posh restaurant. I have a tendency to talk while swaying a food-laden fork and inadvertently flinging morsels onto my attire. Even at home, my tablecloth and wardrobe are stained with splatters.

Instead, Jan took me to a deli. We bought a couple of sandwiches and then walked down to the pier. He was testing my adaptability. The interview was casual; it was more like a conversation with a new acquaintance. We ate our lunch sitting on the ground amidst overflowing trash cans, visited by seagulls and homeless drifters.

On the spot I was given the job. My first trip would be to co-lead a trek in the Everest region. This plan would enable me to learn the company ropes. I was thrilled. It was an ideal set-up—I could work summers for the National Park Service and relax during the winters. During the spring and fall seasons I would be paid to be in the Himalayas as a trekking guide. What could be better? My scheme was to extend my stay in Asia after each gig and then travel on my own.

I was on a flight to Kathmandu in the spring of 1989. My journey came to an unexpected halt during an overnight layover in Bangkok. A revolution was in progress in Nepal. The border had been closed. Planes, vehicles and pedestrians were now prevented from entering the country.

Luckily, the next morning I stumbled upon other Mountain Travel guides at the ticket counter in the Bangkok Airport. We were all scrambling to get information about what was happening in Nepal and when we would be allowed to fly onward. Our clients were scattered around the globe. Some had already arrived in Nepal before its borders were closed. Others were stranded in Bangkok, still flying over the Pacific Ocean, or stuck at an airport back in America.

The next few days were intense. Uncertainty prevailed. We lacked information on the whereabouts of the clients except those in Bangkok, who were all staying at the airport hotel. They were impatient and unhappy. Company tour guides united to find solutions. We created a menu of alternative excursions in Thailand. The challenge would be to arrange everything at the last minute.

Flights to Nepal resumed three days later. The revolution was still in progress, but the political ruckus was calm enough to reopen the airport in Kathmandu. For the next few weeks the military imposed curfews just after sunset. By daylight the streets were packed with people trying to stock up on supplies.

Patricia, the leader of the trip I was supposed to assist, had already flown into the mountains with her clients that had arrived in Nepal before the border had closed. A few days later I arrived in Katmandu with our remaining tour members who had been stuck in Bangkok. We didn't have time to linger in the city since we needed to get into the

Himalayas to catch up with Patricia's group. Our rushed situation wasn't optimal for acclimatizing to the altitude either.

My group took a quick flight to Lukla, a tiny airstrip perched above a cliff at 9,000 feet. This was the same place where Maura and I had flown out of the Himalayas three years earlier. Company porters were waiting for my clients at the airstrip. After they loaded up our gear we headed up the trail. I had no choice but to march these trekkers all the way up to Namche Bazaar, a hike that is usually done in two days instead of one.

There we met up with Patricia. She was visibly relieved to have all sixteen of her clients united into one cohesive group. Now the tour could continue as planned. I was equally pleased to finally meet the leader I would be assisting.

Patricia had shoulder-length, dirty blond hair and beautiful hazel eyes. Around her neck she wore a powder blue scarf made of fine cashmere wool in the fashionable manner popular with Europeans. This contrasted with her other accessories: her hat, mittens, and the socks that she pulled up and over her lower trousers were all knit from coarse, chocolate-colored yak wool.

Patricia introduced herself as Di Di. She had emigrated from California to Nepal a decade earlier. Shortly afterwards she adopted the Nepali word for sister, *Di Di,* as her first name. Di Di was fluent in Nepali. She wasn't particularly athletic or gregarious, but she was a calm, confident and good-natured leader. She genuinely welcomed me as a co-leader for the trek. Each night when she met with the trip's sirdar, the leader of the Nepali field staff, she let me accompany her. This allowed me to participate in planning the next day's logistics and to see how she worked with the local staff.

Our group traversed the same trails that Maura and I had hiked in 1986. It wasn't long before Patricia had me deal with each unfolding calamity. Sometimes this meant leaving the group for days at a time.

Our first high-elevation camp was at 15,000 feet in the hamlet of Gokyo. That evening one of our clients developed serious altitude-related health issues. Before evaluating Charles, I looked through the medical kit that had been issued to us in Kathmandu. A silver box, the size of a carry-on piece of luggage, was packed with supplies. It was full of band aids, dressings, splints, stethoscopes and a blood pressure cuff.

It was a virtual pharmacy too. Even though I was an EMT, my training prohibited me from administering medications. I was shocked that the company would allow their guides to give out prescription drugs without any guidance. Most of the tour leaders had even less medical training than I did. I wondered about the potential liability of working for an American company in Asia.

For now, staying healthy and alive half way around the world trumped all other considerations. I did what needed to be done. I handed Charles a bottle of water and several pills.

"Take these," I said. "The Decadron is a steroid. It will reduce the swelling in your brain. The Diamox is for altitude sickness. It's a diuretic. It will help to re-acidify your blood while serving as a respiratory stimulant. It will also make your limbs feel tingly," I warned him.

Then I gathered two of our porters to pack up his belongings. The Sherpas carried our equipment while I helped Charles down the trail. It was a forced march; we hiked well into the night. Our goal was to descend several thousand feet. It could save the man's life.

Charles became increasingly disoriented and started walking like a drunk. This was a bad sign—fluid was building in his brain. I held on to him as we hiked down the path, stopping occasionally to rest or to let him vomit.

Eventually we were too exhausted to continue. With my headlamp, I studied our topographic map. The terrain was too steep for a tent site and no villages were around. We resumed our slow pace. Later, we stumbled upon a few earthen homes at 13,000 feet. Despite the late hour, the Sherpas pounded on the door and woke up the entire guest house. The lodge was full but the owners graciously heated hot lemon tea for us. This helped to rehydrate Charles since we had run out of water a few miles earlier.

The family in the neighboring shack took our porters in for the night. I set up the tent in the dark and slept next to Charles so I could watch over him. His breathing slowly relaxed and he reported feeling better. Still, I was uneasy. He wasn't out of danger yet. If his situation wasn't markedly improved by morning, I would have the Sherpas escort Charles down the valley while I ran ahead to Namche Bazaar. There I could use a radio to request a helicopter for an emergency evacuation.

The next morning Charles felt much better. We continued trekking downhill at a reasonable pace. He was hoping to acclimatize over the next few days to rejoin the tour. The main group was taking a short cut over Cho La Pass. Our plan was to walk the longer low-elevation route. We would descend to the village Kumjung, go up the other valley and meet up with the others near the Khumbu Glacier.

For several hours I delighted in Charles' company. We enjoyed conversing with each other as we walked down the trail. Occasionally he even shared a joke. Then something changed. He became unusually quiet for a long period of time.

A few miles later he suddenly stopped where the trail traversed above an immense cliff. Next he laid his daypack on the ground. Charles stared into the canyon below. The middle-aged man towered above me with his tall skinny frame. I sensed that something wasn't right. Then he shared with me how unhappy he was with his life. Charles told me that he was going to take his life by jumping over the edge. I was terrified. My heart went out to him, but I didn't know what to say. I chatted with him as he inched toward the precipice.

"Watch me, just watch me," he insisted. "I am going to end it all right here, right now!"

I was nervous. I don't remember what I said. I only remember the rush of anxiety. I felt powerless to help him. I knew I had to do everything I could to change his mind. Apparently, I said something that resonated with him. Soon he calmed down, sat next to me and accepted a snack. After a long rest, he agreed to continue down the path. Our Sherpas didn't understand the whole ordeal. Neither did I. It was the first time I had dealt with someone who was suicidal. I couldn't grasp the notion; it contradicted with my struggle to stay alive on Mount Whitney.

After four days we united with our group. Charles' behavior returned to normal. Our relationship was positive for the rest of the journey. A big smile creased his face when he finally saw Mount Everest from Kala Pattar. It was a great achievement for him to reach the 18,000 foot hilltop.

By the time our group returned to Periche, Di Di was seriously ill. She had a fever and was hacking up phlegm. Early the next morning she came over to my tent.

"I need you to take over the tour. One of the Sherpas can help me back to the airstrip at Lukla.

"No problem, Di Di. Take care of yourself. I will look after our clients."

"Come visit me when you return to Kathmandu," she concluded.

It was trial by fire. Over breakfast I explained the situation to our group. I assured them that they were in good hands with their new leader. Nevertheless, Sharon, a middle-aged woman from Indiana, got lost later that day. Our Sherpa staff were supposed to travel in three groups: one raced ahead to secure a place to camp for the evening; others trekked in the middle of the group and one Sherpa followed behind the last and slowest hiker. I was hiking in the middle of our group while the last Sherpa, Mingma, had stopped for tea at a guest house. Meanwhile fog rolled into the valley and it started to snow. Sharon took the wrong trail without Mingma noticing.

I learned of Sharon's absence only after our arrival in Chhukung that afternoon. The leader of our Sherpa staff managed our camp while I headed back down the trail with Dorjee and Tenzin. We searched frantically for two hours before we found her. Sharon was slightly hypothermic, disoriented and frightened. At the nearest village we plied her with hot drinks and reassured her. Then she hiked with us back up to Chhukung.

The next morning dawned clear. Our itinerary included an optional hike up a nearby 18,000-foot ridge. A small group of us ascended a slope of loose shale to the summit of Chhukung Ri. The view was worth the painstaking effort. The Lhotse-Nuptse massif loomed directly above us. Its formidable black wall rose to nearly 26,000 feet. Across the valley was a fluted icy ridge.

"That is the most beautiful mountain ridge I have ever seen," I said to my clients.

"What's its name?" someone asked.

"It doesn't have one. It's puny for these mountains, but I still think it's gorgeous," I replied.

"Let's name it after our fearless guide," Randy suggested.

I felt embarrassed but accepted the compliment. Chhukung Ri was new terrain for me. It had just become one of my favorite viewpoints in the Everest region.

Over the next week we hiked back down to Lukla. As usual, flights to Kathmandu were backlogged from weather and over-booking. I couldn't take the chance that my group would be split apart; some of my clients could get stranded here for days if we didn't fly out together. In desperation, I bribed airstrip officials to put us on the same flight. All of my clients cheered when they heard that we would be departing on the next in-coming plane.

The following morning my group nearly filled the aircraft. The last passenger to board the nineteen seat plane caught everyone's attention. Countless white silk scarves, known as *khatas*, were draped around his neck as a symbol of honor. The older gentleman sat in the seat in front of me. It was Sir Edmund Hillary. He, too, had been touched by the Sherpa people. After making the first ascent of Mount Everest in 1953 with his Sherpa companion Tenzing Norgay, he dedicated his life to building schools and medical facilities in the area. Hillary was now returning to Kathmandu after another goodwill trip.

Celebrities don't generally excite me, but this one was different. I couldn't resist. I pulled a note card out from my daypack. I had purchased it as a fundraiser for the Tengboche Foundation, founded by Hillary, to rebuild the Tengboche Monastery which had recently burnt down. The temple had personal significance. It was the first monastery to capture my heart. Embarrassed, I sheepishly tapped Sir Edmund Hillary on the shoulder. When he turned around, I asked him to autograph the card. I expressed my admiration for all he had done for the Sherpa people and then left him in peace.

Afterwards I sat back in my seat and watched the Himalayan peaks disappear as we flew towards Kathmandu. A big grin ran across my face; I had lived until morning on Mount Whitney and now I was living a dream.

After arriving back in the city, I called Ken. Our conversation fell flat. Unable to connect emotionally, we only exchanged shallow pleasantries. It wasn't just the difference in time zones; he couldn't relate to the experiences I described. It was as if I was calling from another planet. I realized then that we were living in two very different worlds, both physically and figuratively.

My mood picked up when I visited Di Di in her home for lunch. We reflected on our trek and then prepared a collective trip report for Mountain Travel. Di Di was deeply appreciative that I had taken over the tour when sickness forced her to return home. She promised to put a good word in for me as a guide. I found her intriguing. I wondered how she could feel more at home with a culture so different than the one she grew up with. Over time I would come to feel exactly the same way.

The next fall I returned to Nepal to lead my own trekking tour into the Everest region. Before leaving Kathmandu I met with my clients to discuss trip logistics and safety issues. I also reminded them about the strict weight restrictions for our flight.

"Does anyone want me to look at the gear you're taking on the trek before we depart? It's better to leave excess weight here at the hotel rather than having the airport officials take it away from you," I offered.

A fearful look spread across the faces of several of my clients. Four of them asked for assistance. After dinner I visited each of them at their respective rooms and reviewed the items they hoped to bring on our shared adventure. A few helpful suggestions brought nearly everyone within the maximum weight requirements. Teresa was the exception. Her duffle bag was bulging. Among her excessive clothes were thirty panties, thirty bras and thirty pairs of socks.

"Wow, that's a lot of undergarments!" I exclaimed in disbelief.

"It's just a clean pair for each day on the trek."

"I see that, but you can't bring this much with you on the small aircraft. The plane seats only a few passengers and their gear."

"I know," Teresa replied with disappointment.

"I use the rule of threes with frequent washings," I divulged.

"What do you mean?" she asked.

"Three panties, three pairs of liner and outer socks and well, two bras are plenty while traveling."

"That's not enough. I'll get dirty in the mountains," Theresa insisted.

"Everything is going to get stinky. You might only get one primitive shower on the whole trip. Otherwise, you will be limited to taking kitty baths in your tent when the Sherpa staff brings you a small bowl of heated water each morning."

"That's all?"

"A warm sleeping bag and warm clothes should be your highest priority for high altitude," I explained.

Clearly, Theresa hadn't read the pre-trip planning sheets that had been mailed to her after the company received her deposit for the trip.

"I recommend you take seven pairs of each," I compromised. Theresa nodded with acceptance as I walked out of her room.

Our tour was uneventful once we got going. Theresa turned out to be a real trooper. She never complained and was often bubbling with joy as she hiked along the trails.

For me, the highlight of this trek was being reunited with my Sherpa friends. Lhakpa Norbu was my sirdar, the leader of our Nepali field staff. He had been the sirdar on my previous trip with Di Di. Lhakpa was handsome. He had thick shiny black hair, dark brown slanted eyes and smooth, latte-colored skin. His disposition was sweet and easy going. He was soft-spoken, a good communicator and a competent leader.

For his crew Lhakpa had hired his nephew Pasang Norbu, who had worked for Maura and me on our vacation in the Himalayas. He was no longer the kid with the yak. Now he was a young man. When our group met up with our Sherpa staff at the airstrip in Lukla, Pasang and I were both surprised to see each other again. Over the next month, Pasang and I shared our stories and warm-hearted memories with our clients.

Our trek concluded on a large helicopter. Our ride out of the mountains had been arranged by our office staff in Kathmandu. That evening back in the city, I hosted a farewell dinner for the group at an upscale Indian restaurant. Afterwards I collapsed onto the bed at my hotel. I was finally free. My plan was to trek on my own during my remaining weeks in Nepal, but it wasn't my destiny.

17

SAFARI FROM HELL

A yellow telegram was delivered to me at my hotel the next morning. It was from the Mountain Travel office in California. I was taken aback when I saw the message inside: *Urgent. Our trip leader for the upcoming Elephant Safari is seriously ill. Work with the Kathmandu office to get to Bangkok before November 19. Itinerary to follow.*

Since I was new with the company, I wasn't sure if this was a compliment or a statement of desperation. I wanted to linger in Nepal, but I didn't feel like I could say no. After all, I was one of their newest guides. I confided with another leader that I was doubtful about my ability to lead a trip in Thailand; I had only passed through the country en route to somewhere else.

My colleague Richard tried to boost my confidence. "It will be fine," he said. "That trip can practically lead itself. It's the tour leader's vacation."

"You make it sound so easy, Richard. What if my clients ask me about my previous trips with elephants? I've never ridden an elephant before. I haven't set foot in a jungle either."

"How about taking a quick trip down to Chitwan National Park down by the Indian border before you leave for Thailand? You can ride elephants there. That way, you will at least be able to say you've ridden elephants before," he consoled me. "Your clients don't need to know that you have only a few hours of experience."

The next day Maura returned from guiding her clients on a trek around Annapurna. She enthusiastically agreed to join me to shop for clothes suitable for the tropics. Other than an outfit to wear in town, my travel wardrobe consisted of cold-weather gear designed for high altitude.

Unbeknownst to us, our outing corresponded with another political uprising in Kathmandu. We walked casually through the city comparing notes about our recent treks. All was peaceful until we turned the corner. A huge crowd of energetic crusaders suddenly engulfed us. We were swept up into a demonstration. Supporters of the Maoist rebels terrorizing Nepal marched in the street. Red scarves were tied around their foreheads. Some carried bayonets and others held red flags. They hoisted them skyward and waved them back and forth. Periodically the group thrust their fists angrily into the air and chanted with raised voices.

Maura and I were trapped. The mob made it nearly impossible to move against the flow of humanity; the street was a river of fast-moving pedestrians. Cars could no longer travel the road. Slowly and gently, we pushed our way to the side of the mass, but we couldn't find an escape route. Both sides of the streets were lined by metal fences with sharp, pointed tops akin to spears. Realizing that we were in a dangerous yet absurd situation, we looked at each other in despair. Then we simultaneously broke out and doubled-up with laughter. Our predicament was far from funny but giggling helped to alleviate our fear.

As we moved with the crowd, we periodically sang in unison, "We gotta get the hell out of here. This could turn ugly."

At a corner up ahead we saw a break in the fence. We pushed through the parade of people and then exited from the scene. I was now eager to get out of the city. Maura was too; she would soon depart for a short trek in the Everest region with another group of clients.

The following morning I departed from Kathmandu with a hired driver in a dilapidated jeep. We traversed up and down steep green hillsides, twisting and turning, hour after hour until we arrived in the Terai, Nepal's flat country.

Over the next two days I rode elephants through the jungle with a group of tourists who were staying at the lodge. It was scary sitting on top of those enormous creatures. Their gait also seemed unsteady to me. While riding through the forest we had to duck under tree branches to avoid being knocked down to the ground. Our excursion took us between patches of tall brown grass and semi-tropical trees. The vegetation wasn't as dense or green as I imagined it might be—that would come later in Thailand.

The forest came alive after dark. Countless bugs pulsated loudly through the night with sounds both subtle and thunderous. The pitch and rhythm varied throughout the night. Huge insects in all shapes and sizes crawled and flew about in the lodge's interior. They also came through the gaps in my thatch-roofed room. Since it was still the dry season, I was hopeful about not getting malaria.

A few days later, I returned to Kathmandu to catch my flight to Bangkok. I still had lingering doubts about leading a group around a country I was unfamiliar with.

Once in Thailand, I was excited to meet up with Julie. She had been a client on my recent trek in the Himalayas. Her presence put me at ease; we already had a good rapport. The clientele on this trip were different from my tour members in Nepal. Instead of trekking at high altitude in the cold for a month without a bath, this group had a greater interest in collecting stamps in their passports. I had a hard time relating to them. They came from privileged backgrounds. I was clearly out of my league.

One client had retired from a very high position with the U.S. Marines. The General's wife, Sheri, informed me that her husband had traveled around the world with the armed forces.

With an arrogant voice she shared, "He's quite literally had a red carpet laid out for him everywhere he's been!"

"Not on this trip," I whispered under my breath.

By evening, all but one of my twelve clients had gathered in Bangkok. Margaret was still missing. There was no word of her whereabouts. Since we had a tight sightseeing itinerary, our tour began without her.

First, we visited the Grand Palace. Each of us strolled around the grounds with wide-eyed amazement. The complex was dense with ancient buildings supported by golden pillars and topped with gracefully curved roofs tiled in green and red. Buddhist stupas pointed towards the heavens. They were completely gilded in gold. Exotic statues were placed strategically in the manicured gardens as if they were guardians.

Next our group boarded elegantly painted long-boats. We traveled on Bangkok's Chao Phraya River through a series of narrow canals filled with dirty brown water. Soon traffic came to a standstill. The waterway was completely packed with tourist-laden boats. We could hardly see the skinny Asian-style canoes that carried exotic flowers, fruit and other wares to sell. Boat motors roared loudly. They filled the air with clouds of nauseating diesel smoke. By the end of the morning the group was ready to flee from Bangkok.

Our local travel office continued to search for Margaret while the rest of us took a domestic flight to Northern Thailand. Chiang Mai was refreshing. The city was surrounded by lush rolling terrain. A tapered white building perched on a steep hill dominated the horizon. Our tour bus took us to the summit to explore the Doi Suthep Buddhist temple. While my group took photos, I was drawn to a sidewalk shop selling sparrows. Each bird was housed in a tiny bamboo cage. With great curiosity, I watched the local people purchase the birds and carry them towards the temple.

"Why are they buying so many birds?" I asked our local Thai guide.

"We believe it helps our karma. We give the birds freedom by releasing them. Symbolically, it's like freeing ourselves from suffering."

"I see."

I knew the birds were caught, sold and released over and over by savvy salesmen. Still, I liked the notion of improving my karma. I stepped up and bought one. I realized this was ridiculous, but I hoped it would bring me good luck on this trip.

A plump middle-aged woman with blonde hair was waiting for us when our group returned to our hotel. It was Margaret. She had missed her international flight while still in America. Our travel agent in Bangkok put her on the next flight to Chiang Mai so she could join the tour. Now that all my clients were accounted for, I was ready for the "trip leader's vacation."

Thanksgiving was just a few days away. I was determined to make this holiday memorable for my tour members. I made a shopping list for food that could mimic a Thanksgiving meal in Thailand. Turkey was nowhere to be found. Chicken would have to do. When I asked one of our Thai staff whether yams were available in his country, I received a definitive reply. I was elated. Now I would be able to surprise my clients with a special meal.

"Meet me at the night market at 9 p.m. and we can buy some," Naronsok assured me.

"Great," I replied, "I'll see you there."

After dinner our tour group went to the night bazaar. A huge market filled a building that resembled an airplane hangar. Inside, each stall sold hand-crafted wares made from indigenous tribes in Thailand, Laos and China. Each vendor had their own products. Some carried small metal boxes with hammered patterns, while others sold hand-woven textiles, jewelry, silk or leather.

At the appointed time, I headed to the food section of the market. There I met up with Naronsok to buy yams. He seemed baffled that I was searching among the piles of exotic fruits and vegetables.

Finally he spoke up. "No, no, Madame; they won't be over here," he insisted.

Now I was confused. We wandered aimlessly around the store together. I was getting frustrated. It was almost time to meet our group to take the bus back to the hotel. Then up ahead I saw Naronsok jumping excitedly in the next aisle.

"Here, yams, here!" he shouted with joy.

I was thrilled. I ran over to him. He pointed to a row of shelves lined with glass jars.

"Where are the yams?" I asked.

"Right here!" he exclaimed, pointing to a jar of jam.

"Oh, that's not what I had in mind."

Yams would not be part of our Thanksgiving meal. I thanked Naronsok for his effort and rejoined our group.

The following morning we boarded a tiny aircraft. The puddle-jumper stopped at three small towns en route to a remote airstrip near the Myanmar border. At the end of our flight, our luggage was heaped into the back of two white Toyota pickup trucks. My clients were whisked by mini-bus along a dirt road and into the Golden Triangle, where Thailand, Laos and Burma come together. This region has been infamous through the ages for abundant opium crops and drug trafficking. Along our route we stopped at a roadside waterfall and visited a small Buddhist temple.

During our drive Siam, the head of our Thai field staff, confided in me. "Don't be alarmed if we hear gunfire."

"What? Why would there be gunfire?" I asked with a frowned brow of disapproval.

"Sometimes there are skirmishes in Burma that spill over the border. Ignoring them is the best way to keep our clientele calm."

"I can't just pretend these incidents aren't happening. What about the group's safety?" I inquired.

"It's nothing to worry about. It's never been a problem. There's no gunfire where we are going. Really, it's OK," Siam insisted.

I had to trust him. I heard faint pops in the distance later that day. Surprisingly my clients never mentioned it. Neither did I. It was evening when we arrived at the village of Ban Vanno, where members of the White Karen tribe lived. Our group was immediately ushered into a large bamboo hut perched on stilts. This design kept the structure from being water-logged during the monsoonal rains.

The home was fairly luxurious, at least for an over-sized hut. Mats of woven bamboo covered the floor. A vaulted thatched roof and an open veranda made the shelter spacious. We moved in and unpacked our suitcases. I wondered if the group understood how variable their accommodations would be during this trip. We were far from Bangkok, in villages without $300 a night rooms.

Our group socialized in the living room while our Thai staff prepared dinner. Soon a meal was served. We were each given a tin plate covered with a mound of white Jasmine rice sprinkled with colorful vegetables and flavored with lemongrass. Next a dance troupe from the local village arrived. They wore traditional costumes with streams of colorful yarns hanging from their hand-woven shirts. The women wore headdresses covered with silver coins laced together with bright threads. The tribal men played flutes, drums and a few unfamiliar string instruments while the ladies danced in the center. Our group seemed satiated and happy.

When the entertainment ended, my clients laid their sleeping bags on mattresses on the floor and went to sleep. I went outside beneath a thatched-covered deck. Here I had more privacy and personal space. More importantly, it was slightly cooler outside. Unlike the others, I didn't have a light-weight sleeping bag. I had just come from the Himalayas where my bag was perfect for winter conditions; it was rated for 20 degrees below zero. I draped my red Gore-Tex down bag loosely over me. The high pitch of whining mosquitoes surrounded my head throughout the night. Rather than smearing myself with Deet, I slept all night inside my bag in a pool of my own sweat.

The next morning our Thai staff saddled up seven elephants with double-seated riding platforms mounted on their backs. Before riding, the elephants were prodded to sit on the ground. With various degrees of hesitation, we took turns climbing aboard our assigned beast.

Each animal was driven by a mahout, an experienced elephant driver. The mahout sat behind the elephant's head, steering the creature by nudging his feet behind its sensitive ears. When necessary, the mahout tapped on the elephant's head with a thin metal rod.

It was surprisingly difficult to ride these wrinkled grey animals. Courage helped. Weighing up to 10,000 pounds, the gait of an Asian elephant is uneven and unpredictable. Most of us gripped tightly onto the railings on our riding platforms. A mishap was almost unavoidable—we were riding eight feet above the ground while dodging tree branches in a dense forest.

We spent the next three days traveling on elephants. We traversed up and down rugged hills and crossed rivers. On the steeper mud-covered slopes, the elephants literally descended downhill on their knees. Whenever we broke out of the forest, we encountered patches of cultivated fields and isolated villages.

Something was amiss though. Bird songs were absent. Shouldn't a jungle be full of beautiful calls and titillating notes? When I inquired about the lack of birds, I was informed that most of them had been hunted out for food. I felt sad for both the birds and the hungry villagers.

On our first day out we stopped for lunch next to a spring in a small clearing in the forest. Half the group had dismounted from their elephants when a scream pierced above the constant drone of insects. I hustled over to the commotion. The mahouts were gathered around Margaret. She had just fallen off her elephant and was now lying on the ground groaning in pain. Her pale face contrasted starkly with the vibrant green undergrowth. I grabbed my first-aid kit and assessed her injuries. To be safe, I splinted everything she complained about; her wrist, elbow and ankle. An evacuation wasn't feasible. We were in the middle of nowhere. Margaret would have to ride her elephant for a few more hours to the next village.

That evening we met our Thai support staff in the village of Ban Patong. They had driven our luggage around the jungle on bumpy dirt roads. Before eating, our group strolled over to the adjacent settlement. My clients were curious why the Meo tribe lived in mud dwellings while the White Karen tribes preferred bamboo houses.

The local Meos were also intrigued with us. Hoping for a sale, they dashed out of their homes with armloads of handicrafts. An older Meo woman trailed behind the local residents. She was adorned with silver jewelry and wore rags the color of the rainbow. The crone walked slowly towards us with an intense look on her face. She looked older than her years. Her brown face was covered with deep wrinkles and her pupils were pin-pointed. With the air of authority, she shooed the kids aside. Then she reached into her pocket and pulled out a greasy wad that was the size of an apricot seed. It was opium. In a dazed state, she muttered a few words in English to let us know that it was for sale. My clients seemed surprised that an elderly looking woman wanted to strike a drug deal with us.

"I'll buy it and try it!" Margaret declared, as she limped forward.

My heart sank. I nearly choked. *Not happening on my tour*, I thought. I had flashbacks of walking past a three-story prison in Kathmandu. I remembered the arms dangling out of open, barred windows while inmates wailed from the dark interior. With visions of my client in a foreign jail, I couldn't let this transaction occur.

I asked Margaret to step aside from the group so we could talk privately. A delicate conversation followed. Margaret didn't seem to care that this was illegal, nor did she comprehend the potential risk for all of us. After standing firm, I eventually dissuaded her.

The old lady was smoking opium while talking to us. She was impaired, acted angry and agitated, and seemed desperate to make a sale. She wouldn't take no for an answer. The addict waved her fists as if she was going to strike me, the evil, uncooperative leader. Visibly frustrated, she then enlisted her neighbors by yelling in her native tongue. The Meo villagers came running to her aid. Soon we were surrounded by hostile locals. Our exploratory stroll was turning into an incident.

"Listen to me," I shouted to my clients. "I need all of you, including Margaret, to return to our accommodations right now!"

I was afraid. Siam saw the riot and came running over to help while my group quietly slipped away. He looked worried. Siam and I talked with the aged woman while the villagers screamed behind us. Discussions were heated. After an eternal thirty minutes, the local Meos conceded. Siam and I were free to go. With a sigh of relief, we walked through the fields back to the White Karen home where we were staying.

Our clients were anxiously waiting for us. They were still jittery.

"Hey, everything is OK now," I assured them. "Come on, its Thanksgiving Day. Let's celebrate that we survived our first day on elephants out in the jungle."

Soon a bonfire was lit. Orange and yellow flames spiraled towards the black sky. The campfire was calming. While waiting to eat, we bonded by sharing stories. An hour later our Thai staff emerged from a bamboo shelter with platters overflowing with food.

"Happy Thanksgiving!" They called out in unison.

They served a freshly caught and cooked chicken with yellow squash and rice. It was the next best thing to turkey and yams. Later, the rum and brandy came out with the stars. Our Thai guides serenaded us with a guitar, bamboo flutes and native songs. Soon we were all gyrating around the fire imitating elephants in motion. Our Thanksgiving was special after all. The jungle's loud and ceaseless sounds of humming and clicking insects and our foreign companions made for an exotic holiday.

The next morning we departed from Ban Vanno. Although it was unsafe for Margaret to continue the elephant safari, her condition didn't warrant an evacuation from our remote location. Instead she spent the next few days traveling in the vehicle with our Thai staff. To my dismay, she insisted on riding on top of the luggage in the back of the pickup.

The rest of us continued through the jungle on the backs of our grey, gentle beasts. The air was hot and humid. Occasionally we refreshed ourselves at small streams. We cooled off by plunging our heads under small cascades between the rocks. The elephants got hot too. Our mahouts washed them in the deeper rivers to reinvigorate them. At the end of each day we stayed in the open-aired homes belonging to members of the White Karen tribe.

Our elephant safari ended in the small town of Ban Mae Su. The residents were wealthier than those in the other villages. Our last home-stay had numerous bedrooms and even a toilet. My group was jovial until we discovered that our luggage was missing.

"The bags will be here soon," Siam assured me over and over.

Hours slipped away as the afternoon gave way to early evening. My clients were getting impatient. They expressed concern over the whereabouts of their belongings. Just before dark a single white truck overloaded with luggage appeared outside our compound. Margaret was riding inside the cab to make room for the extra bags. Siam was baffled. He went outside and confronted the driver. The man explained that the other truck had broken down and had been repaired at a roadside village.

"Then it stopped working again," Margaret piped in.

Two hours later a public bus rolled into town. All of us were relieved when our support staff waved from the windows. Siam ran down to the bus stop. Twenty minutes later he and the other staff staggered down the street with the rest of the luggage. I was beginning to wonder what else could go wrong on this trip.

After dinner Siam and I went to the kitchen for a private chat. We discussed our unreliable transportation and the logistics for the rest of the tour. A float trip on bamboo rafts was next on our itinerary.

I probed Siam for details about the Mae Yum River. "How rough is the water?" I asked trying to determine how risky it was for an injured woman who might have broken limbs.

"It's no problem. She can raft," Siam insisted.

Are there any rapids?" I inquired.

His answer typified the Asian desire to please. "It's a big, but gentle river through the jungle."

I wasn't convinced. What if something went wrong? How would we evacuate Margaret?

Margaret was crestfallen when I told her she couldn't join us. I didn't blame her. She had already missed out on most of the elephant safari. The other clients felt sorry for her too. They demanded that I let her go rafting. Then they pleaded with Siam to make me change my mind.

He shook his head. "She's the trip leader. Ultimately, it's her decision and her responsibility."

I stuck to my decision. Margaret's welfare was my burden. While trying to make peace with my group, I noticed Margaret off in the corner taking Percocet and downing a bottle of rum. This made me wonder about her intelligence. That night I went to sleep hoping I made the right choice.

In the middle of the night, Joanne, a fun-loving adventurer, pulled on my arm. "Wake up, wake up!" she shouted with concern.

I was groggy with exhaustion. For a moment, I wasn't sure if I was dreaming. Joanne persisted. She shook me until I acknowledged her. I opened my eyes and saw a panicked expression on her face. Her tone told me something serious had happened.

"Jean, come quickly. Michael is hurt!"

Joanne dragged me by the hand and down the stairs. Her husband was lying on the ground in a small pool of blood. The red liquid oozed out between his fingers as he cradled his head.

"Michael, are you OK?" I asked.

"I am not sure."

"Do you know where you are?" I asked, hoping to determine his level of consciousness.

"I am in Thailand."

"Who are you with?" I continued.

"I am on a tour with Joanne."

"Great. What happened?"

His wife interrupted, "He was on his way back from the bathroom when he hit his head. He didn't see that low beam."

I pointed my headlamp towards the closest beam. Several rusty nails, three inches long, were protruding from the wood. Blood marked the spot where Michael had banged his head. He had missed the nails by only a few inches.

"Joanne, run next door and wake up Siam. Tell him to have his staff boil water immediately. I need sterile water to clean this wound."

Using gauze dressings, I applied pressure on his head until the bleeding stopped. While waiting for the water to cool down, I cleaned the scissors on my pocket knife. Then I gave Michael a less than glamorous hair cut to survey any hidden damage. Luckily, his wound didn't require a twelve-hour drive on a dark and rutted dirt road to the nearest city. Michael whimpered and grimaced while I gently cleaned his laceration. I bandaged his cut and wrapped white gauze across his scalp and around his forehead. He looked like someone in a war zone. Then everyone returned to bed.

By morning Michael had lost interest in rafting and his wife was exhibiting flu-like symptoms. They rode with Margaret and the luggage in our one reliable truck. The remaining Thai staff took public buses to the next town.

Our rafts were waiting for the rest of us on the Mae Yum River. Each of the three crafts was made of several nine foot bamboo stems, four to five inches in diameter. The timbers were lashed together with jute. Before we climbed aboard, I tossed a life jacket to each client.

"You gotta be kidding," Carl snickered at me.

Joe supported him. "Look, Jean, the river is flat and calm, and it's hot and humid. You don't really expect us to wear these, do you?"

"Yes, I do," I insisted.

After we had traveled a mile downstream, the rafts were starting to sink. Soon each vessel was submerged under six inches of water.

"Pull over to the shore so we can check on the rafts," I instructed our Thai oarsmen.

One by one, each group joined us at the river's edge. I ordered my clients to disembark from their boats and on to the shore. By now, we were completely isolated; our only option was to travel down the muddy waterway. Despite their protests, I reassigned passengers to different rafts based on each person's size. Distributing our weight equally among the three vessels was in everyone's interest. It was fortuitous that our group had shrunk from twelve to nine. With our new seating assignments, our rafts were now only three inches under water.

Soon everyone relaxed. Our boats were now close enough for frequent conversations between clients. The tropical weather was perfect; warm and cloudy. The group was soothed by the river as we floated downstream under green vines drooping down from the jungle's canopy.

Our moods changed thirty minutes later. We heard a faint rush of water up ahead. As we drew closer, it turned into a roar. After turning a bend in the river, I got a glimpse of what lay ahead.

"Oh, shit!" I exclaimed.

We were headed into some rapids. Thoughts raced through my mind. *Could the current rip apart our water-logged rafts? Or would the whirling water just sink us entirely?*

My boat was in the lead. We hit the rapids first. The churning water spun us around. Then the raft collided with a rock jutting out of the rapids, sending us ricocheting across the river towards a minuscule island. The impact entangled the vegetation between the slats of our bamboo vessel.

I looked back towards my clients with concern. They were next. Their wide fear-filled eyes told me everything I needed to know.

My attention quickly turned downward. The swirling water had just pinned the tip of my raft under a rock. It was imminent; our boat was going under with three other passengers on board.

My oarsman sprung into action. He pulled a long machete out from under his belt and raised it into the air. With precision, he hacked a foot off the front of our craft. Soon our boat was freed. After witnessing our ordeal, the other rafting guides poled over to the riverbank with lightning speed.

Each of us sighed with relief. Once we were all united on the shore, I turned to my companions. "It's a good thing Margaret is not along with us. This could have been disastrous," I said.

I felt satisfied when they nodded. I was sure that by now they also agreed with my decision about wearing life jackets.

We managed to skirt the rapids by staying close to the shoreline. Gradually the river became wider and calmer. My clients became cheerful again. Near the end of the day we heard laughter in the distance. Farther downstream we were greeted by hundreds of children playing in the murky river. Curious about us, some of the older kids swam alongside the rafts. They greeted us in English and escorted us for a short distance.

Loud speakers soon blared in the distance. The children obediently swam back to shore and returned to the school yard. Once on the rim above the river, the girls squirmed into dry clothes by using their white uniform dresses as personal changing cabanas. This was our welcome to the town of Ban Mae Tia.

The next morning Siam appeared with a second truck and a mini-bus. I wasn't sure how he acquired them, but it didn't matter. Our luggage was loaded into the pickups while our group traveled on a tour bus back to Chiang Mai. My first priority was to have Margaret and Michael examined at the hospital. Margaret's x-rays were normal. She had only sprained her wrist and ankle. Michael checked out fine too. All was well.

After dark we returned to the night bazaar. Shopping for Christmas gifts was on everyone's mind. Silk ties, blouses, and dresses were popular purchases. Margaret's acquisition, an unusual piece of oversized luggage, upset the other clients. Julie was the first to approach me about it.

She spoke with a tone of indignation, "How could Margaret buy a bag made from an elephant hide after we just spent three days riding those wonderful animals?"

I didn't have an answer. I agreed with a passive nod but didn't say a word about it. I wanted to keep peace in the group. My companions penalized Margaret by alienating her during the second week of our adventure. To compensate, I tried to ease Margaret's loneliness by spending more time with her.

I was looking forward to the final leg of our journey. Finally I would get that long-promised vacation at an island resort. We flew south to Bangkok where we transferred planes for our flight to Phuket.

There we boarded a large boat on the Andaman Sea. The crew

arranged our luggage in tidy rows out on the open deck while steel-grey clouds gathered overhead. The threatening sky made me uneasy. I was concerned about the contents in our luggage. Inside each bag were Christmas gifts that my clients had purchased for their loved ones. The weather might ruin them. Without permission, I dragged each bag under the covered deck. I felt a strange twinge in my back while stacking them out of harm's way. It was a warning sign that something had shifted in my back. Instead of paying attention to it, I continued at my task. For the time being, it wasn't enough to set me back.

Minutes later a boatman appeared. He glared at me. Then he hauled all twenty pieces of luggage back to the outside deck. I had lost the battle. The wind started to blow a few minutes later. Sea swells tossed our boat heavily from side to side. It started to rain. Then it poured. All seventy passengers rushed from the boat deck to shelter inside the small ship.

Torrents of water fell from the sky and leaked into our luggage. Hundreds of dollars of silk were drenched and ruined. Their vivid colors bled from one garment to the next. The exquisite attire in each suitcase was soon transformed into tie dyed clothing. By the time we reached the island of Ko Phi Phi Don my group was about to mutiny.

The storm forced us to dock on the back side of the island. We disembarked onto a beach littered with empty water bottles, used condoms and human waste. My clients were disgusted. With our soggy luggage in tow, we trudged across the isthmus on a narrow trail between palm trees. En route we passed several tin houses, pools of toxic waste and piles of burning garbage. The smoky fumes smelled of formaldehyde. Tour groups weren't supposed to see these things. Oddly, I felt a little smug. I thought it was good for my clients to be exposed to the dark side of tourism with its environmental and social consequences.

After twenty minutes of walking we arrived at a resort. Thatched bungalows were tucked into coconut groves. Limestone cliffs and verdant vegetation rose up behind us. A turquoise bay framed with gleaming white sand separated us from the sea. Everyone felt ready for three days of beachside bliss.

The next day a few clients joined me for an excursion to the pristine island of Ko Phi Phi Ley. Carved wooden boats carried us across shallow lagoons. The water was luminous; crystal clear and the color of jade. Tropical foliage draped down the overhanging cliffs that surrounded us.

Our outing included a visit to an immense cave. Inside, tall bamboo ladders were precariously placed against the wall. Thai men clambered up the rungs to harvest swallow nests adhering to the rocky ceiling. Their perilous profession offered an appealing wage. The nests were exported to China for bird's nest soup, a pricey and nutritious delicacy.

That evening we returned to our idyllic resort. It was the perfect place for snorkeling. The water was warm and calm and the cove teemed with brilliantly colored exotic fish. The fragile coral reefs inspired wonder in all of us. Finally I was able to relax while my clients enjoyed exquisite Thai food, and swimming and lazing in the sun.

On our last day on the island, Sheri, the General's wife, walked over to me from her beach-side lounger.

"That's quite a scar showing on your butt! What happened, did a shark get you?" she probed.

I blushed with embarrassment. The long scar marking where the gangrene had been removed from my rump after my fall on Mount Whitney was visible beyond my modest swimsuit. I thought she was rude to point out my obvious deformity in front of my clients.

I responded reluctantly. "I was in an accident once."

Without saying more, I turned away and walked back to my bungalow. I wasn't ready to tell my story.

18

CRISIS AND OPPORTUNITY

My world shattered shortly after I returned home. Just before Christmas of 1990, I made a strenuous hike up a steep, pine-forested mountain near my home. Despite slogging around in my oversized mountaineering boots, I zipped up the snow-covered trail with ease. I was training for an ascent of Aconcagua, the highest peak in South America rising to 22,841 feet. My friend Jackie and I were scheduled to depart for Argentina just three weeks after my return from Thailand, but my hike up Deer Mountain forced me to change my plans.

Pain ran down my legs a few evenings after this seemingly insignificant trek. They twitched and moved uncontrollably. At the time, Ken and I were watching a movie in a theatre in Boulder. I was in agony. Sitting was so unbearable that I insisted we go home immediately. After driving only a few blocks, I was screaming from the pain.

Ken drove me to the nearest hospital. Doctors took x-rays, gave me steroids and pain medication, and then sent me home. During the one-hour drive back to our house, my condition grew worse—it was exacerbated by the medication I had received in the emergency room. I lay in the back of our white Subaru writhing with full-body convulsions.

Several days later, I wondered if my gait had been different in those white plastic boots or if they simply possessed bad juju. They had been worn by a Korean woman who died while climbing on Mount Kenya in Africa. I had purchased them at a used sporting goods store because they were the smallest size mountaineering boots available at the time. They were a rare find and I needed them for my next adventure.

This incident marked a significant turning point. For the next two decades my life slid downhill. I was able to be physically active for only brief periods. I consulted with a string of specialists. Each doctor had a different opinion, leaving me with a variety of possible explanations. I was told that I could have degenerated discs, compressed nerves, fibromyalgia, muscle weakness, nerves trapped in scar tissue, or that the pain was from the uneven hips and rotated sacroiliac joints sustained from my fall. No one knew for sure. They agreed on only one thing: the best treatment was to lie in bed for weeks on painkillers and muscle relaxants until the pain subsided.

At first, Ken seemed genuinely distressed. Perhaps he was fearful that my condition could be permanent. He knew my pain was linked to my accident on Mount Whitney, yet he still didn't want to talk about it. Instead he made it clear that he expected a quick recovery so I could resume my active life. That's what I wanted too, but that's not what happened. The universe had other plans for me.

Friends expressed concern over my physical well-being. They were baffled about my back problems. Everyone told me I was too young to be having these issues. Unless I was consulting with a medical practitioner, I remained silent about my history. I honored Ken's wish and kept our secret.

My past injuries continued to haunt me. Each time I tried to be active the muscles and scar tissue in my left buttock and thighs gradually became excessively tight. Next they pulled on my sacroiliac joints, tweaking them farther out of place. Jolts of nerve-charged pain periodically ran from the scar tissue on my left hip and into the left side of my crotch. With each sudden surge, I clenched my teeth and hopped around the house, as if I was being burned intermittently by a searing electrical current.

I wasn't ready to accept that I might not ever be the same again. Surely I could get past this. I had to; my future looked promising. I had just launched my new guiding career. Mountain Travel had already scheduled me to pioneer a new trek the following spring to a remote, sacred lake in western Nepal.

It was March before I acknowledged that my idyllic job situation was no longer realistic. As the months passed, my dreams and self-esteem slipped through my fingers and vanished. I spiraled downward. It wasn't just the physical pain; I was also tormented with the emotional agony of loss. I had lost my ability to be active and to explore outside. I had lost my new career. My self-confidence and the way I had defined myself was gone. Life had lost the luster and meaning that it once had.

Pain gave rise to self pity. I worried about how my physical condition would affect my future. When I was alone, I sometimes curled into a ball and broke down in a fit of sorrow. I cried so hard, I nearly drowned in my own tears. With a red face and burning eyes, I groaned from my belly and nearly choked on the mucus running down my sinuses and into my throat. I was filled with the kind of regret that comes only with the passage of time and worsening conditions.

I spent the next eighteen years, from 1990 to 2008, consulting with medical experts. I tried nearly every imaginable kind of treatment, physical therapy and bodywork. I was desperate for relief. I begged for surgery even though I was told it wouldn't help. Over time I became disheartened by our inadequate and broken medical system. I was angry. Countless doctors either gave up on me or strung me along while making guesses about how to help.

I struggled to maintain the slightest physical activity. Soon I developed a daily stretching routine. It helped me survive from day-to-day. I took up swimming even though I disliked it and could hardly swim across the pool. On rare occasions I took more Ibuprofen and muscle relaxants than I care to admit. Then, with lessened discomfort I hiked or rode my bicycle.

I also tried Rolfing. Once a week for three months, my rolfer realigned my muscles by separating fascia and scar tissue with super-deep massages. It helped me improve more than anything else I had tried, but still not enough to reclaim my active life.

My pain waxed and waned as the years and decades ticked by. The same determination that kept me alive on Mount Whitney now worked against me. Whenever the pain lessened, I increased my activity until it beat me back again.

It seemed like nearly everyone had given up on me—my husband, doctors and quite a few friends. Nonetheless, I refused to lose faith in myself. I kept a dim, though sometimes flickering, light of hope burning inside my heart. I knew that I would have to find my own way through this maze of pain and confusion.

Since the demons of pain and loss weren't likely to go away, I decided I should try making friends with them. Pushing them aside and ignoring them didn't work. My ordeal on Mount Whitney had taught me that I could survive anything. It had revealed to me how powerful the mind could be. I realized that the hardest mountains to conquer are the ones constructed inside our minds.

But I didn't know how to transform my own experiences of suffering into something positive. My intuition told me that I would find solace in the rich wisdom of Eastern cultures. I recalled the content souls I had met in Nepal who had endured far more hardship than I could ever know. They inspired me.

I bought an assortment of books on Eastern philosophy and read voraciously, as if my life depended on it. In a sense it did. Notions of karma, reincarnation and tapping into the mind's amazing abilities resonated with me.

Over time, I became better equipped to navigate the peaks and valleys of life. Slowly I realized that I had the power to rebuild my self-created universe. It might be different from before it collapsed, but it offered a world of new possibilities.

This realization revived a memory of the first time that I had met anyone in the West with a regular meditation practice. Many years earlier, Ken and I had been invited along with our friend Mary, to have dinner at another ranger's house. Once inside, Paul showed us around his government quarters at Rocky Mountain National Park. He revealed another world when he opened the door to his spare bedroom. The space served as his personal refuge. It was simple yet elegant. My eyes were immediately drawn to the room's centerpiece—a beautiful Tibetan rug made of dyed yak hairs, woven into floral patterns in light blue, navy and cream. On top was a neatly arranged black meditation cushion.

"That's what I need. I think meditation would be good for me." I blurted out upon seeing Paul's special room.

It was years before I acted on this insight. By then Paul had moved to Alaska and there was no one to give me any advice. So I turned to books. The choices were bewildering. There were countless meditation techniques for many different purposes. I experimented with a few until I had the opportunity to get formal instruction in Transcendental Meditation. Later, I switched to meditation practices in the Tibetan Buddhist tradition. I found it both beneficial and meaningful to be connected to something that had a track record for helping countless people for over 2,600 years.

The more I read the more I longed to be back in the East. It wasn't practical. I lacked the income and ability to trek in the Himalayas. So I decided I should work year-round. At least I could help pay off our mortgage. Since I couldn't lead treks anymore, I contemplated working in other sectors of the travel industry. Then I was presented with an unexpected opportunity; the National Park Service offered me a permanent job.

This was the perfect time to employ a lesson that Maura had taught me: ask for what you want before accepting anything. I took the risk. I was excited about this new career but unwilling to make work the focus of my life. My experience on Mount Whitney always kept my priorities in check, reminding me that life was short and that death could come at any time.

My strategy worked. Before accepting the job, I succeeded in negotiating an eight-week furlough each autumn. Now I had sufficient time off, an income to travel economically, and I could work in a beautiful place. Having a chunk of time off each year to pursue my life's dreams was more important to me than having additional income.

I was offered the position only four weeks before the first furlough started. I felt compelled to return to Asia, but I had to do some serious soul-searching first. I wasn't sure if my body could withstand the journey. I had no one to travel with and it was unlikely that I would find a traveling companion with a similar budget, schedule and bucket list. To be honest, I was afraid to travel alone. Nevertheless, I took a leap of faith. My vow to fulfill my dreams helped me to push my fears aside.

Next I needed a plan. I had to think of an accessible and alluring destination that didn't involve hiking. Then I remembered the Tibetan Buddhist monasteries that I had visited on previous trips to the Himalayas. They were the focal point of every village. They served as pillars of peace. Inside, the energy of love and compassion was palpable and nourishing. It was just what I needed.

The night before purchasing my airline ticket to India, I walked around my neighborhood. I was worried about my back and uncertain about continuing with my plans. Distressed, I looked up to the star-filled heavens and pleaded for a sign indicating whether I should go. Just as I cried out loud, a bright star streaked across the black sky. The next morning I booked my ticket.

I survived the long flight by taking muscle relaxants. My mind was in a foggy blur for the entire route. Hour after hour I stood in the aisle; sitting for lengthy periods was too painful. I spent the night in London to take the weight off my back before continuing to Delhi. Then I flew northward to Ladakh in the northwest corner of India.

The sight of the Himalayas beneath the plane filled me with joy. I stared out the window, filled with awe. While flying above knife-edged ridges, I recalled that Indian Airlines didn't have the best safety record. It would only take one mishap for the jagged peaks to tear the plane to shreds. I focused on the scenery instead. Glaciers draped the mountains and poured down into the valleys. Peacock-colored lakes sparkled in the sunlight below. The landscape teased and beckoned me.

Before landing in the town of Leh, the plane flew north, beyond the mountains and into the rain shadow of the Himalayas. It was like entering another world. Politically this was still India, but geographically I had just arrived on the Tibetan plateau.

Buildings blended into the dusty brown landscape. Rolling hills carpeted in short golden grass stretched beyond the city limits. The higher peaks still harbored late-season snowfields while the lower regions were sparsely vegetated. In a few places giant sand dunes nestled against steep, decomposing hillsides.

In the rarified air at 11,000 feet, the late October sun was warm and comforting, but lingering in the shadows even during the daytime was downright chilly. By night, the world turned frigid.

Ladakh is a crossroad of cultures. Tucked between Pakistan, China and Tibet, it is heavily influenced by its neighbors. Before dawn on my first morning in Leh, I was awakened to a hauntingly beautiful melody blaring over the town's loudspeakers. It hailed devout Muslims to prayer. I was quite surprised to hear this Islamic call in Buddhist India. Despite feeling slightly annoyed by the early rising time, the song elevated my spirit.

Leh is full of shops run by Kashmiri businessmen interspersed with Tibetan-style tea houses. Ladakhi men and women dressed in traditional long black robes tied with colorful sashes. They strolled through the alleyways murmuring Tibetan Buddhist prayers. This scene was juxtaposed with helicopters sputtering and circling above. Beyond the city, convoys of open military trucks carried dozens of Indian soldiers. Soon I learned that Ladakh had been invaded by the Chinese in the 1960s. The Indian government is still trying to keep the threat of China's influence from spilling over its borders.

My hired Ladakhi driver was adept in negotiating us through police checkpoints along the highway. Unlike many Indian drivers, he was very cautious. He skillfully navigated our jeep along narrow roads winding up and down steep mountainsides. He extended his warm heart to everyone he met. Throughout the journey his playful nature kept my guide and me in nearly constant laughter.

Periodically we left the main highway to explore smaller valleys. Much of our route followed along the Indus River. The waterway resembled a turquoise serpent snaking its way through chocolate-colored hills.

We stopped along the highway to visit the village of Alchi. It was absolutely magical. Despite its attractive setting on a terrace above the Indus River, surrounded by gold-leafed poplars gleaming in the autumn sunshine, the hamlet's main attraction was a deteriorating old temple. The dark interior walls were covered with thousands of tiny, intricate images of Buddhas. Using fine brushes and natural pigments, the face of each deity was exquisite, vibrant and life-like. I was bedazzled by these masterpieces; they were painted in the eleventh and twelfth centuries using only the light from flickering candle flames.

Over the next week I visited dozens of white-washed monasteries. Red-robed monks almost always welcomed me. They were eager to show me around. Predictably, the men always showered me with hospitality and plied me with cups of Tibetan butter tea. The hot beverage took some getting used to. It's more like a soup; black tea mixed with heaps of butter, salt and roasted barley flour known as *tsampa*. It's a staple in both Ladakh and Tibet.

During this trip something shifted inside of me. I discovered that I didn't just love mountains; I loved this culture. It had a lot to teach me. I was learning to understand life in the West by seeing it through the eyes of another civilization.

The monastery of Lamayuru was the trip's highlight. Perched on the side of a hill, surrounded by stupas and earthen walls, it was mystical and mysterious. My senses were overwhelmed the moment I entered the temple. Inside the air was thick with incense and the baritone of chanting monks. The floor was covered with heaps of ritual instruments, paintings sewed onto brocade cloth, bricks of tea and dishes. My eyes nearly bulged out with wonder and curiosity. I walked quietly along the aisles towards the lama sitting at the front of the room. He sat on a short throne near the altar. While he continued his prayers, I leaned towards him with a white silken khata draped between my outstretched arms. The lama bent towards me. He blessed me in traditional Tibetan style— placing his forehead against mine and then draping the light weight scarf around my neck.

Afterwards, I headed upstairs to the rooftop. For a while I thought about death. I am not sure why. Although the location wasn't as scenic as the Himalayas in Nepal, I decided that this was now the place where I wanted my ashes to be scattered.

I looked longingly at a mountain pass farther up the slope. Light-colored cliffs rose above the monastery. They were pock-marked with caves. My driver had informed me that these caves had been used for centuries by yogis in meditation retreats. I was intrigued.

Something felt familiar and special about this place. I had no way of knowing then that ten years later, Drupon Samten Rinpoche, a lama from Lamayuru, would become my spiritual teacher. He started rigorous studies at this monastery when he was only six years old. He had completed the traditional three-year retreat here in his early twenties. Drupon had also meditated for lengthy periods of time in the caves just above me. I wanted to explore these caverns, but I didn't have the pain tolerance or physical stamina to hike up to them.

After a few minutes on the rooftop, my attention shifted to the sounds rising up from below. Horns blared, and cymbals and bells chimed downstairs inside the temple. Later during a break in the ceremony, the lama to whom I had offered a khata came outside to talk with me. His name was Togden Rinpoche. Although he was well-known in the monasteries throughout Ladakh, I had no idea of his importance. Rinpoche is an honorific Tibetan title used when addressing highly realized or reincarnated lamas.

Togden Rinpoche motioned for me to sit down next to him. He poured me a cup of sweet Indian milk tea from a Chinese thermos decorated with a red and white floral pattern. While I sipped my hot drink, my driver translated a brief conversation between the master and me. The lama asked me to take his photo and then gave me his address so I could mail it to him after I returned home. Before returning inside, Togden Rinpoche spontaneously offered me the Tibetan name, *Thubten Zangpo*, which means noble Buddhist woman.

"Do you understand how amazing this is?" my driver stuttered with excitement.

"No," I replied. "Tell me more."

"This is extremely auspicious. In our culture one doesn't just get a new name out of the blue. High lamas rename a person when it's time to begin a new and needed chapter in one's life," he explained.

Indeed it proved to be a fresh start for me. After exploring Ladakh I spent a week in Bhutan visiting more monasteries. Unlike the dry and sometimes desolate landscape in northwest India, the temples in Bhutan are perched on steep, emerald green hillsides.

Over the next twelve years, I spent each of my autumn furloughs abroad. I explored the Asian continent from Japan to Pakistan and from Indonesia to China and Tibet. There was nowhere else I wanted to be.

One meeting with Death had changed everything—it drove me forward turning dreams into transformative experiences. My travels turned into pilgrimages. I meditated at monasteries along the way and paid homage to both mountains and Buddhas.

These journeys were very hard on me physically. Still, I wasn't going to stay at home and feel sorry for myself. I traveled on a limited budget and with an assortment of things to care for myself. On each trip I lugged countless medications, my own air mattress, foam padding, and self-care tools for muscle and back pain.

Traveling to some of the most polluted places in the world was also challenging for my asthma. Besides using three different inhalers a day, I required a steroid shot before each departure. As an inadvertent benefit, the steroids lowered my pain levels making travel more manageable.

I felt empowered when I was abroad. It was as if I were a new person bursting from a bud. Traveling alone enabled me to discover my strengths and weaknesses, redefine myself, and regain the confidence I once had.

It was a different story when I was at home. My relationship constricted me. During my early travels, I felt guilty for being overseas for lengthy periods of time. Soon I stopped feeling bad about this. I realized that each year Ken spent an equivalent amount of time away on California holidays and evening climbing excursions. Despite the issues in our marriage, I did my best to cultivate contentment.

PART III

DESPAIR
AND
TRANSFORMATION

To face it directly
is to strike against the deepest layer of being
which sleeps within us,
and then one must
listen painfully and lucidly to the sound it sends back.

René Daumal, *Mount Analogue*

19

SURRENDERING TO IMPERMANENCE

My life resembled a tapestry. Each colorful thread was woven into an intricate pattern that created a picture of how I saw myself and the world around me. Then it suddenly unraveled. One morning in 2004, Ken came home from jogging. He looked frustrated and agitated. He had barely gotten over the threshold of our front door when he began yelling at me.

"Sit down!" he demanded.

His tight, red face told me that he had something bottled up inside himself that he didn't know how to say.

"This is it! This marriage is irreparable," he blurted out.

I was shocked. This was so uncharacteristic of him. The tone in his voice gave me the impression that someone else was speaking for him; the words were merely coming from his mouth. Since a few of his acquaintances were dealing with their own dissolving relationships, I wondered how much their experiences had influenced Ken.

His proclamation was harsh, definitive and out of the blue. I didn't know how to respond. My eyes welled up with tears and I swallowed hard. I offered up possible solutions to our problems. Ken just stared at me.

Then he screamed, "This is over now. Nothing can change this."

After twenty-six years together we were finished. I was devastated. I had falsely believed that if Ken and I could survive our ordeal on Mount

Whitney then our relationship could endure anything. I wallowed in regret and sadness for a week. Then it dawned on me: this was my ticket to freedom. Despite the emotional upheaval, the universe was giving me an opportunity to lead a more meaningful life.

It was also the next step toward healing—physically, emotionally and spiritually. My marriage had silenced me. My quelled voice kept me from shedding the invisible shadow that Whitney had cast upon me. Now seemed like the right time to reach out, speak up and move on. One evening, I called a close friend.

"Hey Jude, are you busy?"

"No, what's up?" she asked.

"Can I come over?" I inquired. "I need to talk. I have something important to share with you."

Judy probably thought I wanted to talk about my impending divorce. She was not prepared for the conversation that unfolded. We spent hours lying on the teal-colored carpet inside her log home. For the first time in decades, I dominated the conversation. I shared my secret. I told her why I had chronic pain and back problems. She listened intently while I recounted my ski trip on the John Muir Trail and my fall on Mount Whitney. She was visibly stunned.

"We've been friends for over twenty years. Why haven't you told me this before?" She asked.

"I couldn't. Ken insisted that I didn't tell anyone."

"That's crazy!" She replied.

My face flushed crimson with embarrassment. I took a deep breath from my belly and sighed.

"You're right. I am really sorry. I didn't feel like I could share this until now."

My body felt lighter from our honest conversation. Still, it took me a long time before I opened up and told others the story that had defined my life. By releasing my secret I could move forward and become someone else. Telling Judy my tale was the beginning of this long journey.

Besides dealing with my failed marriage, my sister Debby was facing a steady decline towards death. We were very close. After my parents divorced, Debby and I grew up with my father while my younger sister Mary stayed with my mother. Debby cooked, cleaned, and looked after me while my father worked. Even though she was still a young adolescent, she took on these duties until my father remarried. I always admired her. She was the smart one in the family while I was the athletic child.

Mountains were important to both of us. Growing up in Denver, the Rockies were our constant companions. They were like guardians on the western horizon, visible from the school playground, our backyard and the dining room window. Our family played among the peaks on weekends and during vacations. Our passion for mountains bonded us until the end of Debby's life.

As an adult, Debby visited me in the national parks where I worked. Summer after summer, we shared many hiking adventures. During the winter she worked as a college professor in Ames, Iowa. Most of her summers were spent doing field research on native corn species in Arizona and New Mexico.

Our family was devastated in 2004 when Debby was diagnosed with ALS, or Lou Gehrig's disease. There is no cure; death is the only outcome. Her diagnosis made me pause and once again reevaluate what mattered most in life. Debby did the same. She struggled with the changes forced upon her. Soon she wouldn't be able to control her limbs and bodily functions. With the exception of her mind, her entire body would break down until she either suffocated or choked to death.

Debby displayed the first significant losses from her illness during my divorce. Her hands betrayed her first. She could barely write or hold a fork. This was problematic; she had planned to complete her fieldwork at a research station on a Native American reservation in New Mexico that fall. Since her project corresponded to the time of my furlough, helping her was my priority. We rendezvoused in Colorado and drove south.

I became her hands. I took field notes for her and hulled corn husks on her study plots. I also communicated with the other workers on her behalf. It was hot and exhausting work. I found it utterly boring, but since her passion for research gave meaning to her life, I gave it my all.

When we departed a few weeks later, tears rolled down her cheeks as she looked out the car window towards Shiprock, a massive stone formation on the horizon. I kept silent. Debby needed a quiet space to process her feelings. She knew that she would never return to the place she loved. I struggled to keep my own composure. Our outdoor excursions together were over. Her situation gave me gratitude and perspective about my own challenges. As we drove down the highway, we relished the beauty of each other's company and the desert landscape.

After Debby returned to Iowa, I drove south again. With a month's worth of food, I embarked on my first solo meditation retreat in Crestone, Colorado. The air around my one-room cabin was infused with the scent of pinion pines and gnarled junipers. The San Luis Valley stretched out below me. It was carpeted in sage and yellow-flowered rabbitbrush. The big blue skies and wide open spaces brought serenity and white space into my life, while the jagged Sangre de Cristo Range supported me from behind. The display of light was magical. Rainbows often filled the sky in the wake of afternoon thundershowers. At sunset, golden shafts of light beamed down through grey clouds and streaked across the sky.

In the evenings I frequently left my secluded cabin. I walked up a hill to a large stupa to say my prayers and saunter about. The power of the stupa was palatable; it was filled with the relics of ancient Buddhist masters. Sometimes I was overwhelmed by its strong energy. I could feel it flowing downhill to my shelter. Some nights it even kept me awake. In the stillness, I often heard a faint but constant buzz in the air.

After my retreat I returned home, moved into an apartment, and started my new life. The obstacles were daunting. First, there was the long, agonizing divorce process. I had virtually no money. I had to get smart and savvy, and fast. I hired a lawyer and consulted with experts. I juggled this while working and making regular trips to Iowa to visit my declining sister.

Debby also came to visit occasionally. Her husband or daughter would drive her to Colorado and drop her off at my place. Together we reminisced about our childhood and outdoor adventures as adults.

Sometimes she probed me with questions about Eastern philosophy. She also asked me to teach her to meditate. As her body broke down she became increasingly aware of the value of her mind; it was the only thing she could control. Her mind would determine the quality of her life.

Other times, Debby and I sought the nourishment of nature. I often took her to Bear Lake in Rocky Mountain National Park. During the winter it was nearly impossible to get her to the view point a few hundred yards from the parking lot. With a walker in front of her, I leaned against her back and pushed her across the packed snow.

During the summer we returned to Bear Lake and visited Sprague and Lily Lakes. We spent hours, day after day, sitting along the lake shores just staring at the mountain scenery. Spending time along these accessible trails made me appreciate how important they were to people who have limited access to places that can heal their souls.

I loved Debby deeply, but her visits were hard on me, emotionally and physically. As her body deteriorated, her shell became thin and tightly bound. She lived in perpetual pain. Her suffering touched everyone around her. We all wanted to help, but there was little we could do to alleviate her discomfort.

She needed assistance with everything including getting in and out of her mechanized wheelchair. This was taxing on my back. Once, when she fell onto my bathroom floor it took every ounce of my strength to lift her frame, larger than mine, back into the chair. My back hurt from the effort, but I kept this to myself so she wouldn't feel guilty. At the end of each visit, I wondered if we had just shared our last moments together.

During this time, the lives of my dearest friends were also faltering. Judy was diagnosed with breast and ovarian cancer. My friends Cindy and my life mentor and college professor, Bob O'Brien both grappled with lung cancer. Although I was in my forties, I felt too young to be watching my sibling and close friends die. In the face of death, they each lived the remainder of their lives more consciously. Their life priorities had changed, just as mine had on Mount Whitney.

My needs had also changed since my accident. Since then, sitting had been difficult, not just from the pain in my back and pelvis but from the removal of tissue on my left buttock. I wasn't just lopsided. The missing muscle on one side made me feel like I sat on a bare-boned elbow. In 2006 I decided to have my left buttock reconstructed. I was hoping the surgery would correct imbalances from a tilted pelvis. I flew out to San Diego and consulted with my former surgeon. Plastic surgery had improved enormously in the last thirty years, but it was still impossible to replace subcutaneous tissue. I settled for the best reconstruction available, which used tissue from a cadaver.

While recovering at my sister Mary's house, we received a letter from Debby. It declared her intentions to orchestrate her own death. After a long struggle, she had finally accepted the inevitable. Debby was tired of suffering. Her muscles had severely deteriorated. She wanted to avoid a fear-filled death while struggling to breathe.

Now it was up to me to fulfill her last wish; she wanted to die in my home with a view of the Rocky Mountains. Two weeks before her planned death, Debby and her husband came to Colorado. They shared my bedroom with a view of the high peaks.

Debby could no longer use her limbs; she was completely dependent on others. Her once long, silky brown hair was now cropped short. With so little hair to adorn her head, her brown eyes stood out like the big eyes of a deer.

She seemed most devastated by her inability to speak. Debby could no longer convey her needs or feelings to us. Using a poster board covered with the alphabet, we pointed from letter to letter until she gave us a slight nod. We recorded the letters to spell out her words and sentences. The process was slow and frustrating. Occasionally we perceived her subtle gestures incorrectly. Whenever we couldn't understand her she screamed with anguish. Once she calmed down we resumed our communication.

In 2006 Debby made the Fourth of July her personal Independence Day. Honoring her wishes, we halted the liquid diet that kept her alive and then gave her chocolate ice cream for her last meal. We used a funnel to put melted ice cream into the feeding tube that was inserted into her thin belly. As the cold liquid transfusion entered her body, her eyes twinkled and her lips turned upwards with a slight smile; she was relishing the memory of indulging in her favorite desert.

Debby became weaker with each succeeding day. She spent her last days being driven up Trail Ridge Road, the highest continuous highway in North America. We stopped at overlooks so she could gaze into the bluish, lavender peaks. From a wheelchair accessible van, I pointed in the distance to a rock outcropping on one of her favorite hiking paths.

"That's where I will put your ashes so you can always be in these mountains," I reassured her.

With her weak, now wobbly head, she nodded with approval. As we drove back to my home, I wondered what last thoughts were coursing through her mind. What does one think of when the end is slowly coming? How was her experience different than when I thought I would die on Mount Whitney? What kind of mental processes do the thousands of people on their death bed every day across the world experience before their lives are gone?

A few days later her family surrounded Debby's bedside through the night. No one dared to sleep for fear of missing her final event. She was unconscious from the pain-numbing morphine administered by hospice workers. Gradually the depth and pattern of her breathing changed. She was slowly letting go of life.

Her breathing was barely noticeable the next morning. Then she surprised us. After being unconscious for fifteen hours, she suddenly opened her eyes. With a slow deliberate motion, Debby moved her frail head. She looked at both sides of the bed to make sure that her adult son and daughter were present along with her husband, mother and sisters. My father had not arrived yet; he was still en route from Kansas. I think this gesture was Debby's way of saying good-bye.

Outside Longs Peak was shining brightly, lit by the morning sun with an azure backdrop. Before closing her eyes, Debby looked straight out the window towards the mountain. She took her final breath and released it with the sound of *ah*.

Her death was beautiful, even inspiring. She died exactly as she intended—with purpose and dignity. Her death was a teaching, a demonstration of the mind's power. Despite being completely unconscious, under the influence of drugs and on the verge of death, somehow Debby controlled that final moment in her life to connect with the people and mountains she loved. She, too, had lived until morning to realize an important wish.

After a few minutes, I broke the silence. I tore open a sealed envelope. Then I shared the letter that Debby had instructed me to read out loud upon her death. Debby believed that the deceased returned to nature. Her note instructed her family to see her whenever we encountered beauty in the world, from butterflies to fluttering leaves.

The next day we held an informal memorial service above treeline. Debby was a botanist. She would have been pleased. The tundra was in its glory; alpine wildflowers carpeted the ground, the sweet aroma of pollen permeated the gentle summer breeze, and the sky was radiant blue.

As a tribute to her, I read Debby's favorite campfire story, "The Big Trip," from *A Fine and Pleasant Misery* by Patrick McManus. It was perfect. The title captured the essence of life and the story pointed towards embarking on a new and big adventure into the unknown.

My heart was still heavy with grief a few days later when I heard more gloomy news. Bob O'Brien had just died from lung cancer. He had been an inspiration and an important pillar throughout my adult life.

Over the next forty-nine days I prayed for Debby and Bob each night after work. Tibetan Buddhists believe this to be the maximum time frame before one is reincarnated into their next life.

Thirty days later I bolted upright in the middle of the night. I was awakened by the sound of music. It came from a small Japanese jewelry box that sat on top of my bedroom dresser. Debby had bought it as a child forty years ago while on a business trip with our father. Knowing that I had always coveted it, she gave it to me during the last year of her life. It only played music when someone turned the crank on its bottom.

Upon hearing its sound, I immediately felt Debby's spirit in my room. I thanked her out loud for being such a wonderful sister and suggested she move on to her next life.

"Don't be afraid, Debby. If you see an intensely bright light, head straight into it without any doubt," I advised.

20

BLESSINGS FROM INTERDEPENDENCE

A few weeks after Debby's death, my spiritual teacher, Drupon Samten Rinpoche, came from California to Colorado to teach. His visit seemed timely. Like a close friend and advisor, he had seen me through one crisis after another. He provided counsel during my divorce, prayed for my sister, performed a blessing ceremony for me before my reconstructive surgery, and helped me through the loss of loved ones. Over the years I began to deepen my spiritual practice under his guidance.

I met Drupon in 2003 when he first came to the meditation center where I studied in Boulder. I felt a strong yet unexplainable connection to him. The sight of a real Tibetan Buddhist yogi with dreadlocks stacked on top of his head left me both mesmerized and speechless. Nonetheless, he looked stately in his maroon robes. He had a solid, grounding presence that was like sitting in the room with a mountain.

Drupon spoke English with a soft voice and a thick Ladakhi accent, similar to Tibetan. His eyes were extraordinary. Capped with thick drooping eyelids, they resembled glass marbles swirled in green and brown. Whenever I looked into his eyes I felt transported to a world where everything was calm and perfect. His weathered brown skin revealed a hard life. He had grown up in the Himalayas at 13,000 feet at Lamayuru Monastery in Ladakh, India. This was the temple where

Togden Rinpoche had given me a Tibetan name a decade earlier.

Now three years after meeting Drupon, he joined me and a small group of friends for a hike in Eldorado State Park. It was a beautiful August day. Beneath a clear blue sky, red sandstone cliffs towered above us, bird songs filled the air with melodic notes, and laughter and conversation bounced back and forth between my teacher and closest friends. Since it had only been a few months since my reconstructive surgery, I was a bit hesitant about hiking up steep terrain again. Nevertheless, I charged up the mountainside to keep up with the group.

After our trek, pain returned with a vengeance. For the next few months I could hardly move. I could barely hobble the twenty feet between my bed and the bathroom. I ate simple, pre-made meals right next to the kitchen stove to avoid walking ten feet farther to the dining table.

Once again I frustrated medical experts. They couldn't seem to help me. Sometimes I ventured to the larger cities of Boulder and Denver and stayed with friends while getting treatment. Still, nothing seemed to work. Between seeing doctors and physical therapists, I spent the next three months in bed.

Life hardly seemed worth living any more. I wondered if my life would ever flow effortlessly like a stream moving down a valley, carving through rocky obstacles with persistence and grace. While in bed, my fits of despair alternated with philosophical musings. Reflecting on the nature of reality helped me understand how much of life is defined by the connections between thoughts, decisions and actions. Even tiny actions can have huge consequences. In the East they call this *karma,* or cause and result.

I didn't like being bedridden, but I knew I had control over how I approached it. To improve my own karma and to make this experience meaningful, I used this period, as best as I could, as a meditation retreat.

My solitude was occasionally interrupted when friends graciously dropped by with groceries. When no one was available, I shopped on my own. Like an invalid, I moved through the aisles of the store at a snail's pace, leaning heavily on the cart for support and requiring help to get food both into my cart and out the door. I needed assistance with nearly everything but since I was living alone, I often had no choice but to fend for myself. Every task seemed daunting, taxing and painful. Occasionally my family physician, Dr. Fonken, called my home in the evening to check in on me. This small gesture meant the world to me. Knowing that someone cared uplifted my spirit and gave me strength to continue on.

With Christmas fast approaching I worried about my mother. Debby's absence would be conspicuous. She had always spent the holidays with our family, while I disappeared into the mountains. For the sake of my mom, I rallied forth. It was an exceedingly difficult journey, but I flew to California anyway.

It was a week from hell. I couldn't make it up the stairs to the spare bedroom in my mother's house. For most of my visit I lay on her couch groaning in agony. Desperate to help her second daughter, my mother took me to a local pain specialist who prescribed even more drugs including the lowest dose of Fentanyl. Unbeknownst to me, this synthetic opioid, delivered by a skin patch, is fifty times stronger than heroin. The physician added this medication to my existing daily regime of Percocet and morphine that had been prescribed by my pain doctor in Denver.

My pained presence didn't exactly bring holiday cheer into my family's home. It may have even intensified my mother's sadness rather than serving as a distraction from Debby's absence.

Later that week, my own discomfort was eased with a visit from my spiritual teacher, Drupon. He lived in a small monastic community at a retreat center just forty-five minutes away. The day after I called him to say hello, he and one of my friends, a Western Buddhist nun, showed up at my mom's place. They brought a giant box of candy topped with a stuffed penguin. His presence warmed my heart, but it was bit strange for my family to have a lama in their house. My mother had met Drupon several times before and had always appreciated his kindness. Now that he had shaved off his once-abundant hair, it was easier for her to interact with him as a simple, bald man dressed in red monastic robes.

After the holidays I had to return to work—I had used up my entire furlough and years of accumulated sick leave. I was only in my forties, but I felt geriatric—immobile, helpless and drowsy. I moved around the office with a walker. I don't know how I managed to function, and I honestly don't know how productive I was either. Nonetheless, I was grateful to live only a few minutes from the office and to have supportive coworkers. Sheer determination, the same resolve that kept me alive on Mount Whitney, was the only thing that enabled me to stay employed.

I often saw Ken on the days when I staffed the visitor center at park headquarters. He always avoided me. Whenever he saw me en route to the restroom, he darted down the hallway and into the nearest office for refuge. During these moments, I pondered what was going on in his mind. Did the sight of his helpless ex-wife, pushing a walker across the floor evoke painful memories of our time together on Whitney? Or was there something else that compelled him to avoid contact with me? Each time this happened, I hoped that he had tried to heal his own emotional wounds. Despite being divorced, I still cared about his well-being.

One day, when I was staying in Boulder with my ill friend Cindy after a doctor appointment, I checked my email on her computer. An auspicious letter was waiting for me.

"Cindy!" I called to her. "My friend Paul is coming back from India."

"What has he been doing there?"

"He's been studying Eastern philosophy and trying to learn Sanskrit and Tibetan." I exclaimed.

"What's he going to do now?" she inquired.

"I don't know. He's out of money and probably needs a job."

"Ask him to come help you," she insisted.

"I am not sure what his plans are. I don't know him well enough to ask him just to drop everything. He might want to resume his former life as a yoga instructor in the Bay Area."

Cindy walked across the room and stood behind me.

"I am not leaving this room until I see you email him and ask for help," she insisted. "Seriously, you need someone to assist you around the house and to take you to on-going medical care. It will make a world of difference. Ask him to come to Colorado right now."

I knew she was right. It was hard to acknowledge that I couldn't do everything by myself anymore. I was slowly learning the importance of asking for help. I carefully crafted a response to his email and read it out loud. After Cindy's approval, I hit the send button.

Paul replied favorably. He flew to Denver on a snowy day in March of 2007. We rendezvoused at the Boulderado Hotel in Boulder. Paul greeted me with a warm hug. He was as handsome as ever, with a muscular frame and straw-colored hair. His sincerity was revealed in his aquamarine eyes. I enjoyed listening to his gentle, soothing voice over a cup of hot tea.

I was thrilled to be in Paul's company again. We had a lot in common. Besides being park rangers we both loved mountains, Eastern philosophy and traveling in Asia. We had met in 1986 when he started working at Rocky Mountain National Park. Shortly afterwards Paul inspired me to learn to meditate.

We had stayed in touch after he left Rocky. He later got married and worked in national parks in Wyoming, Alaska and California. Paul was divorced a year before me and promptly went to India. During his three years abroad we had regular email exchanges. I often advised him of the locations of secret and sacred meditation caves tucked away in the Himalayas. Now Paul had returned to Colorado to help me recover. His arrival coincided with Garchen Rinpoche's visit to Boulder to give Buddhist teachings.

I had met Garchen several times before when he traveled from his Arizona home to teach in Colorado and New Mexico. As a monk who joined the Tibetan resistance during the Chinese invasion in the late 1950s, he was incarcerated along with hundreds of other monks, nuns and lamas for their religious beliefs. Garchen Rinpoche was radically transformed during his twenty years in confinement. He was forced into hard labor and frequently tortured. He gave away most of his food rations to fellow inmates. At night when everyone else was asleep, he studied in secret with his spiritual teacher, said his prayers quietly under his breath, and meditated until the wee hours of the morning. He even befriended the Chinese soldiers who guarded the jail.

Garchen Rinpoche is an advanced being. Instead of getting bitter and harboring hatred, he used this horrible experience to develop his mind and heart until he had unconditional love for everyone. His kindness is almost overwhelming.

I was at a retreat center near Santa Fe with Garchen Rinpoche a few years earlier, when my sister Mary called to tell me that Debby had been diagnosed with Lou Gehrig's disease. The retreatants were all on a break outside in the courtyard. When it was time to go back inside all eighty participants lined up at the door. I was sandwiched between people with my back toward the entrance. I was too shell-shocked to cry and I wasn't showing any obvious signs of distress.

Soon Garchen and his attendant walked across the compound to the temple. Rumor had it that high lamas are sometimes clairvoyant. And then I experienced it. Garchen couldn't see me or my facial expression, yet he stopped just before entering the door, turned around and walked back along the line of people until he reached me.

He spoke to me via his translator. "Move your tent. Bring it across the ravine and set it up next to my retreat cottage," he instructed. "It will be good for you to be close by," he concluded before walking into the shrine room.

I was dumbfounded. Somehow Garchen knew that I had just received traumatic news. He also understood that resting near his strong meditative energy would be soothing for me.

Now that Paul was in back in Colorado, I was eager to have him meet this amazing lama who had touched my life a few years earlier. Paul drove me up a canyon just beyond Boulder to listen to Garchen Rinpoche's teachings. We gathered with a hundred students at an octagonal building in the woods. Paul carried me across the snowy parking lot and then blew up my air mattress so I could lie on the floor at the front of the room. During the event Garchen mumbled something in Tibetan. Then he pointed at me, and then sternly at Paul.

"I think I just got my marching orders to care for you," Paul whispered to me.

Apparently he did. Over the next few months Paul drove me countless times, from the mountains down to the plains for medical treatment. During these long drives, he insisted that I read to him from the journal that I had kept while skiing the John Muir Trail. He thought it would be healing for me to revisit the trip while undergoing physical therapy.

One day, while I was recounting my adventure, Paul interrupted,

"Wait a minute. Those solo ski tracks that you and Ken crossed at Thousand Island Lake could have been mine."

"What makes you think that?" I asked.

"The date in your journal—that was the same time I skied alone to climb Mount Ritter. I was working in Mammoth Lakes for the Forest Service that winter. It was the last backcountry ski trip I did before leaving to work on the trail crew in Grand Teton National Park."

I could hardly believe the coincidence. Later Paul confirmed the dates of his employment and compared them to the dates of my journal. Indeed we had crossed ski tracks decades earlier without knowing it. This discovery felt like karma unfolding. Over the decades our lives had crossed paths several times; it was as if we were meant to be together.

Each time we drove to medical appointments, I read from my diary. My trip journal ended with a disturbing entry made in Room 32 at the hospital in Lone Pine. After describing what had happened on Mount Whitney, I concluded with:

I can hardly wait for the next challenge, the next dream, and the next mountain.

Was I crazy? Had the morphine made me forget the pain? Perhaps I was a different person three decades later, shaped by the challenges that come with old injuries and age. Decades later, I viewed my ski trip on the John Muir Trail as a grand yet regrettable adventure. Like most life regrets, I would do anything to undo that segment in my personal history.

Eventually Paul and I found a talented physical therapist. Lori Duncan explained how the body's natural tendency to protect us from pain actually makes the discomfort worse. Moving stiffly to guard hurt areas decreases blood flow, causes muscles to spasm further, and increases pre-existing levels of pain. During each session of physical therapy Paul accompanied me into a special pool and helped me with the therapeutic movements guided by Lori. Finally, after several months, I noticed that my condition was improving.

My pain lessened as I became stronger. One of my doctors suggested I get off medications. My pain specialist in Denver insisted that withdrawal symptoms could be avoided. His advice was to increase the dosage of the less powerful painkillers while reducing the stronger opioids. His confidence boosted my own. Unfortunately, he was wrong.

I took a week off from work and followed the suggested regime. My addicted body revolted. Within twelve hours, withdrawal symptoms turned my inner world into a hell realm. Even with the blinds open during daylight, I felt as if I lived in perpetual night. I was tormented around the clock. I couldn't regulate my body temperature. Sweat oozed out from my pores, trickled down my skin and burned my eyes with each salty drop. My body oscillated between freezing and feeling as if I were on fire. Whenever I shivered violently with cold, I buried myself beneath a heap of blankets. Even the children laughing and frolicking in the sunshine outside failed to bring a smile to my face.

My stomach churned repeatedly. Hoping to keep my bowels from an untimely explosion, I crawled out of bed and across the floor to the bathroom. After each of these episodes, I heaved over the toilet bowl trying futilely to vomit. Periodically my body convulsed. I writhed and moaned in agony. Withdrawal sucked the life right out of me. I felt like I was going to die, and there were moments when I actually wanted to.

How could this have happened to me? I wasn't a likely candidate for drug addiction. In my entire life I had never puffed on a cigarette, tried marijuana or experimented with recreational drugs. I didn't even have a sip of alcohol until I was in college, and I drank only a few glasses of wine a year. Painkillers never made me feel high or pleasurably mellow; they merely dulled the intensity of my physical discomfort.

Nonetheless, this first-hand experience gave me perspective and compassion for those struggling with addictions. Dependency starts as an innocent attempt to escape one's physical or emotional suffering but ultimately creates a vicious cycle of more misery. While thrashing about, I prayed for everyone who was imprisoned by their own afflictions. And I practiced patience. I knew that this state was impermanent – with time, I would emerge from the darkness and out to the other side.

I was fortunate to be supported though the ordeal. Paul was now working again at Rocky Mountain National Park. Several times a day, he slipped away from his nearby office to check on me. He cheered me on and cradled me in his arms when I screamed in despair.

After a wretched week I re-emerged into the working world. Then I gradually reduced my other pain medications. Finally I was free of narcotics. Slowly my mind shifted from fuzzy to focused. Constipation became a thing of the past. My body no longer reeked of medication. I still had pain, but it was more tolerable. As time progressed, I learned to accept and relax into physical discomfort. One evening over dinner, Paul suggested that I consult with a talented healer and physician that he knew in Nepal.

"I think you would greatly benefit from Dr. Shrestha's treatment. He's amazing. He even volunteers one day a week at a monastery treating monks with chronic pain. I've seen his patients get incredible results," Paul said in a slow and thoughtful manner.

At first, I was skeptical. Then Paul highlighted the physician's credentials.

"He's a Nepali who was trained in Western neurology. The government of Nepal also sent him to China to study Eastern medicine for twelve years."

"That's impressive, but it's also a long journey half way around the world. I am not sure I can endure the pain to get there," I replied.

"I've seen him transform lives. Please, seriously consider making the trip to see him."

I had nothing to lose and everything to gain. The plane ride couldn't be worse than withdrawal from painkillers. I sent my medical history to Dr. Sarbottam Shrestha via email. He agreed to see me during my upcoming furlough. The physician would treat me three times a week over the course of seven weeks.

Friends thought I was crazy to go to a third world country for medical treatment. I ignored their expressions of disapproval. Instead I listened to my own inner voice. I trusted Paul's advice and his intention to help me. During the time that he nursed me back to health, our friendship had transformed into a deep love. At last, I felt truly supported.

21

THE INTREPID PATIENT

I returned to Asia in the fall of 2008. To manage pain, I stood in the aisle for most of the flight across the Atlantic and overnighted at the halfway point in Frankfurt. The next morning I met a matronly German woman at the ticket counter. She pushed me in a wheelchair across the international airport and left me in a long line of elderly, frail and disabled passengers waiting to be conveyed to another terminal. I felt out of place. The group gazed sternly at me. Their verbal reprimands in German informed me that they didn't think I belonged with them either. I wasn't sure if they were reacting to my age or wondering why I was in a wheelchair. I felt humiliated. I looked away and waited in silence until I was moved to my departure gate.

After enduring another eight-hour flight, I arrived in New Delhi shortly after midnight. I was tired and groggy from the medication I had taken to survive the flight. Paul, who had arrived a few weeks before me to continue his Tibetan language studies, had made arrangements for a tour company to pick me up and take me to an ashram on the outskirts of the city.

As I limped off the plane, a short skinny airport employee, dressed in a matching grey cotton shirt and pants, waited for me at the gate.

"Welcome to India," he said in a sing-song voice.

"Namaste," I replied using the traditional greeting of simultaneously pressing my hands together in the gesture of prayer while lowering my forehead.

The attendant helped me into a creaky, dilapidated wheelchair. His kind demeanor enabled me to be patient. The wheels on the chair occasionally halted and turned uncontrollably as we traversed through the airport hallways. My assistant wasn't fazed by the inadequate device. Later, he waited for me while I got my passport stamped. From there, he took me to baggage claim.

"Madam, can you describe your luggage?"

"Look for two bags, one forest-green and the other grey. Both have lime-green ID tags," I instructed him.

He parked me on the side of the room and then headed for the spinning carousels. While waiting, I amused myself by watching the luggage spew down to the floor towards anxious on-lookers. After a long wait, my helper enthusiastically returned with my property in hand. Like a pro, he juggled my bags and pushed me along in the uncooperative wheelchair. We passed through customs and into a long corridor lined with a metal fence.

A sea of humanity greeted us. Indian men held white placards bearing the last names of their expected passengers. Each one tried to capture the attention of the passengers who had arranged to be transferred to their hotels. From behind the barricade, they waved their hands and shouted loudly. I was overwhelmed by exhaustion and discomfort. All I wanted was to find my driver, lie down, and get off my aching back. My head bobbed back and forth, searching from side to side, for a white sign with my last name scrawled on it.

Then I spotted it. In a hallway filled with brown-eyed men with dark skin, there was a single pale male with eyes the color of the sky. He was holding my name tag. It was Paul. He had bribed a travel agent in Delhi to give him access to this part of the airport so he could surprise me. I lit up when I saw him. My attendant transferred me to the end of the fence where Paul and I were reunited. After tipping my Indian helper, Paul assisted me outside. We weaved our way past throngs of noisy, jostling people. It was a relief when we stepped into our pre-arranged taxi.

Despite the late hour, the roads were busy between the Indira Gandhi International Airport and the ashram. Each time I arrived in India I had the same experience. It was always in the middle of the night and the atmosphere was chaotic with beeping horns trying to compensate for the lack of traffic rules on congested streets. Dusty roadsides were filled with closed tea stalls, homeless people slept under shawls pulled over their heads, and sacred cows wandered about. Strangely, this scene was always welcoming. It told me I was in Asia again. It meant that I had returned to the home of my spirit.

In the dark humid night the ashram was a cool quiet haven. The compound was gated and walled off from the noisy activity on the streets. Inside the temple, ornate but simple living quarters created a tranquil atmosphere. Everyone in this peaceful Hindu community was fast asleep. Our room was inviting. It was ornamented with graceful archways made of cement blocks and stones. Paul and I collapsed onto a comfortable bed covered with wrinkled saffron-colored sheets.

The next morning we ate a buffet breakfast in a large communal dining hall. The space was nearly silent. People spoke in whispers or not at all. Although a few Westerners were staying as guests, most of the ashram's inhabitants were young Indian men and women. These gentle people came to practice meditation and the generosity of serving others. They stayed for months and even years.

Paul and I wanted to linger in the ashram's beautiful gardens with its bright flowers and lovely water fountains. Instead we exchanged US dollars for Indian and Nepali rupees, and finalized our onward travel arrangements. The next morning we flew to Kathmandu, Nepal. I couldn't wait to be back in my favorite city. In addition to coming for medical treatment we were going to attend Buddhist teachings at a new monastery in the hills just beyond the city. I hoped that our arrival would coincide with Garchen Rinpoche's flight.

After passing through customs, Paul dashed ahead to claim our luggage. I moved slowly down the stairs towards the carousels. Then I spotted Garchen Rinpoche. He stood at the bottom of the stairway tucked against a corner wall with two lamas on either side of him. I was overcome with joy. I whipped out a white silk khata from my pocket. I draped it over my out-stretched hands, and then bowed and offered it to him. Garchen Rinpoche blessed me by touching his forehead to mine, and then wrapped the scarf around my neck. Like a loving grandfather, he held me close, with my back pressed against his chest and both of his arms wrapped around my waist, until Paul returned with our bags.

After we claimed our luggage the maroon-robed entourage departed for the distant monastery. Paul and I caught a taxi to the Lotus Guest House near the stupa in Boudhanath. For nearly two months this would be our home away from home. We purposely stayed in Boudhanath, the center of Tibetan culture in Kathmandu. It was the one place outside the Himalayas that could feed my soul between doctor appointments.

Each day during the next week, we made an arduous journey beyond the Kathmandu Valley. Our daily commute took an hour and a half each way. The final leg of the trip was especially hard on my back. Our taxi had to traverse up a very steep incline on a rough, rutted road to get to the newly constructed temple. Here we joined hundreds of Buddhist monks, nuns, and Westerners to listen to Buddhist teachings given by Garchen Rinpoche and several highly respected incarnate lamas. Their words of wisdom were translated from Tibetan into English, Nepali and Chinese. I listened intently while lying atop my air mattress on the cold floor.

Breaks were more challenging. The only access to food and restrooms was down a long cement staircase cut into a steep hillside. It was difficult, painful and time-consuming for me to get up and down this path. One day while stopping to rest on the way back up, I noticed Togden Rinpoche walking towards me. I was elated.

"Paul, let's wait here a minute. There is something I want to say to Togden Rinpoche."

As the man stepped up towards us, I gently stopped the lamas who accompanied him.

"Could any of you translate for me?" I inquired.

One of the bald men in robes nodded. "Sure, go ahead."

"Please tell Rinpoche how much my encounter with him fifteen years ago affected me. He invited me for tea at Lamayuru Monastery in Ladakh. Then he blessed and renamed me. As he requested, I took a photo of him and mailed it to him."

The lama turned to Rinpoche and translated.

Then I continued, "Togden Rinpoche sent me a thank-you note for the picture. That meant a lot to me. In fact, I still have his letter. Please tell him that shortly after meeting him at Lamayuru, I started seriously studying Buddhism."

A big grin split across Togden Rinpoche's face.

"I wanted to express my gratitude to Rinpoche. It seems as if he planted a seed in me that grew after our encounter," I concluded.

A warm fuzzy feeling arose in my heart. The joy came from communicating my appreciation. Unfortunately, I couldn't walk with the lamas. Instead I trudged slowly up the long stairway, with one hand on the railing and the other hand grasping Paul's arm.

After three days, I decided to stay behind at our guest house in Boudhanath while Paul attended the teachings for the rest of the week. It was difficult for me to accept that taking part in the event was more than I was up for. With the Himalayas on the horizon beyond the valley, it was equally heart breaking that I couldn't go trekking in the mountains.

Instead I was here to further my physical healing. A few days later I called Dr. Sarbottam Shrestha for directions to his office. I felt anxious about my first visit to see him. I had no idea how long the journey would take in rush hour traffic, how far I would have to walk, or what Dr. Shrestha's treatments would entail. To be safe, I gave myself several hours to get to his office.

From the Lotus Guest House I walked haltingly next to Paul in a dense fog through a maze of dirt alleys. Each path along the way was lined with small eateries, lodges, Tibetan shops and monasteries. The labyrinth of earthen roads converged into streets that led, like spokes on a wheel, toward a huge circular compound—the great stupa of Boudhanath. The structure towered over the surrounding buildings. It spread over a space larger than a football field.

The three-dimensional edifice is a monument to the Buddha of compassion, *Avalokiteshvara*. The stupa attracts crowds of devout Buddhists and intrigued tourists. Foreigners touring the city dominate at mid-day. At dawn and dusk, devotees infused the place with a sacred atmosphere. They whispered prayers and chanted mantras while walking around the stupa. Some prostrated around the complex. The air was permeated with the scent of juniper incense. Yellow-flamed butter lamps and marigold flowers were scattered as offerings along the pilgrimage route. The energy was magical and intensely transformative.

En route to the doctor, Paul and I joined a throng of people along a broad avenue that surrounded the stupa. Together we circumambulated the structure. We followed the local custom of walking in a clockwise direction. As I plodded down the path, I often grimaced with pain. At the far side of the complex, we passed through a gateway leading to paved streets.

Stupa at Boudhanath

Here the roads were jammed with cars. Everyone choked on diesel fumes. Immediately we encountered an onslaught of aggressive taxi drivers. Paul and I ignored their pestering inquiries about where we were going, if they could give us a ride, and how much we would be willing to pay. We knew the drill. If we walked farther from the tourist site, we could haggle a reasonably priced ride to the town of Patan.

Soon a driver whisked us into Kathmandu's morning rush hour. My love for the city made the journey tolerable. Forty minutes later we were dropped off at Durbar Square in Patan. As soon as we exited the cab we were bombarded by beggars and salesmen.

Since we still had plenty of time, Paul and I wandered over to the plaza to admire the ancient architecture. The square was filled with red-bricked Hindu temples shaped like pagodas. Each tiered roof was held up by intricately carved wooden struts that portrayed multi-armed goddesses. I was happy to see Patan again; it had been seventeen years since I had last visited this historic city.

Next we needed to find the physician's office. I pulled a folded piece of paper out from my pocket and tried to make sense out of the scribbled instructions. From Mangal Bazaar we trekked slowly for several blocks. Occasionally I had to stop and rest. This made the pain more tolerable before continuing onward.

There were no signs or street numbers along the way. We were surrounded by a jumble of shops and nondescript brick buildings. We walked through alleys lined with stores selling cheap jewelry, Indian fabrics and hammered metal wares. Along the way we inquired with shopkeepers and pedestrians to see if we were on the right street or getting close to Dr. Shrestha's clinic.

Responses varied. There were shoulder shrugs, blank stares, and the undefined Nepali head tilt that teeters from one side to the other. These gestures left us mystified. None of them indicated which way to go. Paul and I asked a multitude of strangers. Eventually someone pointed toward a small plaza off the narrow street. After dodging local shoppers, businessmen, and sacred cows, we found the correct building.

A dim, dusty staircase led from a courtyard up to Dr. Shrestha's office. I paused for a few seconds on the second floor to ponder what might unfold once I was inside. With a bit of trepidation, I turned the handle and opened the door. Inside, a small waiting room was packed with people.

Patients waited quietly on long wooden benches against drab, pale-green walls. A receptionist sat behind a small wooden desk at the back of the room. As I came through the door the young woman wrinkled her brow with a quizzical expression. She looked at me as if I were from outer space. This made me wonder if Dr. Shrestha had mentioned that I would be coming for an appointment that morning. She riffled through some papers but couldn't find my name. In faltering English she pointed toward the wall, indicating that Paul and I should take a seat and wait.

Sitting for forty-five minutes on a hard, narrow wooden bench was the last thing I wanted to do; my hips and back were throbbing from my journey across the Kathmandu Valley. I sighed and sat down. Waiting patients focused their attention on us. Self-conscious, I smiled. Then I looked away for a moment to compose myself. When I looked up again, all eyes were still pointed in our direction; chocolate-colored, fixed and curious. They stared for a very long time. As foreigners we were out of place here. I looked back with a gentle smile until their tan Nepali faces finally relaxed.

The patients were just as interesting to me. Older women were dressed in traditional garb. Their bright-colored saris were trimmed with ornate borders. They were half-shrouded in color-coordinated scarves and cloaked in an abundance of brightly colored fabric that piled up in pleats around their shoulders and into their skirts. The younger ladies were outfitted in salwar kameez; knee-length shirts draped over matching pants. Bright metallic threads were woven into the fabric worn by the higher caste clientele. Other patients were dressed in stained, worn-out clothes.

A closer look revealed an odd assortment of patients. Each had different needs. Kids fidgeted in the laps of their parents. Adult children accompanied their older parents for treatment. Their faces and bodies revealed stories of suffering. Tormented by discomfort, we all shared a sense of hope. Everyone in the waiting room was seeking restored health from the good doctor and trusted in his reputation as a healer.

For me, being here was a leap of faith. In the past I had given doctors too much medical authority over deciding what was best for me. Through experience, I learned that a collaborative approach to healing was more effective. Yet I had chosen to come half way around the world to surrender to an unfamiliar treatment from a stranger. I was driven by both conviction and desperation.

Soon an elderly man clutching a cane emerged from the treatment room. Then the receptionist rattled off a few words of Nepali. She pointed her chin up and towards the door. A mid-aged woman dressed in a saffron-colored sari with blue and red flowers stood up. Now my eyes were on her. She was beautifully adorned with a gold necklace, earrings and a large nose stud. Her wrists were covered with thin colorful bracelets that jingled as she walked into the doctor's office.

We had yet to spot Dr. Shrestha. Instead we watched one patient after another disappear behind his door. After a long wait, the receptionist got up from her desk and walked over to us.

"Come with me," she directed.

Paul remained in the waiting area while the young lady escorted me into his office. Inside there was a dark wooden desk, a shelf covered with books and a treatment table. The walls were plastered with posters of acupuncture meridians. A plastic skeleton stood in the corner. Dr. Shrestha turned from his desk and greeted me with a warm smile and a soft spoken voice.

"Welcome, Jean."

I was delighted to finally meet the saintly doctor whom Paul had spoken so highly of. I reached out and shook his hand.

"Thank you for seeing me," I said. "You have a very busy practice. Were you able to use the x-rays and medical history I sent by email?" I inquired.

"Yes, it was no problem. You have quite a list of fractures and injuries. Let's see what I can do for you."

Then he gestured for me to sit up on a thinly padded table covered in black vinyl. I was embarrassed—I couldn't get up on to it. Dr. Shrestha slid a step stool next to the table, gently assisted me on top, and then rolled up the sleeves of his blue shirt so he could work on my fully clothed body.

"Lie on your left side first," he instructed.

The table felt rock-hard. I moved my pain-filled body very slowly into position.

"This might hurt," he warned me.

I swallowed hard and took a deep breath. Then he repositioned my legs at a 90-degree angle. With the full force of his weight, he dug his elbows into the joint of my hip. I nearly hit the ceiling from the jolt of pain. Tears welled up in my eyes while I clenched my teeth.

Oh, my God, I thought, *this really, really hurts!*

It was excruciating. I wasn't sure if I could continue. He dug deeper into my back and legs. Then he twisted me in a variety of poses. I reminded myself that I had traveled to the other side of the globe just to get these treatments. This first experience with Dr. Shrestha gave me the impression that I had committed myself to twenty-one sessions of torture.

Just suck it up, you can do this, I coached myself.

While lying in agony on the table, I remembered my physical therapist Lori Duncan's vital lesson: *It's natural to tense up and guard our injured areas. Yet this actually creates more pain. It prevents us from releasing the area that hurts.*

I first discovered this in 1996 at Kopan Monastery right here in the Kathmandu Valley. At one point during a month-long group meditation retreat I was unable to leave a room jammed with people. Despite sitting upright in a chair, my legs were going numb and my back throbbed. Nothing seemed to help. Out of anguish, I decided to experiment with another approach. Instead of trying to push the pain away, I used it as the object of my meditation. Without identifying with it personally, I focused on every detail; its sensation, location and intensity. Doing so actually helped to bring open curiosity to the pain. By bringing full awareness to the pain something amazing happened; it became easier to work with. As the years passed though and my pain increased, I stiffened up and forgot what I had discovered here over a decade earlier.

Now Dr. Shrestha's treatment forced me to relax with the raw and sharp sensations he induced. To survive, I turned his treatments into a meditation session. Instead of squinting my eyes and tightening my body in response to the discomfort, I intentionally opened up. This allowed him to treat the deepest levels of my body's tissues. I also surrendered to whatever odd position he put me in.

After forty-five minutes, Dr. Shrestha helped me off the table. He gave me a few words of dietary advice for the time I was in Nepal. To my dismay, this included not eating papayas, one of my greatest weaknesses.

Then I tottered unsteadily towards the door.

"See you Wednesday," he said.

I paid the receptionist in Nepali rupees. To my amazement, I was charged the same price as the locals. I reminded her that I would be coming at the same time every Monday, Wednesday and Friday for nearly two months. She nodded with a warm smile as I headed to the door.

Slowly, Paul and I proceeded down the stairs. Outside, people gathered around a small Hindu temple in the center of the courtyard. Curious, we walked over to the structure and joined the crowd. A Hindu priest dressed in a citrus-orange gown and a white cap was conducting a *puja*, a session of devotional prayers of worship. He rang a small bell and chanted in Sanskrit. Wafts of sweet incense filled the air. Occasionally he made mysterious ritualistic gestures with his hands. I was captivated until the brief ceremony was over.

Afterwards, Paul and I found a small cafe for lunch. I felt an intense soreness settling into my bones while waiting for my meal. Then we haggled for a taxi ride back to Boudhanath.

Paul joined me for the first few visits to the doctor. For the rest of our stay in Kathmandu, he meditated at the stupa, took courses on Buddhist philosophy at some of the nearby monasteries, or went hiking in the mountains.

I carried on with my regular appointments. After each treatment, I shuffled slowly, like an old lady, back to the guest house. Still, I experienced pure delight every time I walked through the gateway leading into the stupa complex. On each return trip, I completed the circumambulation of the stupa that I had started earlier in the morning.

I repeated the same pattern each time I visited the doctor. Along the way I sought out small ways to uplift myself. Before each appointment, I limped up a short staircase to the top of an ancient stone ruin near Mangal Bazaar. From here, I could occasionally see distant snow-capped Himalayan peaks piercing through a dense layer of smog. When the mountains were visible, they yanked at my heart. As the weeks passed I slowly resigned myself to being in the city. After accepting that this was where I needed to be, I developed a deep connection to Patan.

Each visit with Dr. Shrestha was its own adventure. I witnessed an endless parade of injured and ill patients coming and going from the waiting room. I endured more stares and more smiles. Once in a while someone pressed their palms together and mumbled *Namaste*. On rare occasions, a patient attempted to communicate with me.

Dr. Sarbottam Shrestha put his magic touch on everyone; those who had suffered anything from strokes to twisted ankles and broken hips. He was unassuming, calm, and caring. He wasn't particularly talkative. Instead he focused on his work. He used his hands, head and heart to heal others. His treatments were unlike anything I had experienced before. Despite his degree in neurology, he employed an assortment of bodywork techniques. Each session was analogous to being treated simultaneously by a chiropractor, an osteopath and a rolfer. The talented physician was equally adept in traditional Chinese medicine. He used acupressure with the precision of a surgeon to work on my subtle energy channels. Dr. Shrestha also relied on *tui na*, a powerful form of Chinese massage. And he always twisted and pulled on me to manipulate my spine and hip joints.

Lastly he drew on the 2,500 year old practice of cupping. Miniature domes of clear glass were placed on my muscles. A small device was then attached to the top of the cup to create a vacuum inside. This raised the skin beneath the cups to stimulate blood flow, elevate pain, and promote healing in scar tissue, muscles and connective tissue.

Dr. Shrestha's healing modalities were intense for my delicate body. It was just as well that he didn't chat much with his patients. Once I was on his treatment table, I followed his instructions, surrendered to his treatments and focused my mind in meditation.

The tissue surrounding my sacrum, sacroiliac joints and the scar tissue on my left buttock, were extremely sensitive. The significance of this triangular area was noted by ancient cultures. Greeks referred to the sacrum as the "strong bone" because it is the central support for the entire body. The English word "sacrum" comes from *os sacrum*, Latin for "sacred bone."

To receive such powerful medical care in a place where the people perceived everything as holy was a blessing. It was healing on many levels. I felt supported everywhere I went. I was surrounded by an amazing landscape and touched by a kind and gifted doctor. And, Paul's love, encouragement and altruism soothed my worst days.

Over time I saw improvement from Dr. Shretha's treatments. Each week I walked farther and with greater ease. I began lingering in Patan after sessions. First, I paused outside in the courtyard to watch and listen to the chanting Hindu priest. He was always surrounded by an assortment of pedestrians. They came to have him comfort their souls. Afterwards I ate lunch at my favorite restaurant near Durbar Square. Then I wandered through the city's intriguing passageways.

Durbar Square in Patan

Patan is one of the oldest Buddhist cities in the world. Temples abound. It's also home to expert metal craftsman. Metallic echoes of *tap-tap-tap* filled the air. As I passed through the narrow streets, I watched artisans at work. Sitting on dirty cement floors, they pounded copper, brass and gold into exquisite shapes. Some alleys specialized in brass and copper pots. Others sold handcrafted bells, scepters, lotus flowers and Buddha hands made of metal. Endless shops and showrooms featured statues of Hindu deities and Buddhas.

Sometimes I shopped for statues of specific deities. I wanted their faces to be perfect; both exquisite and life-like. Eventually, I acquired three statues, each eight inches tall, made of gold, silver or bronze.

Patan was alluring for other reasons too. Buddhist and Hindu shrines are tucked into recesses throughout the town. With a little imagination, I could get past the juxtaposition of elegant fountains and statues surrounded by stone-lined pools that brimmed with filthy water, garbage and sludge. Instead I imagined Patan's rich past. It must have been paradise. I could easily picture the temples and greenery with a backdrop of towering white peaks and cobalt skies. I fancied the notion that I had lived in such a place in a previous life. Sometimes I wondered if this were mere fantasy or if that explained my insatiable attraction to this part of the planet.

Between treatments I rested at the Lotus Guest House. Sometimes I strolled around the stupa to work the soreness out of my muscles. For inspiration I meditated near prostrating pilgrims.

I encountered the same beggars each day. Each one had a different story of destitution. Two men in particular touched my heart. They were never aggressive in seeking donations. One was confined to a wheelchair; both of his legs were missing. He was a heavy-set man with a head of slick black hair and big brown eyes. He was a bright, friendly and talkative thirty-year old. He begged on a busy street near a shoe repair stall. The man was gifted. He spoke English and connected easily to people. During our conversations, he shared what it was like to live on the street. He stayed only on the busier paved streets; his wheelchair couldn't negotiate the majority of roads which were unpaved, rutted and filled with potholes.

One day he vanished. Paul and I worried about him. Later we learned that he had been hospitalized; he had developed kidney and bladder issues from not drinking enough water. His disability and the lack of facilities made it difficult for him to find a bathroom.

Nearby, an older man begged for a living in a dirt passageway near the stupa. His bald head was covered with a navy wool cap with red trim. His face was endearing. He had large almond eyes and a gentle smile. His legs were missing too. His body looked like a stump with a head and two arms. To move from one alley to the next, he hoisted his trunk onto a thick wooden board with small metal wheels resembling a skateboard. In the face of hardship, his quiet yet cheerful demeanor was heartening.

Boudhanath was an ideal place for beggars to gather. The stupa naturally evoked a feeling of compassion. Tourists and shopkeepers could spare a few rupees for those in need. I sometimes wondered if the serene atmosphere of this holy place affected the vagrants as much as it did me. I felt at home here. With over sixty Buddhist monasteries and nunneries nearby, the ether was both charged and calming.

During our stay, the Sakya Monastery behind our guest house held a special ceremony for ten days. From the rooftop, we watched monks engage in rituals. Music was offered to the divine with the choreographed use of bells, drums, trumpets, gongs and colliding cymbals. Deep male voices chanted in rhythmic mantras. Except for the burning of plastic water bottles and the acrid clouds of toxic smoke rising from the fire beneath our room, it was magical. Instead of looking for another guest house during peak visitation, we sealed our windows with cloth, plastic sheets and duct tape. Then we went outside to enjoy the event.

22

MEETING A MYSTIC

One evening Paul and I walked to a Hindu temple for a performance of traditional Indian music. With the help of our headlamps we rambled through dark alleyways near Pashupatinath, a temple complex on the Bagmati River. The atmosphere was surreal; silhouettes of pagoda-shaped temples lined the riverbank and the scent of wood smoke lingered in the air. Families came to Kathmandu's holy river to cremate their loved ones. They believed that it would help the deceased have an auspicious rebirth. The ashes would be dumped into the water and carried hundreds of miles downstream to merge into the Ganges River in India.

Just beyond Pashupatinath, Paul and I stumbled upon a ghat, a raised platform on the riverside used for cremations. A small pile of smoldering wood was evidence that a body had been burnt earlier that day. Paul and I stopped. We said a prayer for the departed stranger. While gazing into the apricot-colored embers, we noticed small pieces of bone and wondered about the deceased's life story.

A large black statue overlooked the fire pit. It was a figure of the Hindu deity, Hanuman. Depicted as a human with a monkey head, he represents the qualities of courage, power and selfless service. Smeared with vermillion powder, the stone monolith glowed neon orange under the bright light of our headlamps.

Paul and I walked down to the river's edge. I dug out the plastic bag from my daypack that contained some of my sister's ashes. Before dying Debby had asked family members to spread her ashes around the globe. She was delighted when I assured her that I would scatter them at sacred sites in Asia. Paul and I said another prayer as we released Debby's ashes into the Bagmati River. We had stumbled upon the perfect ghat at which to do this; Hanuman also symbolizes the connection between the body's life force and the divine.

The dark and foggy night and the strange odor in the air cast an eerie atmosphere across the land. It reminded me of a pre-dawn boat ride I had taken years earlier while on a pilgrimage in India. I was on the Ganges River, where flames had reached towards the sky from the countless funeral pyres that lined the riverbank. Families and Hindu priests stood nearby whispering prayers at the ghats. The air was thick with an otherworldly stench—the burning of human flesh. White specks of ash were carried away by the warm rising air. Throughout the day, ash from human remains was carried upwards by the wind. Later, it fell from the sky and onto the sacred city of Varanasi.

This flood of memories made me think about how different cultures deal with death. Wherever one is on the Indian subcontinent, the living are always reminded that death is not far away for any of us. Here, death is part of the daily drama, openly displayed on the stage of life.

At first, I found this heart-wrenching. American culture hadn't prepared me to witness this kind of suffering. Women stand in the streets holding their deceased babies, mourning and begging for money. Heroin addicts lie in the gutter with a needle protruding from their arm after an overdose. Processions of people traverse the streets carrying their loved one shrouded in white to the riverbanks for their journey onward. Here, death has traditionally been regarded as a transition from one life to the next reincarnation.

Whenever I returned to the West, I was bewildered by my own culture's failure to accept death. I noticed how an obsession with youthfulness, coupled with an unwillingness to talk about and prepare for death, created fear and agony over the inevitable.

My own near-death experience had profoundly altered my life. Before my encounter with Death, I avoided thinking about dying because I was busy living. I was young and felt entitled to a future. But when Death actually hovered over me, it forced me to confront it, not just during that moment, but over and over again. During that initial experience, I realized that my mind could interpret dying as either terrifying or peaceful. Nonetheless, I resumed my earlier angst about dying once I had survived. I viewed death as a threat to accomplishing my dreams. Gradually this shifted.

Contemplating death on a regular basis as part of my Buddhist studies, enabled me to accept it. Later, the passing of my sister and friends helped me to see that death could be my ally. It reminded me of the preciousness of life and to use each moment in the pursuit of something meaningful. Today I see death as a passage to another life into a different place in time and space.

I was deliberate in where I chose to scatter Debby's ashes. One evening we took some of her remains to the stupa at Boudhanath. There I found an arched niche, lit a candle on her behalf and placed her powdery remains inside. Paul and I also took her ashes with us to Pharping. I had always wanted to visit this sacred site on the southern end of the Kathmandu Valley. Here, in the seventh century, Guru Rinpoche, who brought Buddhism from India to Tibet, became enlightened. We left Debby's ashes near his meditation caves. Many devout pilgrims had done the same. A gully nearby was packed with *tsa-tsas*, miniature shaped stupas made from a mix of human ashes and clay. Back home, my lama-teacher Drupon Samten Rinpoche, had created several *tsa-tsas* from my sister's ashes. Once dry, he painted them ornately in gold and maroon.

Even though Debby never saw the Himalayas, she smiled when I assured her that her remains would be near the world's highest peaks. Since I could no longer hike, Paul took her ashes on a trek into the Langtang Himalayas. After bathing in a holy lake, he scattered her grey powdery remains into the icy water.

While Paul was away I heard rumors that a very learned lama, Khenchen Gyaltsen Rinpoche, was staying in a monastery on the far side of the Kathmandu Valley. He was the founder of the meditation center in Boulder where I studied. I met him years later when he visited Colorado again to teach. It would be auspicious to see him again. It wasn't possible to call the monastery to find out if he was actually present. Instead I had to take a chance. I made the long journey, hoping that he would be there and if not, that my trip would still be worthwhile.

Before departing the guest house, I carefully wrapped my three newly purchased statues. I was hoping that Khenchen Gyaltsen Rinpoche would bless them. I struggled through the alleys of Boudhanath with this heavy load in my daypack and then hired a taxi to drive me out of town.

Finding the monastery proved challenging. My driver inquired with the locals for directions, but no one seemed to know about a Buddhist monastery in the area. I was bewildered. Monasteries are often fairly large, ornate structures. Was it really possible that the residents in this small village were oblivious to its presence? Despite driving around town and inquiring countless times with the people on the street, we couldn't find it.

The taxi driver was visibly frustrated. Both of us were baffled. Perhaps the building wasn't on the radar of the Hindu townsfolk. Eventually, my driver sighed, threw up his hands and gave me a look of exasperation.

"Madam, we must be at the wrong village. There is no monastery here," he insisted in broken English.

"This is the right village. Let me just think for a minute. There must be somewhere else that we could look," I insisted.

Sitting quietly in the back seat for a few minutes, I thought about the hundreds of monasteries I had visited in Asia. Often they were built on areas of high ground. I tuned into my intuition. Then I made my best guess.

"Go back to the dirt road that we saw when we first entered town," I instructed.

The driver turned the cab around and headed down the highway.

"Here, make a right turn and go up this small hill," I directed.

After driving a few blocks, we found a three-story, amber-colored building. Fluttering prayer flags outside confirmed that we were in the right place. Filled with excitement, I leapt out of the car, grabbed my pack and paid the taxi driver.

He wrinkled his brow for a moment and then offered, "Madam, shall I wait for you?"

I paused for a long time. I was far away from Kathmandu. Other than knowing the name of this village I had no idea of where I actually was. The monastery was quiet and there were no signs of anyone around. It was uncertain if Khenchen Gyaltsen was really here. I wondered if there was anyone inside who could speak English. I didn't know if I would stay for a few minutes or several hours.

In all my travels, lamas had always welcomed me with kindness. I trusted the universe; somehow a lama would materialize out of nowhere and make sure that I got back to the city, or at least give me a place to stay until the next day.

"No thanks. I am not sure how long I will be here."

"Madam, I am happy to wait for you," my driver reiterated.

"It's OK, go on without me."

The taxi sped away. I took a deep breath, walked over to the front door and banged on it. I waited and then knocked some more. No one answered. All was silent. Next I tested the door. Since it was unlocked I went inside. No one was visible. Dim hallways gave me the impression that the building might be vacant.

"Hello, Tashi delek," I projected in both English and Tibetan. "Tashi delek. Is anyone here?" My voice bounced off the walls of the hallway.

Soon a pair of young monks, dressed in flowing maroon robes, appeared. After I rattled off a few words in English, they shrugged their shoulders. Clearly, they didn't understand me.

"Is Khenchen Gyaltsen Rinpoche here?" I asked.

They recognized the name and nodded. One of them gestured for me to follow him. We went down a hallway and then upstairs to the second floor. The monk knocked gently on a closed door. There was no answer. He knocked again and waited. Then a voice responded cheerfully from the other side.

"Ah, come on in."

I recognized it immediately. Just hearing Khenchen's voice made me smile. The monk opened the door. Inside was a large room with minimal furnishings and drab walls. Gorgeous hand-woven Tibetan rugs covered the floor. I walked towards Khenchen who was sitting on a red meditation cushion. I was overcome with exuberance to see him again. I bowed down and gave the lama a white silk offering scarf. He reached out and draped it over my neck. Then he put his forehead against mine. For a few minutes, time stopped. Our hearts had merged. I was at a loss for words. Then Khenchen asked the monk to bring us tea. To fill the silent gap, I took my daypack off, placed it on the table, and gently removed the three statues.

"What do you have there?" Khenchen inquired.

"Statues—will you bless them?"

"Of course!" he exclaimed with a loud voice that echoed across the room. "Which statues do you have?"

"It was hard to decide which ones to buy. They are all so beautiful. I bought the ones that would be most valuable for my practice. I have Vajradhara, the Buddha of all Buddhas, and Vajrasattva for purifying karma. Oh, and there's one more. I couldn't resist this statue of Guru Rinpoche, the founder of Tibetan Buddhism."

A huge smile split across the lama's face. Then he roared with laughter. The folds in his robes jiggled like jello. Khenchen was known for his hearty and jovial laugh. Regardless of one's circumstances, Khenchen could lighten them. He was gifted at pointing out the comical side of any situation. He always helped his students to perceive the world through a positive lens.

"These are lovely," he said.

I sat quietly as Khenchen picked up each statue with reverence. He examined their exquisite facial features. Then he held them up and put his head to the base of each figure. He whispered Tibetan prayers and blew on them as a blessing.

"You should get these statues filled with written prayers and precious substances when you can," he advised.

"Yes, I understand. I don't have time to get that done before my departure. I will ask my teacher to do this when I return home."

Just as I finished my last sip of tea, a monk in his early twenties entered the room. He was carrying a large serving tray with two aluminum plates heaped with rice, lentils, curried vegetables and chapattis. The monk served the food and then disappeared. Steam rose from the meal, carrying the aroma of delicate and pungent spices. The food was sumptuous. Khenchen's company was so engaging that several hours slipped away in conversation before I even looked at the time.

Beneath his charismatic charm there was a palpable presence. Khenchen's awareness was steady and vibrant, wise and loving. These qualities were cultivated during his many years in retreat. It was therapeutic for me to connect with the spirit of a great master again. He was a bridge to an indescribable energy; immeasurable, vast and beautiful.

While chatting with Khenchen, I felt an emanating field of energy much stronger than anything I had ever detected before. I thought it was coming from him. It made me wonder if Khenchen was doing a special meditation practice. I knew it would be inappropriate to comment on it. True yogis keep silent about their inner accomplishments. Still, the energy was incredibly powerful. It prompted me to inquire about one of the greatest living Tibetan Buddhist practitioners.

"Khenchen, how's Drubwang Konchok Norbu Rinpoche's health these days?"

"He's ninety-three years old now. He doesn't get around much anymore. He's upstairs. Would you like to see him?"

My brown eyes nearly popped out of my head. This explained the mysterious, intense field of energy that I felt. It was coming from Drubwang's powerful mind.

"He's here?" I asked with disbelief.

"Yes, on the third floor."

"I would love to see him. I thought he lived in India at Jangchub Ling Monastery in Dehra Dun."

"Come with me," Khenchen said. "I'll take you to see him now."

I wasn't prepared to have a private moment with one of the greatest living yogis on Earth. For a Tibetan Buddhist this was akin to a Catholic having a personal audience with Mother Theresa. Khenchen stood up and gestured for me to follow. A wide staircase led up to the next story. At the top, we went behind a large glass door and into the lama's private quarters. An attendant, a yogi with his hair tied up in a thick topknot, greeted us. Speaking in Tibetan, Khenchen asked him to take me to see Drubwang. Then his assistant escorted me into another room.

His Eminence Drubwang Konchok Norbu Rinpoche looked dignified yet peaceful. He was in a deep state of meditation. His eyes gazed slightly downward, just like a Buddha statue. His lips murmured prayers while he spun a hand-held prayer wheel. A soft white light radiated around him. Wrapped in a small blanket, Drubwang sat on a wooden throne topped with a cushion made of gold-colored brocade. Despite his advanced age, he sat upright with perfect posture. His legs were crossed beneath his elderly frame. His skin was smooth and shiny.

I hardly recognized him. He was bald now. He was no longer weighed down by the long dreadlocks that he had worn on top of his head for much of his life. Instead he looked like an ordinary lama with red robes and a shaved head. Nonetheless, he was a true yogi by definition. He was one of the few people in modern times that had spent many, many years in isolated retreat. During that time he engaged in secret, self-transforming practices that enabled him to develop extraordinary mastery over his body and mind.

I walked in, prostrated in front of him, and offered him a white khata. He placed his prayer wheel on the seat cushion next to his knee, before draping the silk scarf around my neck. Next he gently placed both of his hands on my crown and whispered a lengthy prayer to bless me. After a few minutes, he gestured for me to sit down.

His energy was overwhelming. While sitting on the floor below him, I searched for something meaningful to say. I wasn't able to think. His profound and powerful presence left me speechless. Then a few thoughts bubbled up from my mind. I talked to Drubwang about my meditation practice. His attendant translated for me. Drubwang advised me to persist in my efforts. I asked for a blessing that my practice would bring great benefit. The yogi paused for a moment. Then he resumed his prayers. Sitting silently with him for a few minutes was a tonic for my soul. I wanted to sit with him forever, enveloped in his loving field of energy.

Instead, I was reverent. Following the Tibetan tradition, I stood up, bowed with deep respect, and scooted myself out the door while facing Drubwang. Khenchen was waiting for me in the next room. My eyes were wet with tears of gratitude. I was so choked with emotion, I could barely speak.

"Thank you," I whispered with appreciation.

That brief encounter was a gift of a lifetime. Khenchen Gyaltsen took me back to his room and helped me pack up my statues. The afternoon was getting late. A young monk escorted me to the nearest bus stop. He sat dutifully with me for over an hour while I waited for the next bus.

My mind was still and silent on the return trip. I watched the view change from the window; villages gradually converged into the hustle and bustle of Kathmandu. Nonetheless, I felt an incredibly deep inner peace.

Paul returned to the city a few days later. Excitedly, I shared my adventures at the monastery with him.

"You will never meet such an enlightened master. Make it your highest priority to see him," I insisted.

Paul took my advice. He was grateful that he made the journey. Drubwang Konchok Norbu Rinpoche passed away three weeks later. At the Dalai Lama's request this great master lived longer than he intended; advanced yogis are known for controlling the exact timing of their deaths.

Shortly after this encounter, I concluded my medical treatments and flew back to Colorado. Dr. Sarbottam Shrestha had done wonders for me. The improvements in my health enabled me to finally get results from other practitioners. Eventually I found a skilled chiropractor in Boulder, Dr. Evan Katz. He restored a curve in my spine that had been flat for decades and helped me become active again.

23

EXPLORING INNER TERRAIN

After my treatments in Nepal, I pondered what it means to heal. Was it possible to feel whole after experiencing trauma and a permanent loss? What does healing look like, if one can't be fully restored? These were difficult questions for me to grapple with. Healing occurs on so many different levels. It's a long journey of self-discovery, acceptance and finding positive outcomes from difficult circumstances.

Decades of physical pain made me feel like I was riding on an emotional roller-coaster. My fall on Mount Whitney had redirected my life. Pain followed me everywhere like an invisible shadow. That mountain had changed me. At first, I felt broken. My shattered bones had literally fractured my life. No matter how hard I tried, I couldn't put all the pieces back together.

Intuitively, I knew I had to heal on every plane. This included addressing the most subtle issues that still needed resolving. My healing had been sabotaged by suppressing and silencing my story, first while convalescing in bed with mind-numbing painkillers and later, in my marriage to Ken. Our secret disaster had kept me from feeling supported and fully recovering. Ken was a master at avoiding the painful aspects of his life; he denied their existence to himself by not acknowledging them. I wanted to live my life differently.

Time had taught me how harmful it is to conceal what needs to be released. The more I opened up and told my story, the more progress I made. I discovered that unresolved issues from emotional and physical pain are held not only in the subconscious mind but in every cell, like a pacing tiger locked inside a cage. Until released, the tiger feeds on us from the inside out. Over time the tiger takes a toll on one's well-being.

So I took a candid look inside myself. I invited my secrets and skeletons out into the open and carefully examined the sorrow and joy that were etched in their bones. This was the beginning of slowly illuminating my dark emotional clouds with traces of light.

To further my healing, Paul suggested I investigate the emotional entrapments around trauma. After reading Peter Levine's book, *Waking the Tiger: Healing Trauma,* I decided to meet with a somatic trauma counselor. This therapy helps to release emotions and adrenaline from a past traumatic event that have become physical blockages inside the body.

The therapy revealed how fear had paralyzed me since my accident. It was as if I were still clinging to those cliffs to keep myself from falling, or still trying to hold my bones together while dragging my nearly dead body out of the mountains. Behind this struggle was the lurking fear that I might not make it out alive. After thirty years, I was still unconsciously stuck in survival mode. It was illogical. Not only was I safe and sound, I was fully alive—I had survived.

Yet that psychological trauma had frozen into the cellular memory of my body. The normal survival response of fleeing hadn't been an option for me on Mount Whitney. Instead, I froze, ran out of strength and fell. The freezing response decreased my life force; welding fear permanently into my nervous system.

My trauma therapist, Paul Chubbuck, suggested that I write a book. He thought it would help me heal. Maybe it could even benefit others. I pondered this briefly—nearly everyone who had heard my tale had given me this advice. The time had finally arrived. I dug out my trip journal and started writing.

Reading my notes, reviewing pictures and recounting the journey brought up a lot of unresolved emotions. One morning while Paul and I were lying in bed, I told him that I regretted skiing the John Muir Trail. Paul mentioned that I could have waited for Ken to return with the rope instead of down climbing through the rocky band. I didn't need reminding. It was the biggest regret of my life. Nonetheless, his statement triggered me. I screamed from my core. Anger rushed through my veins as I felt the flames of self-rage explode inside me.

I leapt out of bed, turned away from Paul and punched my fist up into the darkness. The pre-dawn quiet was broken as my hand smashed through the bedroom window, sending shards of glass flying across the room. I felt shattered too. The tiger had awakened from within.

Paul jumped up, turned on the light and came over to check on me. Blood oozed out of a long gash on my wrist. I was shaking and crying. I was both angry and ashamed. I had never responded to anything in such a violent manner. Outwardly, I was upset with Paul. Self-inquiry revealed that I was really furious at myself. The specter of Mount Whitney wasn't just about my encounter with Death; it was also about regret, fear and self-loathing.

Paul washed my wrist and bandaged it. After being treated at an urgent care facility, we went to see my trauma therapist. I was humiliated. I hardly looked at my counselor for the entire appointment. Yet in some indescribable way my action had released something. It also forced me to acknowledge the need to exonerate myself. Forgiveness heals.

During this time, I also became preoccupied with revisiting Mount Whitney. In my head, I recalled every detail of my accident. Intentionally, I remembered the felt-sense of fear and injury in my body. To my surprise, this process sparked a desire to make a physical journey back to Whitney. I finally felt ready to confront and make peace with my adversary. Standing on the mountain again would enable me to make face-to-face contact with my own emotional shadow and thus, to look into the depths of my soul.

And there was still the question of my abandoned skis. I wondered what had happened to them. Were they still littering the mountain? Was it possible I might be able to find and retrieve them?

The answers remained elusive. It was still winter. My body wasn't yet capable of an arduous trek. Instead, I visited the north face of Mount

Whitney on Google Earth. It was scary at first. I had to master navigating the terrain on a computer. One wrong move on the keyboard sent me plummeting over virtual cliffs; the very precipice that I had equated with death. Each time this happened, I felt a reaction in my body. Fear returned. I became tense and my chest tightened. Then I sucked in air and gasped loudly, as if it might be my last breath. Using Google Earth got easier over time. Soon I appreciated the peak's innate beauty again.

In a sense, Mount Whitney had given me an unexpected gift. It was the psychological shadow of this mountain that had cast me down the path of exploring other worlds and perhaps most importantly, the world within. Nepal was the starting point. The immense mountains lifted my spirit towards the sky, grounded me with solace and led me into the depths of my being. Here, the local people viewed every living and non-living thing as sacred. The rarified air was filled with a spiritual essence that was ineffable. All of this changed me—I became a seeker.

While trekking beneath the ice-laden Himalayan peaks, I felt grateful to be living the dream which had inspired me to stay alive on Mount Whitney. However, it wasn't just this goal that had kept me alive—it was the power of my mind. I carried that realization into the rest of my life.

Eastern philosophy reinforced my discovery. For thousands of years Asian cultures have focused their development on understanding the intricacies of emotions and the profound capacities of the mind. My studies taught me that I was the maker of my own perceived reality. I could choose to let pain imprison me in a state of perpetual misery or I could let it change me into something better.

During my divorce I decided to take the development of my own mind to the next level by doing a classic three-year Tibetan Buddhist retreat. It's a formidable undertaking. Many monks and nuns traditionally spend three years, three months and three days in a continuous retreat, guided by an experienced and learned lama, or spiritual teacher. Why would anyone want to do this? During a three-year retreat the mind undergoes an inner alchemy; a self-transformation with ripple effects that can benefit oneself and the people around us.

These retreats involve a methodical exploration of the mind's nature. During this process I saw my habitual mental tendencies and the mind's remarkable capacity for self-deception. I learned that the conceptual mind's activity of constantly interpreting the world around us results in mistaking our perceptions and views for reality. This skews beliefs about ourselves and changes our reactions and behavior towards others. It's the human condition to judge everything and to compare ourselves to others, but doing so leads to the deluded thinking that one is either superior or inadequate. I fell for this too. For decades, I interpreted chronic pain and disfigurement from my accident as something that had made me imperfect. Like most people, I had yet to discover that I wasn't really lacking anything. Instead I hadn't developed my attributes to their greatest potential.

In the story of *The Wizard of Oz*, Dorothy and her companions on the yellow-brick road are the perfect examples of this. Like me, they were looking for happiness outside of themselves, believing that once they arrived at the Emerald City the Wizard would deliver what they each longed for. Only then could they each live happily ever after.

But the Wizard turns out to be a charlatan. He wants the residents of the Emerald City to believe in the images and projections he displays. In a similar way the conceptual mind convinces us that our thoughts, ideas and perceptions must be accurate interpretations of the world around us.

When Dorothy clicks her ruby slippers together and says, "there's no place like home," her intention transports herself back to Kansas. It isn't until she wakes up that she realizes that her journey to the Land of Oz was merely a dream.

This story makes me ponder what Dorothy was really looking for. Was it to return to the familiar structure of her house or to find the elusive state over the rainbow where inner peace and happiness prevail? Like most people, Dorothy longs for a trouble-free life. Sadly she can only wish for it. She doesn't know that taming her thoughts with mindfulness is the secret to abiding in the extraordinary state of lasting tranquility.

My meditation practice taught me that the mind can be either a friend or foe. The conceptual mind doesn't serve us when it engages in repetitive thoughts. Instead it keeps people up at night or drives them crazy during daylight. This unnecessary overthinking of events and situations is often the cause behind much of our dissatisfaction. It can also result in emotional and physical stress that can lead to disease.

But there is an alternative. Through long periods in retreat, I've discovered that it's possible to gradually harness the mind's power, uproot the distracting thoughts that don't serve us, and transcend the perceptions and mental patterns that perpetuate our own suffering.

Meditation is about paying attention to the thinker behind the curtain. By noticing when the mind is caught up in discursive thoughts, we expose our own *Wizard of Oz* and take back the controls. Once the mind is no longer obscured by useless thoughts it can operate with the clarity of wisdom.

This is one reason why the Dalai Lama is so popular. He has spent his whole life training his mind and changing his energetic state. He oozes the inner peace that everyone else longs for.

I want this too. And I am willing to put effort towards that end. That's why I am doing the three-year retreat. It doesn't matter that I am a woman living in the West in the twenty-first century, immersed in the workaday world. Nor am I required to take monastic vows. Still, the necessity of working for a living makes such a lengthy retreat daunting, if not impractical. Few Western Buddhists would entertain the idea. Recognizing this, my teacher encourages serious practitioners to do this retreat over a long period of time while continuing to work.

Much of my free time is committed towards doing the three-year retreat. In fact, I've been engaged with it for over twelve years! Once I have completed all the training, I will continue to dedicate my life to mastering what I have learned.

All forms of meditation, secular or religious, provide various benefits. Scientific studies confirm this. Meditation creates a profound inner serenity where body, mind and spirit come together to reach a greater state of well-being.

It's been a worthwhile but difficult journey. I've learned the value of staying power to develop my inner spirit. Practicing meditation daily has become my refuge and kept me more grounded.

While balancing my practice with a demanding job, I've persisted through a divorce, decades of pain, and the death of family members and friends. Looking back, I can see how my meditation practices enabled me to get through all of these challenges and maintain perspective.

Like my physical healing, it's been a slow and steady process that has yielded results. Through meditation, I entered another portal to healing. I found an expansive, calm and energizing inner space. Tending to my heart and my mind put me on the path to restoring my body in a more holistic way. By connecting to my larger self, where I am always whole, retreats helped me to realize that my body was only a small part of who I actually am. I was then able to redefine myself and my relationship to pain.

Exploring my inner universe also prepared me for the next leg in my personal odyssey—returning to Mount Whitney, the place where my psychological landscape would merge with the physical terrain.

24

PASSAGE TO THE PAST

While seeing my trauma therapist, I had a powerful, almost prophetic dream one night. I dreamed that I was hiking on the flanks of Mount Whitney's north face on a warm summer day.

In the first part of my dream, the mountain appeared different from how it is in reality. Instead of cliffs and heaps of loose stones, the alpine scenery was lush and inviting. In my dream, the scene was reminiscent of a Zen garden. A narrow, earthen path meandered through neatly arranged boulders next to a small gurgling stream surrounded by emerald-green moss. Ken and I were hunting for our missing skis.

Out of the blue he exclaimed, "There they are!"

Ken scampered up a series of granite ledges to retrieve the skis. Then he suddenly disappeared into space—he was gone forever. Next Paul appeared where Ken had vanished above me. As he scrambled down towards me, Paul held a bizarre bouquet in one of his hands. It was made of the broken tips of red and yellow skis interspersed with the fractured ends of blue ski poles. With a big smile on his face, Paul handed me the mangled gear. It was an offering for healing and closure. It made me giddy. I giggled with joy and danced with prancing feet.

Then everything in my dream changed. My mood became somber. Summer faded into autumn. The cool blue shadows of afternoon crept across the slope and the terrain transformed into an expanse of grey talus.

Paul and I scampered up the rocks searching for the exact location of my fall. I stopped when I reached a precipitous ledge—the place where I had tossed my skis before down climbing. It was the site of my ill-fated decision three decades earlier.

I was shocked by what I found. At my feet was a small white wooden cross. It marked a grave—mine. This was the spot where part of me had symbolically died. My body shook with fear, regret and sadness.

In my dream a moment later, my emotions shifted. In the vast space between Mount Whitney and Mount Russell, the sky was filled with rainbow-colored light. The light was shaped into an image of Guru Rinpoche, Tibet's patron saint. The figure plucked me away from my gravesite. My dream ended with him holding and comforting me in the radiance of a bright blue sky.

This dream was rich with layers of symbolism. Clearly, it was time for me to return to Mount Whitney. Going back to the site of my accident held the hope of reconciliation. It required an enormous amount of courage. The mere thought of this trip evoked emotions in me as complex as the mountainous terrain; sometimes tears streamed down my face and trepidation pervaded my body. At other times, I felt joy and peace.

I also wanted to find my beloved red skis. I envisioned our reunion. I would hug them as if reuniting with a long-lost friend. After all, we had been separated for decades. Just thinking about the possibility of finding these old, useless skis brought me a strange sense of delight. The skis held memories; they had transported me to some amazing places. In addition to their personal significance, I felt an ethical responsibility to remove my trash from the wilderness.

Paul and I departed from Colorado to revisit Mount Whitney in the fall of 2012. At Montgomery Pass, on the border between Nevada and California, we got our first glimpse of the Sierra Nevada Mountains. The sight of them after so many years made me jubilant. Then my heart sank—the peaks were plastered by an early autumn snow. Up high, the snow was too deep. It would be dangerous, if not futile, for us to hike through trail-less terrain across unstable, icy and buried rocks. As a consolation, we soaked in hot springs scattered about the Owens Valley and hiked on the trails near Bear Creek Spire.

Afterwards we drove to Lone Pine. A deluge of memories gave me a heavy heart. The town looked the same. I walked around looking for the Southern Inyo Hospital. I was curious to see how the facility had changed since 1982. I expected a larger medical center. Over the last thirty years, demand for emergency services had increased—there was more traffic on Highway 395 and more hikers on Mount Whitney.

Yet only two obvious changes had occurred: a new front entrance and the addition of a helipad. Patients could now be flown to more advanced facilities in Los Angeles. Over the years I often wondered how my physical recovery was affected by not having access to a major medical center. Today, Lone Pine's hospital still has only two rooms set aside for acute patients. The remaining thirty-five beds housed geriatrics in a nursing facility, just as it did during my stay.

From the desert floor in Lone Pine we drove up to Whitney Portal. Rising above the forests were steep granite cliffs. They were just as impressive as I remembered. Still, I was disoriented when we arrived. The layout of the parking lot had changed and the trailhead had also been relocated. I couldn't find the willow shrub at the old trailhead where Ken had laid me before he went looking for help. I was determined to retrace our steps. Yet another year would pass before we could return.

Over the winter, I continued to build strength. I never lost sight of my goal. With every step I took on the elliptical machine at the gym, I imagined that I was hiking up the steep canyon of the North Fork of Lone Pine Creek.

Slowly I reclaimed my ability to ski. I was ecstatic to be gliding through the Colorado backcountry again. As winter melted into spring, I rode a bicycle. In summer I trained on hiking trails. After years of gradually increasing my endurance, I finally saw results. I had less back pain and more confidence. At last, I enjoyed the outdoors again.

We were ready to tackle Mount Whitney again in August 2013. Our good friend Jonathan from the Bay Area joined us for the expedition. He was the perfect companion; a trained counselor, an experienced mountaineer with a strong constitution, and a compassionate, kindred spirit.

The three of us gathered in a small parking area in Lone Pine. Under the sweltering sun we organized our equipment and supplies. We were optimistic. The weather was in our favor. It had been stormy and wet in the high country just before we arrived, but now a four-day window of mild weather was forecast—it was all we needed.

Since we couldn't leave our car at the campground while we were away, we parked it at the trailhead the night before our departure. The next morning we trekked up a path that connected the campground to the Mount Whitney Trail. This was the worst part of the trip for Paul. He later confessed that during the first half mile, he had one dominant thought: *This is a really heavy load! It's going to be a long, long day.*

He graciously kept his thoughts to himself so he wouldn't contaminate the group's enthusiasm, but Jonathan and I were thinking the same thing. I had barely gone three hundred yards before I was feeling miserable from my pack bearing down on my uneven hips. I wondered how I was going to carry my load 4,000 vertical feet up a rugged canyon. Instead of letting my thoughts destroy my confidence, I advised myself to just get used to it.

When we reached the trailhead parking lot, we detoured to my car to retrieve the bathroom scale I had brought from home. I pulled it out from under the seat and placed it on the asphalt. Jonathan heaved his rucksack onto his back and stepped onto the scale. His pack weighed fifty-five pounds. Before we could weigh the other loads, a car appeared around the corner.

"Quick, grab the scale!" Paul yelled.

It was too late. A second later we heard a loud *crunch*. Passengers in the car gasped with shock. The driver brought the car to a screeching halt. Paul walked over to assure him that all was well—they had only run over a bathroom scale. We tossed the crushed parts into my Honda and walked over to the trailhead.

The start of the route up Mount Whitney was marked by a series of tall wooden posts just above the parking lot. The contraption was an eyesore. Nonetheless, we were pleased to see a heavy-duty scale hanging from one of the robust wooden beams. We took turns hefting our packs onto an enormous metal hook. While our packs dangled in the air Jonathan recorded their weights. Paul's backpack weighed fifty pounds and mine, twenty. This was all I could carry on my once-broken back. Our packs were stuffed with supplies: four days of food packed in plastic bear-proof canisters, a rope, climbing hardware, helmets, warm clothes, a tent and overnight gear.

The exhilaration and uncertainty of what was ahead kept us in suspense during most of our trek. Questions bounced around in my head like balls in a pachinko machine. Was I really capable of this hike? Would we find any skis? How would it feel to stand beneath the cliffs where I should have died?

The dusty trail climbed back and forth across the hillside through shrubs and open forests. A mile later we stopped for a short break. The temperature was already hot. We dipped our sun hats into a small waterfall to cool our hot, sweaty heads. Next to the small creek, a faint narrow path diverged off the main route to Mount Whitney. It headed straight up the steep canyon of the North Fork of Lone Pine Creek. Warning signs indicated that this direction was for experienced mountaineers only. We turned and followed the less traveled track.

As we toiled under heavy loads through willows towering over our heads, I watched for landmarks from my epic descent in 1982. Although the landscape was familiar, I had only a vague sense of where I was. Things had changed. In addition to the taller vegetation, this time I was traversing the canyon from the bottom up, and without snow and ice.

A few things had remained the same. The trail still split frequently into multiple paths, and it was necessary to ford back and forth across the stream to stay on route. Despite the drought, there was a considerable amount of water gushing down the valley.

The canyon narrowed farther upstream. White granite cliffs towered on both sides of us. We followed a fleeting path that hugged the north side of the canyon until it ended at the base of a massive stone wall interspersed with broken ledges. Paul insisted we rope up as a precaution before scrambling up and across the rocks. After all, the cliffs dropped several hundred feet below us and our backpacks were heavy and unwieldy. We were safe, but I still felt edgy while climbing upwards.

Higher up, we unroped. While Paul and Jonathan traversed the wider ledges ahead of me, I occasionally stopped to catch my breath. Each time I paused, my eyes scanned across the terrain trying to pinpoint the ledge where Ken had lowered me, many years earlier, by rope. I looked over and over again, but my efforts proved useless.

Lower Boy Scout Lake was an enticing place to eat lunch; a green meadow tinged with blades of gold autumn grass surrounded the shimmering blue water. Nearby, a lone deer grazed next to a large boulder. Although painful memories were present, I was thrilled to be back in the High Sierra again. This was my first summer hiking trip into these mountains; my previous expeditions had always been in the winter. Now, both the weather and the scenery were inviting. Rocky terrain was interspersed with subalpine trees. Sharp crags rose above us. At the head of the valley, Mount Whitney beckoned us onward.

Just past the lake a subtle trail wove between boulders. Soon we encountered evidence of a recent landslide. A deep gash had sliced into the slope. We had no choice but to hike tenuously on a narrow trail zigzagging across a steep hillside with loose soil and enormous, unstable rocks. To get through them, we took huge steps, lunged forward, and climbed up and down between refrigerator-sized boulders.

Nearby, silver ribbons of water cascaded over a massive sheet of stone. Then the trail became intermittent. To stay on track we meandered back and forth through the waist-high willows lining the stream. Keeping the soles of our boots dry was paramount. None of us wanted to slip on the glacially polished slabs that angled away below us.

Higher up, we detoured to Upper Boy Scout Lake. Ken and I hadn't visited this glacial cirque during our exit from the mountains. Back then, we were just trying stay to alive. Now in the August heat, the lake was appealing. Beneath a ring of granite towers, blue water sparkled in the late afternoon sunshine.

An array of tents added splashes of color to the stark landscape. Climbers relaxed on the lakeshore after their strenuous hike up the canyon. They were now poised for their early morning ascent of Mount Whitney the next day. Farther up the trail hikers trudged past us on their way back to Upper Boy Scout Lake. Most of them had just climbed the Mountaineer's Route which traverses from the east to north side of the mountain.

By now, the weight of my backpack was unbearable. I plodded slowly along. I tucked my arms behind my back to lift my rucksack off my once-shattered sacrum. The discomfort made me question whether I could actually make it all the way to Iceberg Lake. My companions also complained about their loads. Our pace gradually slowed. As exhaustion set in, the distance between us grew.

Up ahead, beams of afternoon sunlight poured through the silhouetted spires of Keeler and Day Needles. Gigantic grey shadows crept across the cirque. The sun slipped behind Mount Whitney and the temperature turned from comfortable to cold. A faint trail passed through a jumble of unstable boulders, large and small. We were passing through "the trough," the valley where Ken and I sank helplessly through hip-deep snow during our escape. Now it was just a dry valley filled with rocky glacial rubble.

Ahead of us, countless paths braided through the gorge. Soon we were off-route. Paul was in the lead. He stopped just below a broken headwall interspersed with miniature gardens—alpine flowers, moss and tiny rivulets of water. Darkness was fast approaching. Instead of wasting daylight trying to determine which of the vague trails would lead us up to Iceberg Lake, we opted for the direct route.

Paul pulled out a short 8-mm climbing rope from his pack. I tied the rope into the climbing harness around my torso. Then Paul scrambled up the broken wet ledges without his pack. Once on top, he anchored himself to the rocky band to safeguard our climb.

"On belay!" Paul yelled from above.

I clambered upwards. It felt strange to be climbing again. After ascending a short distance, I became uncomfortable. I could barely reach the next hold. A mild rush of adrenaline was accompanied by a sense of déjà vu—the memory of my fall instantly returned. Here I was, once again in the shadows of Mount Whitney at twilight, trying to make a move to the next handhold with fear coursing through my veins. But this time I was safeguarded by a rope.

With some encouragement from Paul and Jonathan, I successfully mounted up and over a problematic move and continued the short distance to the top. Then Paul hauled our heavy backpacks up the rocky ledges and belayed Jonathan to the crest.

In the fading light we dashed towards Iceberg Lake. A different kind of thrill filled my heart. Now I was realizing my long-held dream of camping in this alpine setting. This had been my wish when Ken and I passed by the frozen lake in 1982.

Only a few other parties were camping at 12,600 feet. Surrounded by sheer spires and rocky ridges, Iceberg Lake was exposed to the wind and cold. The best campsites were located behind walls of stacked rocks. While the men set up camp, I pumped lake water through our filter and into our bottles. I felt rushed to get the task done—it was nearly dark, I was shivering from an alpine breeze, my hands were numb from the frigid water, and my blood sugar was low.

Back at camp I huddled with the men around our tiny camp stove. Assertive mice joined us. They darted about the stove for warmth and looked for crumbs. After our meal, we crawled into our sleeping bags. Despite exhaustion, I lay awake. I was sore and elated from the day's exertion. It had been quite a feat for me to hike into these rugged mountains again. My newfound strength and courage opened up a whole new world of possibilities. I listened to the wind swirling outside our tent and wondered what tomorrow would bring. Soon the day I had spent years training for would dawn.

25

THIRTY-ONE YEARS AT 13,000 FEET

I was up at daybreak. Despite the chill, I dashed out of the tent and trotted between the granite boulders to a hill east of our camp. As the sun rose, Mount Whitney and the surrounding peaks lit up with hues of pink and orange. Iceberg Lake was still in shadow. The water resembled a dark jewel set against brightly lit rocks and a sapphire sky.

After savoring the sunrise, I prepared for the big day. First, I squatted behind a boulder. It was awkward and unpleasant to poop into a "Wag Bag," a plastic pouch whose use is required by the Forest Service. Otherwise, the abundance of backpackers would spoil the landscape and contaminate the water. After sealing the bag, I shook it to activate the digesting gel inside. After one use the bag became foul. It was gut-wrenching to reuse it over the ensuing days.

While organizing our gear, several guided groups arrived from their camp down at Upper Boy Scout Lake. They were bound for the summit of Mount Whitney via the Mountaineer's Route. Our nearest neighbors, four men from San Diego, were celebrating their friend's fiftieth birthday by climbing the sheer eastern face of Whitney. Today, both of our groups marked significant life events. It wasn't my birthday, but I was celebrating being alive by returning to the site where I had nearly died in my early twenties.

I was curious about what experiences awaited us on the north side of the mountain. First, we had to climb up to the Whitney-Russell Col. We traversed along Iceberg Lake's rocky shore to the base of the 500-foot slope. The distance between the lake and the pass was greater than I remembered. Perhaps it was the difference between descending on snow and ascending over loose rubble.

Paul led. Like a mountain sheep, he hopped upwards through the boulder-covered hillside. Jonathan and I lagged behind. As a safety precaution to avoid dislodging a rock onto the person below, we each took a different route up the pass. Airborne stones are like missiles. Flying rapidly downslope they have the potential to injure and even kill anyone in their path. It had been a long time since I had hiked through such unstable terrain. Nonetheless, I remembered to push the stones inward as I climbed upwards so that fewer rocks would move out from beneath my feet and tumble down the mountainside.

While stepping from a granite slab onto scree-sized rocks, I felt something fall from my wrist. The string on my Buddhist mala had broken. Beads made of fragrant sandalwood, suffused with nearly two decades of daily prayers, scattered across the rocky jumble. Many of them disappeared into the crevasses between the stones. I was crestfallen.

It was my first Buddhist rosary. I had purchased it in Kathmandu for a long retreat at a monastery in the 1990s. Later, it accompanied me to sacred sites throughout Asia. I had brought the mala to Mount Whitney hoping that it would bring me good luck. Instead, it gave me another Buddhist lesson in impermanence. Now my broken mala was a reminder of the suffering that comes from attachment and loss. I could only hope that the blessings contained in each bead would consecrate the mountain and bless all who passed this way. I was retrieving some of the beads when Jonathan caught up to me.

"Oh, no!" he exclaimed.

He sorted through the boulders to reclaim a few of the lost beads.

"Let it go, Jonathan. We will never find all the beads. Besides, this slope is too unstable for us to linger on. Let's keep moving."

Paul gave us a congratulatory yelp when we finally reached the top of the Whitney-Russell Col. On the other side, Mount Russell dominated the skyline. The peak was just as beautiful as I remembered. After my fall, I thought it would be the last thing I would see before dying.

Now I was more intrigued by the view to the west—a sea of brown talus interspersed with cliffs, stretched across the lower flanks on the north side of Mount Whitney. It was radically different without snow. Stones of all sizes were stacked on top of each other. With each step for the next half mile, rocks teeter-tottered back and forth, shifted under foot and banged loudly against each other. Each stride had the potential for a sprained ankle or broken leg.

Farther ahead I recognized some of the features on Whitney's northern slope. The cliffs where I had fallen were just beyond the second rocky spine on the horizon. Paul and Jonathan followed as I led them to the exact spot at 13,110 feet where Ken and I had camped during a storm.

In summer this was an inviting, high-altitude campsite. It was the only place flat enough for a small tent and the ground was covered with soft sand. In winter, the site was buried under a deep snow drift that collected beneath a rocky rib.

Now, standing at our former campsite, I perceived something strange. Energetically, it was heavy. I closed my eyes. I focused my attention on the ground beneath my feet. This act, in this place, re-connected me to the energy of death. Death's presence was all around. It was also in the cellular memory of my body. It was a bit unsettling. I sensed it in the way that one feels changes in the moisture levels in the air before a storm. This time though, Death's energy seemed lighter. The energy of life and death were equally pervasive in the atmosphere. Now they seemed to balance each other.

Still, memories of Death burst into my mind. I remembered lying in the tent in 1982 when I felt Death's presence. It wasn't evil or negative. It felt like a shadow made of tar—dark and dense, hovering directly above me. It tugged gently at my life force. Without taking me away, Death had touched and changed my life forever. Then it took my sister and several close friends—Bob, Judy and Cindy.

Over the last few decades, I occasionally wondered about the dying process. The world is full of stories of near-death and after-death experiences. Many people report seeing a bright light and experiencing feelings of peace. I wondered if one has to actually die before the light is revealed. From my perspective, life is full of emotional and physical experiences that are like dwelling in shadow or light. I've learned that the darkest times in life have the potential to be transformative.

Now that we stood at the place I referred to as "Death's campsite," I was eager to look for my missing skis. After we drank some water Paul dug through his pack and pulled out a map, photographs and binoculars. We put our climbing helmets on and scanned our surroundings.

Before embarking on our search, I looked up the mountainside. Looming just beyond us were the cliffs over which I had fallen decades earlier. An expanse of convex granite was topped by a steep band of rocks. It stretched horizontally for a quarter of a mile. Even though it was late August, a large frozen cascade draped over the stony wall. In other places, water trickled down the slabs.

Jonathan stood quietly off to the side while Paul and I discussed our next move. After a few minutes, Jonathan spoke up.

"Look, there's a ski right over there," he said calmly, pointing to the west.

A hundred feet away was a single yellow ski. It had been exposed to the elements for thirty-one years at 13,000 feet. The mere sight of Ken's abandoned ski evoked a cathartic response. I frowned in agony and disbelief, then groaned and bawled out loud while tears streamed down my face. I could hardly swallow. Something had ripped loose from deep within my belly. I felt like I was going to choke on an invisible rush of energy; it gushed upwards through my chest and out my mouth with the velocity of water coming out of a fire hose.

Events from the past had just collided with the present moment. Above were the fateful cliffs. Ahead was Ken's ski. These were tangible reminders of what had happened here. It was one of those *Oh my God moments* when you feel your most painful wound tear wide open again. It was overpowering, tormenting and raw. I grieved for a million things simultaneously. I felt a devastating sense of loss—loss of my once-active youth, loss of confidence, loss from nerve damage and physical injuries, loss of my marriage, and loss of my beloved skis. I regretted that my wonderful adventure with Ken had concluded so horribly.

I rushed over to the ski. It looked as if it had been intentionally placed atop a small angled rock adjacent to a larger white granite boulder. The ski was gracefully aligned with the curvature in the rock. The brand name and model, Epoke 900, had faded away. Yet the yellow fiberglass sheath on the top of the ski was still in excellent condition. However, the bindings had taken a beating; the metal bail had ripped away and the plastic heel guide was broken. The ski's underside had been weathered by the elements down to its wooden core. Huge splinters covered the plank along with a few strips of meshed fiberglass in silver and black.

Mount Russell and author with Ken's ski

This was the ski that had fractured forty miles before the end of our trip while crossing chunks of avalanched snow. The top of the ski and the metal pot gripper that had splinted it together was now gone. During Ken's fall, the upper part of the ski was ripped apart at the repair site. The lower end remained only because it was lashed securely onto the side of his pack.

Now it was easier for me to piece together the events from our tragedy. Before my fall Ken had down climbed a rocky wall and traversed eastward along a ramp above the cliffs. Once on talus, he hiked around a rocky spur, our future campsite, and over to his abandoned pack at the base of the precipice. From there he watched me hurtle over the cliffs.

Next Ken dragged me across the slope, removed his broken ski from his pack, and placed it on the rock before setting up our tent. He was probably frantic. It was nearly dark, snow was falling heavily, and his injured fiancée lay bleeding in the snow in a state of medical shock. Over the next few days Ken's useless ski was buried in the accumulating snowfall, forgotten and left behind. His poles and other ski had ripped off his pack and scattered during his fall.

While holding Ken's broken ski I reflected on all the unanswered questions I had from our epic nightmare. Since we never talked about it I didn't know Ken's side of the story. What thoughts had raced through his mind while he fell down the mountainside? Had he been afraid of dying or was he too occupied with trying to stop himself? What was it like for him to watch me bounce through the cliffs and then stay awake all night wondering if I would slip into a coma or be dead in the morning? How had our tragedy affected him? Did Ken feel guilt, anger or remorse? Or did he, as I suspected, push his own tiger of trauma into the cage of denial by not talking about it? Now that I was on my own journey of healing, I wondered how Ken's life could have been different if he had tended to his emotional wounds.

For decades our catastrophe had filled me with regret. Now I had returned to Mount Whitney to make peace with my own remorse. I had to feel these intense and complex emotions to let go and move on. Besides anguish, I felt self-admiration, something rare for me. Even though I had made a foolish decision and paid the consequences for many decades, now I was impressed by my own capabilities.

While hiking back up to the north face, it didn't seem possible that I had crawled out of these mountains. The terrain was extremely rugged, the snow was deep, my body was broken, and I was on the verge of death. Discovering Ken's ski near our campsite gave me clarity and perspective on our struggle to survive. It was empowering. It was a tangible and meaningful connection to my past. It also reminded me of the marvelous times that we had shared.

What I really wanted to find though was my own red skis. They had transported me on many wonder-filled trips in the Sierras. In a sense, they had become part of me. Now we had perfect conditions to search for them—the weather was pleasant and the drought had completely melted the snowfield at the base of the cliffs.

We first searched through the talus field and low-angled slabs below the cliff band. As I combed through a field of stones, I moaned aloud in hopeful anguish, "Where are my skis? I want to find my special skis!"

Paul and Jonathan searching for my skis

We spent hours looking through the rocky debris. Small stones and fragments of ice occasionally rolled down from above. It made me jittery. Fortunately, the rockfall was minimal. We carefully examined every nook and cranny where skis or poles might have lodged. Paul and Jonathan looked along the base of the bluff. Then they climbed up the lower cliffs to peer behind huge rocky plates that had peeled away from the steeper slabs.

While they searched higher up, I examined the talus below and a low-angled, slippery slope that had been polished by the former snowfield. Then I spotted something—a long, dark shaft. Excited that this might be one of my missing ski poles, I pulled the rod up and away from the small

255

stones that buried it. To my surprise and disappointment, out popped a full-length ice ax. It wasn't mine, but I claimed it and took it with me.

Then Jonathan stumbled upon a broken 35-mm camera. We contemplated the relationship between the two items. Perhaps this was evidence of someone else's ordeal on the cliffs above. We wondered what their story was.

Today, extreme skiers using high-tech equipment occasionally descend the gullies on Whitney's north face. Before reaching the lower end of their run they traverse farther east to avoid the cliffs where I had fallen. Ken and I had hoped to go that direction, but the slabs that separated us from the safer slope were glazed by new snowfall. We unknowingly proceeded downward into more risky terrain.

Now while searching for my skis, I found the improbable. Wedged between fist-sized rocks was a flat, black piece of rubber. Curious, I picked it up. It was the heel of a small shoe. I stared at it in the palm of my hand. A vague recollection came to me. Hadn't I resoled the heels of my boots after my accident? The heel looked as if it had come from an old Nordic Norm ski boot. It was about my size. Just in case, I slipped it into my pocket.

Author's Nordic ski boots and heel

I dug my old ski boots out after I got home. They had indeed been re-soled after my fall. The found heel was a perfect match on my size 36 Norwegian boot. It gave me shivers. It was as if I had found a needle in the proverbial haystack. The heel must have loosened during my fall and popped off as Ken dragged me across the snow. Its location also gave me a better idea of where I had landed after my accident.

Yet I still wanted to know exactly where I had fallen through the cliffs. The view above me was too foreshortened to determine precisely where I had been. My search on Google Earth had narrowed the location to two possibilities. The uncertainty remained. For a time, the question nagged at me. Then Paul approached me with an announcement.

"I am going up there to look for your skis," he said.

At the moment, I didn't understand exactly where he planned to go next. As Paul headed upslope, Jonathan continued his search farther west. I poked around the boulder field below 13,000 feet. Perhaps snowmelt had carried my skis farther downhill each year. My poles were less likely to have traveled any distance. I looked behind each and every boulder. Nothing was found.

It was unlikely that someone would have stumbled upon my skis. We were on a remote section of the peak. They would be buried under snow when extreme skiers were in the area. The Mountaineer's Route was farther east. If someone had gotten off route and discovered my skis, they probably wouldn't have bothered to carry them out of the backcountry. The terrain was too rugged to remove something useless and awkward.

As I continued wandering through the rocky debris, it hit me. I finally understood where Paul had gone. He had hiked up and around a rocky rib and then behind the stone tower that accessed the ledge used by Ken before I fell. When I looked up, I saw Paul walking across the ramp between the steep slabs and the cliffs. A surge of anxiety rushed through me. Intellectually, I knew he was safe, but emotionally I was overtaken with fear. I trembled, cried, and yelled at him to come down, but Paul was too far away to hear me.

Jonathan, a trained psychotherapist, heard me yelling and sobbing. He abandoned his search, came over to me, and comforted me. I bawled like a baby in his arms. Then he made a loud whistle. After getting Paul's attention, he waved at Paul to come down and join us. I was embarrassed and disgusted by my reaction, but the sight of Paul on that ledge was more than I could bear. Fortunately, Paul had seen enough of the rocky shelf to be certain that my equipment wasn't there. I calmed down when we were reunited. Then I probed him for more details.

"What was it like up there?" I inquired.

I was curious about the terrain. After all, I had been unconscious during my fall. A broken escarpment with a 50-60 degree angle and steep gullies rose above him. The ledge was five to ten feet wide and inclined gently outwards. It spanned across the slope for nearly fifty yards. The shelf was covered in rocky debris. Beneath it was a sheer fifteen foot cliff. Farther below, a 75-degree angled slab dropped away for over a hundred feet to the bottom of my fall.

My skis were nowhere to be found. They were probably buried. Rocks had exfoliated down the mountain and accumulated on the slope beneath the cliffs for decades. Perhaps my red skis were meant to stay with the mountain.

After our search, we returned to Death's campsite. While resting on a rock, I thought deeply about my missing skis. What had I really hoped to find here? Was it the skis, or was I searching for something else? Perhaps I was longing to reconnect with my twenty-two year old self. She wanted to be forgiven for making a regrettable decision during desperate circumstances. Perhaps she also wanted acknowledgement for her gallant fight for life, and for blossoming from a personal tragedy. After a few minutes of silence, I looked up at Paul.

"This is where I looked Death in the eye," I said with wet eyes and a choked up voice.

"And it's also the place that you made your vow to live your most important dreams," he reminded me. "Your lama-teacher, Drupon Samten, once told me that your experience on Mount Whitney ignited your interest in the spiritual path," he continued.

Paul's comment made me pause. My encounter with Death was the shadow that had influenced my life's choices. It forced me to define what was most important. I embraced my personal dreams with the same vigor that many people put towards climbing the career ladder. My dream to see the Himalayas spun new dreams. I grew and changed with each goal that I accomplished. Now I pondered what dreams still held meaning. After decades of pain, I wanted to free myself from all forms of suffering. I also wished for everyone to be able to cope with whatever ailed or haunted them. On the spot, I revived my determination.

Just before leaving, I recalled lying here in the tent. I was penned in by a storm and unable to urinate due to the nerve damage in my bladder. Now, I pulled down my pants and peed gleefully in the open. This act gave me a small degree of revengeful satisfaction. Today I still have to bear down to push the urine out of my bladder. Nonetheless, I felt giddy peeing on the very spot where it had once been impossible to do so.

Afterwards, I thanked Mount Whitney for sparing my life. I thanked my skis and wished them well, like a dear friend whom I'd never see again. Then I hugged my two friends, Paul and Jonathan, and expressed my gratitude to them for all their support. I strapped Ken's broken ski onto my pack and carried it out of the mountains with me.

As our threesome hiked back towards the Whitney-Russell Col, I felt a sense of reconciliation; I pranced across the stones with a joyful lightness in my step. I had confronted my demons, forgiven myself, and reclaimed a few lost treasures.

As we scrambled across the unstable terrain, I turned to Paul. "I feel like I should bring something back from Whitney to give to my teacher."

Moments after I spoke, something caught my eye. Below my feet, in a crevice between golden granite boulders was a clear, fist-sized quartz crystal. It was the most beautiful rock that I had ever seen in the Sierras. The transparent stone was layered with thin white lines and shaped like a cube. That was it. I picked up the precious rock and put it into my pack.

Paul and Jonathan left Iceberg Lake early the next morning to climb Mount Whitney via the Mountaineer's Route. It was a personal victory for both of them—their first ascent of the peak. I was tempted to join the climb. Instead I rested at base camp; one time on top of Mount Whitney was enough for me. Besides, I still had several thousand feet to descend through the canyon before finishing our trip.

When we arrived back at the Whitney Portal Trailhead, we located the old trail. It switched back and forth across the hillside beneath the Jeffrey pines and down to the parking lot. Just past an immense grey boulder was the once-small willow where Ken had laid me before looking for help. Now that my steps were retraced, I felt a sense of completion.

26
THE LIGHT WITHIN

Shortly after we returned to Colorado, I ran into Ken at work. For the first time since our marital parting, he stopped and waited for me to speak. I reached out with my heart and my voice, as I always had since our divorce.

"Hi, how are you?" I inquired.

I was surprised when he greeted me back. He had spent the past eight years avoiding me. His predictable pattern was to act as if I were invisible and walk quickly away in the opposite direction. Perhaps it was his way of not dealing with his pain or shame.

I wondered if I should ask him if he would like to have his old ski. But I knew it wouldn't interest him. Nor would he want to know that I had just returned from the place that had once bonded and later broken us. Still, it was nice to hear his voice again. My recent trip had renewed my appreciation for Ken.

It also changed my perspective towards the peak. Mount Whitney was no longer just a personal symbol of regret and pain. Now the mountain inspired me. I could emulate it; standing strong again and reaching upwards towards new possibilities. Facing my trauma had created space for yet another level of healing.

A few weeks after my encounter with Ken, Paul and I returned to California to our teacher's meditation center. After only a few days in retreat, one of the nuns from Ladakh interrupted my silent contemplation. Ani Dolma quietly entered my room during the evening. The solemn expression on her face confirmed my suspicion. Something was wrong. Despite her dignified appearance in burgundy robes, she struggled to maintain her composure.

"There has been an emergency," she said with a quivering voice.

Then she handed me a small piece of paper with a phone number scrawled on it.

"We received an important phone message today. Call this friend right away."

I stared at her in disbelief.

"After your call, you can come to the house and talk with Drupon if you need to," she added. Then Ani Dolma disappeared out the door.

A million thoughts raced through my once-peaceful mind. What was this all about? What had happened, and to whom? I sat on my bed and made the dreaded phone call. Mary, my life-long friend, delivered the disturbing news with grace. Ken had just died of a heart attack. I was shocked; another life-long friend, gone. He was a fit and active fifty-five year old. Having survived the impossible on Mount Whitney, I was surprised that death had taken him at such a young age.

I was too sad to sleep much that night. I still cared about Ken. Despite our divorce, we had been through a great deal in our twenty-six years together. That night I dreamed that I was in the home that we had shared. Ken's belongings were neatly arranged and his personal papers were all boxed up. The scene looked like someone was preparing to move. It gave me the impression that Ken knew he was about to part from this world.

As the dream continued, an image of a dark, angry gorilla appeared. It was lying on top of me. It squeezed me as if it was trying to suffocate me. The ape-like creature resembled Ken; it had short legs and long arms. Like the figure in my dream, Ken had a slight hunch in his back from his work as a computer programmer at the national park.

I woke up with a tight chest. Sweat dripped from my body. I felt Ken's presence, and his fear. I wondered if this was what he had experienced in his last moments of life.

I kept Ken in my prayers during the next six weeks of my retreat. Each morning I lit a candle on the altar for him. I thought of him off and on during the day. Sometimes I cried. My tears were for his shortened life, his unfulfilled dreams, and for the loss that his absence had created in this world.

Occasionally I sensed his presence in the retreat cottage. I spoke to his spirit. I thanked him for the wonderful times we shared and expressed my gratitude for helping me off Mount Whitney. I told him that he had been a good man and that he had done his best as a husband. I encouraged him to move on to his next life and wished him well. Then I prayed for his reincarnation.

Over the years I had gained compassion, insight and understanding about his inability to cope with his own unresolved issues. Each night before going to sleep during my retreat, I lit another candle for him. It wasn't just to illuminate the darkness of night, it was also to brighten Ken's emotional shadow.

The timing of Ken's death was eerie. He passed away shortly after I had revisited the site of our shared tragedy. Now his life had slipped away, just as quickly as he had disappeared down the mountain in 1982. His sudden death reminded me of the dream I'd had before Paul and I departed for the Sierras. In that dream, after searching for our skis on Mount Whitney, Ken evaporated into space and vanished into eternity. Now he was gone forever from my life.

A few days before Ken's demise and before we went into retreat, Paul and I were gathered around the dining table with our lama-teacher, Drupon Samten Rinpoche. We frequently lingered after meals to ask him questions about life, and to ponder his insights and advice. During a break in the conversation, I spoke up.

"Rinpoche, I have something I want to give you."

My teacher scooted his chair next to mine.

"It's a piece of Mount Whitney. That's where I met Death over thirty years ago," I explained.

From the pocket of my fleece coat, I pulled out a silk, indigo-colored pouch. I paused for a moment. Then I sheepishly handed it to him.

Wrapped inside was the square crystal that I had found on Mount

Whitney. The situation felt slightly awkward. I was embarrassed to be giving him something as simple as a rock. Drupon carefully untied the small package. While he admired the stone in his hand, I pondered what he would do with it. The crystal's only value was based on the meaning that my mind had given it. Otherwise, it was worthless.

Since Drupon already had countless rocks decorating his beautiful gardens, he didn't need another. I thought perhaps he would just politely accept it, and later put it outside. He knew my story. He also understood how difficult it had been for me to acquire this crystal. While he examined the stone, I looked into Drupon's rich greenish-brown eyes. They were kind and calming. His eyes were like a gateway—they revealed a vast timeless world beyond my limited self.

With a heavy Ladakhi accent and a gleam in his eye, he uttered softly, "We'll put this crystal inside the stupa that we are going to build here at the meditation center."

His statement infused me with joy. A huge smile creased my face. In a sense, Drupon had just sanctified my entire experience on Mount Whitney and the pain that I endured for decades.

Since a stupa is a Buddhist symbol for enlightenment, I couldn't imagine a finer resting place for the transparent rock. For me, that crystal was a physical link between the place that had once defined me and transformation.

My experience on Mount Whitney had become part of me. From it, I've learned that I can choose whether suffering holds me captive or becomes an opportunity for transfiguration. Whitney's shadow has also compelled me to live my dreams. Despite the pain, I've tried to savor the sweet richness and beauty of life. My personal journey wasn't just about finding my own voice; it was about discovering my own inner light.

The crystal in Drupon Samten Rinpoche's hand wasn't just a brown piece of granite, like most of the stones that make up Mount Whitney. Instead I had chosen to bring him a transparent rock from the mountain. That stone held the luster of light.

I had learned from Drupon that humans express the vibrancy of light when they abide in pure love. It's a product of selflessness, wisdom and compassion. Love helps everyone. Unconditional acceptance and love have the power to heal. I believe that at the subtlest level, our physical being is made of pure conscious light. It's the light within us that illuminates the shadows we each carry in our souls.

Soon my teacher called out to Ani Dolma. She was at the kitchen sink washing the breakfast dishes. The young nun looked up, dried her hands on a towel, and came to the table.

"Take this crystal and put it with the precious items that I brought back from India and Nepal," Drupon instructed her.

Ani Dolma nodded as she accepted the gift. She moved with grace, like a gentle breeze, towards the adjacent shrine room. Her small frame parted the rainbow-colored curtains covering the doorway to the monastery's private sanctuary. Inside, she placed my rock onto a collection of sacred items in the corner of the room.

During construction, the crystal from Mount Whitney will be buried inside the stupa along with holy treasures. Relics from enlightened masters, precious stones and paper scrolls printed with prayers will imbue the structure with sacred energy. The stupa's exterior will be made of tiered layers of white-washed mortar.

Stupas and mountains are both metaphors for the human spirit's potential to reach new heights. It's human nature to yearn for something better. Lasting inner peace and happiness are at the top of humanity's wish list.

In Buddhism this state of well-being is a product of enlightenment. To realize this advanced state one must experience the inherent oneness of all things and the mind must abide continually in non-dual awareness.

Stupas remind me of mountains. They have the same shape with tapering towers that extend towards the sky. I am reaching for the sky too. I am still inspired by mountains, but the summit I long for the most is enlightenment itself. I am determined to follow the path towards the loftiest of aspirations, the very pinnacle of human achievement, and the ultimate form of healing. It's my greatest dream, and the gift from living with the specter of Mount Whitney.

May all beings have happiness and be free from suffering

YOU can help me make a difference!

If you enjoyed this book, please write a review. I am an independent author with the aspiration to benefit others. Honest reviews help other readers to discover this powerful story. I am also donating 100% of my proceeds from this book to non-profit charities

Leaving a review is easy. Log onto your account on Amazon.com and type *If I Live Until Morning* into the search box. Click on Customer Reviews, then on Write a Customer Review, write your review and then click Submit. Even a brief review can make an impact.

Thank-you

ACKNOWLEDGMENTS

For encouragement and/or assistance in writing this book

Leanne Benton

Debra Denker

Andree DuPont

Mary Ann Franke

Ruth Greider

Maura Longden

Carol Naff

Dave Pillmore

With gratitude for help in surviving, recovering or healing

Drupon Samten Rinpoche

H.E. Garchen Rinpoche

Padmasambhava

Jim Asher

Mary Carroll

Paul Chubbuck

Kyle Duncan

Lori Duncan

Dr. Paul Fonken

Cindy Haney

Jonathan Kabat

Dr. Evan Katz

Dr. Ambrose P. McLaughlin

Paul McLaughlin

Forrest McVicar

Debby Muenchrath

Fred Muenchrath

Bill O'Brien

Bob O'Brien

Kelly O'Brien

Alice Reinig

Dr. Sarbottam Shrestha

Ken Unitt

The family at Whitney Portal

Manufactured by Amazon.ca
Bolton, ON

28219684R00159